The Campaign Manager

The Campaign Manager

Running and Winning Local Elections

SECOND EDITION

Catherine M. Shaw

Westview Press
A Member of the Perseus Books Group

Copyright © 2000 by Westview Press, A Member of the Perseus Books Group

Published in 2000 in the United States of America by Westview Press, 5500 Central Avenue, Boulder, Colorado 80301-2877, and in the United Kingdom by Westview Press, 12 Hid's Copse Road, Cumnor Hill, Oxford OX2 9JJ

Find us on the World Wide Web at www.westviewpress.com

Designed by Heather Hutchison

Library of Congress Cataloging-in-Publication Data
Shaw, Catherine, M.
  The campaign manager : running and winning local elections / Catherine M. Shaw
    p.   cm.
  "Revised and expanded edition."
  Includes bibliographical references and index.
  ISBN 0-8133-6848-0 (pbk.)
    1. Local election—United States—Handbooks, manuals, etc.   2. Campaign
management—United States—Handbooks, manuals, etc.   I. Title
JS395.S43   1999
324.7'0973—dc21   99-034784

The paper used in this publication meets the requirements of the American National Standard for Permanence of Paper for Printed Library Materials Z39.48-1984.

10   9   8   7   6   5   4   3   2

Dedicated to my children, Daniel and Sarah,
who have shared me, nearly all their lives,
with the community I love.

A special thanks
To my mom, Dr. Ruth Schifferle,
for her stellar clipping service
and
To my husband, Rick, of Rickshaw Productions,
for his support and invaluable contributions to the
media sections of this book.

Contents

Tables and Illustrations

Box

Preface

Running for local office can be one of the most demanding and exhilarating experiences of your life. Your house will be cluttered and chaotic, your children ignored, and your partner, whether involved or not, will be stressed. And yet, seeking office or pushing through a ballot measure gives you an opportunity to be a leader, effect change in your community, and repay something to the city, county, state, or country you love. You will also find that the campaign experience offers an opportunity for you to grow personally. You will be challenged and stretched as never before. When all is over, win or lose, you will be a different person, with a different outlook on our political process and a new respect for those who run and serve.

When I first ran for mayor of Ashland, Oregon, I had no prior government or management experience. Many felt I should start at the council level and work my way up before taking on the position of CEO of a multimillion-dollar municipality. However, having little or no experience allowed me to see things with a fresh eye. Now, eleven years later, the council, city staff, community, and I have implemented dozens of programs, including open space, water conservation, community composting and recycling, affordable housing, voter-approved strict air quality standards, wetland wastewater treatment, forest management, and specialized school funding. We also divested our hospital and acquired a ski resort and an ambulance service. Recently we placed a dark fiber ring in our city to provide high-speed Internet service and are preparing to offer cable TV services. By community and government working in partnership, we've been able to create and act upon opportunities normally available only to large metropolitan areas.

There are over a half-million elective offices in the United States. If you have an inclination to serve and a desire to be a leader in your community, do it. Being in a position where you have a positive impact on your community and bring about change is more rewarding and fun than you can imagine. Ultimately, the only real credentials you need are integrity and a caring heart.

> "You have to be smart enough to understand the game and dumb enough to think it's important."
> —Gene McCarthy on how politics is like coaching football.

Since 1985 I have worked on or run many campaigns in my region. Through years of experimentation and collaboration with other seasoned campaigners, I found organizational techniques that worked in political campaigns and began to apply them to the campaign process. This book is the culmination of campaign trial and error. It gives you the tools needed to organize the efforts of others on your behalf. Whether you are a novice or a seasoned campaigner, you will find information here that will make your efforts more organized and effective.

Good luck and enjoy the process.

CATHERINE M. SHAW

> "Politics—good politics—is public service. There is no life or occupation in which a man can find a greater opportunity to serve his community or his country."
> —Harry Truman

How to Use This Handbook

In this section
The Framework
The Layout
Know the Law

Running a local election can seem a bewildering, complicated process. It involves recruiting volunteers, raising money to run the campaign, analyzing how best to allocate people and money, projecting the best image and message, and getting-out-the-vote.

This handbook breaks a campaign down into manageable units for easy implementation. If you are the candidate, you will find the necessary tools to run your own campaign. If you have either a paid or volunteer campaign manager, this handbook will organize and guide the two of you and your team through the campaign process.

Because of the complexity of the campaign process, take time to read this entire handbook, especially before you design your campaign flowchart or campaign calendar. A campaign makes more sense as a whole.

The Framework

In local politics, there are generally three types of political campaigns:

- Partisan: Democrat versus Republican versus Independent.
- Nonpartisan: Two or more candidates, with no party affiliation, square off. These elections usually have no primary, only a general election.
- Ballot measure or proposition: These represent single issues brought to the voters by a governing body. An initiative or referendum is a single issue brought to voters by a citizen group. Neither involves candidates.

A partisan race differs from other campaigns only in how the precinct analysis is performed for the primary. For example, if you are involved in a partisan race in the primary—that is, two Republi-

> "...the seeds of political success are sown far in advance of any election day. ... It is the sum total of the little things that happen which leads to eventual victory at the polls."
> —J. Howard McGrath, Former Chairman, Democratic National Committee

cans running against each other—you will look at the voting trends of
your party only, just as you will if you are a Democrat running against
another Democrat. In all nonpartisan or ballot measure races, you look
for past voting trends on that issue, regardless of party affiliation.

"Behind all politi-
cal success is at-
tention to de-
tail."
—Larry O'Brien,
advisor to John F.
Kennedy

A campaign measure differs mainly in how it starts. If it is being
referred by the voters' initiative or referendum, it will begin with
signature gathering. However, if a government body places the measure on the ballot, this campaign is run exactly like any other.

The "formula campaign" that is the basis for this book is a way of
systematically organizing other people's efforts on your behalf. You
provide the guidance in setting up volunteer systems for phoning,
clerical support, fund-raising, lawn sign dispersal, and canvassing.
Within each of these areas, critical organizational work is necessary
to accomplish a variety of tasks. These tasks include such things as
putting together your campaign team and volunteer organization,
developing a campaign theme and message, designing campaign
brochures and lawn sign art, performing precinct analysis, designing direct mail, handling the media, presenting the candidate, following a flowchart, and overseeing campaign clean-up.

After reading this manual, determine what your campaign is capable of, then use this book to provide the blueprints for completing those tasks successfully. By breaking a campaign down into
manageable units and organizing the activities within each component, you will never overload your workforce. Once you have decided what you can or want to do in organizing your campaign, you
will need to plot these activities on a campaign flowchart or campaign calendar. Many campaigns use a "campaign plan" as a way to
track the necessary upcoming campaign activities. Instead, I prefer a
more visual "campaign flowchart" because it presents a campaign
time line at a glance. However, any campaign flowchart can be con-
verted into a campaign plan.

The Layout

Chapter 1, "The Campaign Team," covers the small, select group
that will develop campaign strategies and lend the support and expertise needed to win. Chapter 2, "The Campaign Brochure," details
the single most important thing the campaign team will do in the
campaign: develop a campaign theme and message. It is also the
first task of the team.

Chapter 3, "The Volunteer Organization," gives you the basis for
organizing your phone banks and clerical workers. Chapter 4,
"Fund-raising," helps you raise money in a variety of ways using
your volunteer force. In Chapter 5, "Lawn Signs," I discuss the design, placement, and maintenance of signs. Chapter 6, "Precinct

Analysis," gives you a step-by-step methodology for directing campaign resources where they will do you the most good. If your campaign has an especially busy schedule, precinct analysis is actually something that can be done months ahead of the campaign kick-off. However, I have placed precinct analysis in Chapter 6 because it must happen prior to canvassing and getting-out-the-vote, which are outlined in Chapters 7 and 8.

Chapters 9 and 10, "Direct Mail" and "Media," cover what have become the most expensive aspects of a campaign. Along with all the necessary information to make the most out of direct mail and media, you will also find tips in each of these chapters for stretching your campaign dollars. Chapter 11, "The Candidate," is about projecting a positive image before the voters and thereby minimizing the potential nit-picking that the public might do. Chapter 12, "The Issue-based Campaign," covers initiative, referendum, recall, and school and library money issues as well as a couple of monsters in the night: the double majority and the super majority. Chapter 13, "The Campaign Flowchart," puts in chronological order all that you will need to do to win. Although laying out a flowchart is one of the first things you will do to organize your campaign, without a baseline knowledge of the first eleven chapters, it would make no sense. I have also included in Chapter 13 a campaign calendar, which I often use in place of a flowchart.

Finally, Chapter 14, "After the Ball," is simply about winning and losing gracefully, putting your campaign to bed, and election night. For ease in applying this handbook to a campaign, I have included all forms mentioned in the text in Appendix 1, additional information on the state initiative and referendum process in Appendix 2, and campaign Web sites in Appendix 3.

Know the Law

Visit the county clerk and/or city recorder to become familiar with state and local election laws. For example, in my city, you are not allowed to place lawn signs more than thirty days prior to an election. You also are not allowed to place them on the median strip between the sidewalk and street. Although the homeowner may plant, mow, and care for this area, it is, in fact, public property. To place a lawn sign here could be interpreted in one of two ways: Either you feel you're above the law or you don't know it. Either interpretation is a problem if you hope to be in government.

It is against federal law to place campaign literature in and around mailboxes. The federal government owns your mailbox even though you bought and installed it, and it can be used only for the U.S. mail. Also note that, because publicly owned buildings are

> "Play for more than you can afford to lose and you will learn the game."
> —Winston Churchill

maintained, lit, and owned by the taxpayers, they may not be used for campaign purposes.

The county clerk or city recorder will also draw attention to filing dates that you and your treasurer must know. Missing a campaign expenditure filing deadline will almost always get you media coverage, just not the kind you need or want. Other than the legal materials that you will want to get from the county clerk, city recorder, or Secretary of State, everything you need to run a successful campaign is included in this handbook.

"One thing I know: The only ones among you who will be really happy are those who will have sought and found how to serve."
—Albert Schweitzer

1
The Campaign Team

In this chapter
The Campaign Committee
The Treasurer
The Campaign Manager
The Campaign Chair or Co-chairs
Finding Volunteers
Matching Volunteers to Skills
Potential Volunteer Sources
Volunteer Sign-up Sheet

Your "campaign team" is everyone who helps organize your efforts. It is made up of the campaign committee, the treasurer, your volunteers, and the individual teams that oversee a portion of the campaign. Your media team, for example, may have a liaison to the campaign committee, but this team should be looked upon as part of your overall campaign team rather than part of the committee itself. Aspects of the campaign team will be covered in this chapter. Campaign efforts that involve large numbers of people and independent efforts, such as lawn signs, media, brochure development, and fund-raising, are covered in separate chapters.

The Campaign Committee

The relatively small campaign committee serves two functions: First, it is a support group, for both itself and the candidate, measure, or initiative; second, it is the primary source of expertise for the campaign. This small, select group maneuvers and steers a campaign while drawing on the resources of the community. The committee should consist of individuals with different personal strengths and areas of ability.

> "The impersonal hand of government can never replace the helping hand of a neighbor."
> —Hubert Humphrey

Your campaign committee is a real insiders' group. The candidate and each of the members must feel safe to speak candidly without fear of recriminations. Treat them like insiders and keep them informed of any campaign developments. You would never want a committee member to learn about a problem with the campaign in the newspaper. Welcome their criticisms. Call your committee members often. Encourage them and support their individual efforts in the campaign. Listen carefully to determine when they might need additional help. Be clear about their tasks, expectations, and time commitment.

Take time choosing the right number of people for a campaign committee. I have worked on county-wide campaigns with four committee members (including the candidate), which was too few, and city-wide campaigns with twelve members, which was too many. I have found that six or seven committee members for a city with a population of up to 20,000 is perfect. In county-wide campaigns a successful committee also might include members from each city who oversee teams within their respective cities.

You want only enough committee members to cover the pertinent campaign activities. Keep in mind that not all campaign activities occur at the same time, so it is often possible to have more than one task assigned to a single committee member. For example, the campaign brochure is written and printed at the beginning of the campaign, whereas the demands on the canvassing coordinator are greatest at the end of the campaign. Fund-raising responsibilities and clerical worker coordination, however, are both ongoing and should *not* be the responsibility of one person.

Once the campaign starts, I meet with my committee each week for one hour. For city-wide campaigns where people are not traveling great distances, I like to do this in the evening after 8:00 or 8:30 P.M., after children have been taken care of and the day's work is done. Up to a point, the later you meet the better. Why? Because people are ready for their day to be done, so they arrive on time and get right down to work. Few people function well after 10:00 P.M., so by 9:30 you're ready to call it quits. Never let a meeting go beyond one hour unless it is the first meeting and you're setting up the campaign. If this is the case, allow additional time by starting the meeting earlier or move the first meeting to a different time; for example, a morning retreat followed by lunch where the campaign becomes official. For county-wide campaigns, it works well for the committee to meet in a central location at the end of the work day before dinner.

Your committee may quickly break down into specialized campaign functions. Once specialized groups are formed, keep track of their progress by getting reports back each week. When the committee meets, I want meetings to be productive and people to feel time is well spent. I always have an agenda on an easel or in front of me and will sometimes have a task for the committee members to do while we are covering the agenda (for instance, brochures can be

> "The time to win a fight is before it starts."
> —Frederick W. Lewis

folded or envelopes stuffed). It is important that all meetings begin and end on time.

Besides the weekly meeting for the full committee, it is necessary to get together occasionally with individuals responsible for specific campaign tasks. Sometimes, for example, I will meet with my ad person to hammer out two or three ads. I will then bring these to the regular committee meeting to have them critiqued.

Other than the treasurer, the makeup of your committee is optional, and you must decide how many people will be needed to plan and supervise the campaign. You will depend on those you invite to join your campaign committee, so they each should be capable of organizing and directing some particular aspect of the campaign. In addition to a treasurer, your committee may include a campaign manager and one or more people to oversee letters-to-the-editor, canvassing, clerical work, brochures, the media, lawn signs, phone banks, fund-raising, getting out the vote, and your volunteer workers.

The Treasurer

Campaign treasurer is almost always a volunteer position. Selecting the right person is one of the most important things you will do. The name of your treasurer will appear on every campaign publication. He or she will be called from time to time by the press, or even the opposition, and asked questions. Like a vice-president in a presidential election, the treasurer should balance the ticket. For example, if you are a retired senior, get a prominent, involved young person of the opposite sex. If you are a young progressive man and relatively new to your community, consider an older conservative woman who has been in town a number of years. Find a person who complements rather than merely repeats your strengths. If you're a Democrat, find a respected Republican. Ideally, if you are working for more taxes for schools, get someone who is conservative and who may have sometimes spoken against tax increases.

If possible, find someone willing not only to represent the campaign and discharge the official duties of treasurer, but to perform other tasks as well. For example, I try to get someone who will handle all the treasurer's responsibilities and oversee the thank-you notes for contributions.

The treasurer is usually responsible for obtaining and completing the registration forms required for participation in an election. The necessary forms can be obtained from the city recorder's office for city races, from the county clerk's office for county races, and from the Election Division under the Secretary of State for state legislative races. Don't be afraid to use these offices. The people who staff government offices are often extremely helpful and accommodating.

> "If you want something done, ask a busy person."
> —Benjamin Franklin

Not all the forms and information in the election packet are necessary or applicable to every race or election. Ask the clerk's or recorder's office what exactly you need to read, what is required, and when it is required. Ask either the clerk or the recorder to direct you to the pertinent dates for filing your campaign contributions and expenditures. While the filing of these reports is the principal job of the treasurer, it is a good idea for both the candidate and the campaign manager to be aware of them. These tasks can be placed on your campaign flowchart or calendar as a reminder. (See Chapter 13 for more information on flowcharts.)

> "Making the simple complicated is commonplace; making the complicated simple, awesomely simple, that's creativity."
> —Charles Mingus

Contributions and Expenditures

Your treasurer should be a stickler for detail. The opposition will be examining your Contributions and Expenditures (C&E) filings for mistakes to report to the state elections office. If a mistake is found, it is bound to make the paper. That sort of damage is preventable.

Following the filing of the C&E forms, local papers generally do a story on who spent how much on what. If you are running a modest campaign and your opposition is funded by outside money, make sure your committee points that out to the media. Running a visibly hard-working campaign with modest funds gives people the sense that you are fiscally responsible. That trait is desirable in office, and people will make the connection.

While it is difficult to work on a campaign when the opposition has unlimited funds, this fact can also work in your favor. In a small community election with no television involved, there is just so much ad space to buy in the newspaper, just so much direct mail that can be sent to homes, without voters realizing that the election is being bought. In one campaign I ran, we were outspent nearly five to one by the opposition, and we publicized this spending discrepancy to our advantage. When the newspapers ran the usual C&E article, many in the community were stunned by the amount of money coming in from outside interests. Because we had a pretty good idea of how much the opposition was spending, we were ready when the press called for our reaction. Supporters wrote and sent letters-to-the-editor for those who missed the newspaper articles when they first appeared.

In that particular race, the opposition was convinced that the accounting in our campaign was wrong and sent people to the recorder's office on a regular basis to check our C&Es. This is where having a meticulous treasurer paid off. Finally, convinced of foul play, the opposition called the paper and suggested there must be something amiss. When the press called me, I explained that we were in fact spending a normal amount of money for a small-town race and that it was the opposition whose expenses were excessive. We got another great newspaper story.

Committee to Support

Given the importance of a good treasurer, what do you do if you can't find the right one for you? Not to worry. You have two options. First, you can place a short list (six to nine) of carefully selected supporters at the bottom of all your literature and ads. This "Committee to Support" should represent a good cross-section of the community. Although some of these people might be working on your campaign, this is not your work crew. The primary job of this group is to give your cause credibility by lending it their names. Depending on the issue, the committee may include people in business, environmental groups, real estate, labor, and so forth.

Using a Committee to Support works well if you have broad support up front, but not at all if your support is marginal. I once worked on a campaign that was so controversial that I could get only three people to sign the Committee to Support list. Rather than have such a short list, which didn't cover the political spectrum of the city, I dropped the notion of listing the committee. In fact, it was valuable to find out about the level of controversy early in the campaign. It made us work that much harder.

Let me caution you here: When you are working on a very controversial campaign and have a listed Committee to Support at the bottom of all your literature, you face the risk that community members who do not embrace the initiative or measure will get to one or more of those who are listed and undermine their support for you. The newspapers may also call these people and grill them on the cause. This can get a little dicey. I find it best to use a Committee to Support for relatively unknown candidates or difficult yet uncontroversial initiatives or measures.

Another option you have if the right treasurer cannot be found is to simply press on. Continue to look for someone who is thorough, honest, easy to work with, trustworthy, and committed to your cause or candidate. Ask friends and associates to suggest people who work with numbers to support you. Talk to an accountant or the person who prepares your taxes. Certified public accountants have good community credibility, and they may be willing to provide report preparation on a pro bono basis.

> "Putting a bunch of people to work on the same problem doesn't make them a team."
> —Gerald M. Weinberg (*The Psychology of Computer Programming*)

The Campaign Manager

Of all the tasks in a campaign, the most demanding is that of the campaign manager. Where other jobs have finite responsibilities and time commitments, the job of campaign manager is open ended. It is a lot to ask of anyone, especially on a volunteer basis. For this reason it is usually the first and sometimes the only position to be paid.

"Even the highest towers begin from the ground."
—Chinese saying

A campaign manager will interact with your volunteers more than any other person in the campaign, so good communication skills are a must, especially phone skills. The duties of the campaign manager vary greatly depending on the number of individuals working in the inner circle. In general, he or she will do such things as attend coffees, debates, and events with the candidate and set up sign-in sheets while lending moral support. The campaign manager also *must* give candid feedback to the candidate without being too blunt.

If you are running a county-wide partisan election campaign, a manager is critical. You will need someone to oversee it all and to be a source of support for the candidate. If your campaign is to pass a local ballot measure, you can serve as the campaign manager with the help of this handbook. If you are running for office in a small city, you probably don't need a manager. However, without one you will need capable people to head up various campaign tasks such as lawn signs, canvassing, and letters-to-the-editor. The most effective campaign teams I have employed have been volunteer teams I supervised myself.

Potential Sources for Campaign Managers

I highly recommend teachers as campaign managers. They are smart, organized, articulate, and personable. They are able to speak to large groups of people and ask for things in simple, understandable ways. They tend to know computers, have a nice collection of presentable clothes, work hard, and are generally politically savvy. They are also likely to be available all summer. If you choose wisely, a teacher who is a campaign manager will force you to get everything ready during the summer so that your fall campaign goes much easier. The drawback of using a teacher is that he or she may be overwhelmed with school responsibilities in the fall and not be available to the campaign.

Other potential sources for campaign managers or workers are fund-raisers or development directors for local charities, private schools, or nonprofit organizations. These people might consider short-term work for a candidate, and they will have a proven track record. Other leads: people who have worked on other political campaigns, for a United Way campaign, or for a Heart/Lung Association fund drive; those who have organized local parades, 4-H fair shows, music concerts, or county fairs; and individuals who have served as development chairs on local boards.

I have always structured my own election campaigns so that my manager and I run the campaign together. This setup makes it a lot easier to ask someone to take on this huge responsibility. In general, a good campaign manager is hard working, organized, intelligent, self-confident, and loyal. And, because appearance is important, this person should reflect the values and style of the candidate or campaign.

Maintaining Control

Recently, I was a campaign advisor in a campaign where the campaign manager became a problem. He was parking illegally on city-owned land and then hassling the police with a "do-you-know-who-I'm-working-for" attitude. To make matters worse, volunteers were complaining to the candidate that the campaign manager was being unnecessarily rude. The candidate was at the end of his rope and called me to help find a way to let this volunteer go.

Although a candidate obviously does not need this kind of stress in a campaign, firing a volunteer who wants to work on a campaign can cause more headaches than it cures. So short of firing the manager, what can the candidate do?

First, the candidate always has the option of reorganizing the campaign so that the manager has less involvement and responsibility. Second, the candidate could deal with the campaign manager and the situation in a clear and straightforward manner. He or she could kindly explain that the manager's actions were being interpreted negatively by others and that they were reflecting badly on the campaign and the candidate. Because campaign managers are so closely affiliated with the candidate, there is an assumption that their activities are both known and endorsed by the candidate. A problem situation like this must get immediate attention. While campaigns are a way for the community to see how a candidate will perform both publicly and under pressure, they are also an opportunity for the candidate to get some experience dealing with awkward situations and people. Once in office, these things materialize all the time.

> "We've run into a couple of problems, but nothing minor."
> —Brenda Collier

The Campaign Chair or Co-chairs

When working on an issue-based campaign, the messenger is the message. Who heads it up is therefore critical to the success of the campaign. You have a choice to use either one or two people, serving as either one campaign chair or as co-chairs. These people should be noncontroversial leaders in your community. This person (or couple) may serve in name only as a figurehead or as the campaign co-coordinator. Most times, other than at the speakers' bureau, these people become the face of the campaign. They meet the media, meet with the campaign committee on a weekly basis, and work the endorsement circles of the community: the Rotary Club, the chamber of commerce, business leaders, and more. They gain power and stature when they seemingly have nothing to gain personally by the passage of the measure. So avoid using someone as a campaign chair who has a vested interest in the outcome of a campaign, such as a county commissioner for a county tax base.

> "Loyalty is more important than experience."
> —Bill Meulemans

Choose your co-chairs carefully. They should be people who are well respected within the community, and they should have established relationships with other prominent local leaders. You will depend upon these existing relationships to establish your ballot measure, raise money, and activate volunteers.

Well-selected, hard-working chairs can win a difficult campaign for you. I like to have co-chairs and prefer they be a man and a woman. If it is a county measure, I will look for someone who is respected and involved in the urban community and for another person who is involved in the unincorporated area. Selection of your chair or co-chairs is completely dependent on the ballot measure. For example, if the measure is for school taxation that augments revenues for extracurricular activities, bring in two individuals who have different interests and involvement in the schools. One might be a big supporter of sports and the other of foreign languages. A nice touch here might be someone who has been outspoken in the past against school funding measures coupled with someone who has been very involved in supporting school programs.

I have worked on ballot measures with co-chairs and no chairs. Each alternative has its strengths and weaknesses. If you cannot get someone you feel would be the right chair or co-chairs, don't use anyone, but be sure you have top people to respond to the press and who are willing to debate the opposition.

Finding Volunteers

Finding and directing volunteers is almost the same for each campaign task. Although the tasks vary considerably, only a small modification is necessary to organize your volunteer force for each specialized campaign activity.

Regardless of the activity, as with your campaign committee, there are a number of important things to remember about using volunteers:

1. Don't waste the volunteers' time. Have everything laid out and ready to go the moment they walk in the door. Begin

and end on time. Do not encourage late arrivals by delaying the start of the meeting.

2. Be prepared with anything the volunteers might need. If the task is to stuff envelopes, make sure there are enough stamps, sponges, pens, staples, and other necessities.

3. Call the volunteers ahead of time and let them know what they need to bring, for example, extra staplers, clipboards, good walking shoes, a truck.

4. Be clear about tasks, expectations, and time commitments. Give clear written instructions and deadlines.

5. Pick the right people for the job. Don't ask out-of-shape people to canvass hillsides; don't ask counterculture people to canvass conservative areas.

6. Keep your volunteers informed; support them. When you call, let them know how the campaign is going. Be sensitive to their schedules.

7. Treat your volunteers as you would highly paid employees.

Some people tend to value volunteer time less because it is free. This is a serious mistake. When you are disorganized and waste your volunteers' time, they are bound to feel frustration and irritation. If this problem happens more than once, they may not be back. Even if it happens only once, you could lose your best people and have trouble getting the support you need. To prevent such problems, assemble a clerical team to help set up other tasks. For example, a clerical team could staple lawn signs in preparation for the lawn sign team who will be putting them up or look up phone numbers before phone bankers arrive. This is actually more important than you might realize; different types of people agree to perform different types of jobs, and looking up phone numbers and phoning are very different tasks. This pre-planning is vital to volunteer success.

Matching Volunteers to Skills

Although a small campaign can be run without volunteers, it would be a mistake to do so. When people work for you, they have an investment they want to see pay off. Volunteering in campaigns is also a terrific part of the political system because it gets people interested and involved in government. There is one caution, however. If workers tell you they do not want to do a particular activity or that they are not good at something, believe them.

"Nothing is particularly hard, if you divide it into small jobs." —Henry Ford

I once placed a woman on the phones who told me she didn't like to phone. I found it hard to believe that anyone would have trouble talking on the phone; I was also desperate for callers. What a mistake. She was painfully uncomfortable calling people she didn't know and projected a poor image of the campaign. I couldn't take her off once I saw my error because that would have called further attention to the problem, making her more uncomfortable. I left her on the phone for about one-half hour and then told her that I had finished my work and asked if she would mind if we shared her phone. She gratefully gave it up. Similarly, if someone says he or she hates to canvass, believe it. It is better for the campaign to have people doing tasks they enjoy.

It is possible to place people who are unwilling to call or canvass. Some who say they do not like to work phones actually do not like to make "cold calls"; that is, they do not like to call people who may be opposed to the candidate or measure. Quite often, these same people are willing to make calls if they are calling voters who have already been identified as supporters, as in a get-out-the-vote effort. Similarly with canvassers: Some do not like to canvass because they dislike knocking on doors and talking to residents. However, these same people may be willing to do a literature drop or a door hanger where no knocking is involved.

I try to supervise my volunteers to make sure I do not bring back poor workers a second time. For example, if while I am supervising a phone bank I see people struggling, I simply note it on their 3 by 5 inch volunteer worker cards and pull the color circle that indicates "phone volunteer" (see Chapter 3, "The Volunteer Organization"). That way I will not call those persons again to work the phones, and everyone will be much happier. Similarly, if I discover workers who are great at a task like phoning, I try to keep them away from other campaign activities to avoid burning them out because I hope to use them again in tasks at which they excel.

The same kind of supervision is necessary for each volunteer activity. For example, if a canvasser returns without notes for lawn signs, no impressions of voter attitudes, and a partially covered area, I know I have a volunteer who isn't particularly good at knocking and talking. I remove the canvassing color code from his or her 3 by 5 inch card, make a note about why, and move that person over to something like lawn sign placement and maintenance. You never want your volunteers to have a bad time if you can avoid it. You want to keep people working for you in election after election.

Potential Volunteer Sources

If you're involved in politics, you have to be able to find people who, for whatever reason, are willing to help you. Finding volunteers can be a lot of work. Remember, however, that the only people you can be absolutely certain will not help you are those you do not ask. You should approach the following:

- Your family, friends, and business associates
- Women's rights groups
- Former candidates, office holders, and their volunteers
- Local service groups
- Labor unions
- Teachers or school associations
- Any special interest groups dealing, for example, with the environment, human services, hunting, or fishing

In nearly every election there is an issue so controversial that people you would not normally count on will decide to vote for you based solely on a position either you or your opposition holds. These issues are called "ticket splitters" because they pull people away from their normal voting pattern. Such an issue will motivate a voter to work or vote *against* a candidate rather than *for* a candidate.

In general, ticket splitters can translate into both volunteers and money for your campaign. Following is a list of some groups that are more inclined than most to let a single issue influence their votes:

- Veterans
- Sportsmen, fly fishermen, hunters
- River guides
- Environmentalists
- Timber, logging advocates
- Clean air advocates
- Pro-choice, anti-choice supporters
- Fire fighters
- Bicyclists
- Land use advocates
- Seniors
- Tax and anti-tax groups
- Gay rights activists
- Anti–gay rights activists
- Public union employees
- Identifiable work groups such as teachers and fire fighters.

> "Nonpolitical issues are the most political."
> —Bill Meulemans

Volunteer Sign-up Sheet

In addition to finding volunteers in the groups listed above, you can use the form in figure 1.1 for sign-ups at coffee meetings and debates once the campaign is under way. (A full-sized form for photocopying is included in Appendix 1.) The information gathered on the sign-up sheets is then transferred to the 3 by 5 inch volunteer card described in Chapter 2. Using a volunteer/donation card is another way to get people to sign on to work for a campaign (see figure 1.2).

VOLUNTEER SIGN-UP SHEET | *I would like to volunteer for the following (please check all that apply):*

Name (please print)	Home Phone	Canvass neighborhoods	Phone Banks	Lawn Sign Location (address)	Donation	Letter to the Editor	Endor. ad?

FIGURE 1.1   Example of Volunteer Sign-up Sheet

Last Name   First Name   Mailing Address

Phone: Daytime   Evening   City   Zip   Precinct #
                                                                     (if known)

I would like to volunteer a total of   ❑ 2 Hours   ❑ 5 Hours   ❑ 10 Hours
                                        ❑ 20 Hours   of work on the campaign
I will (Please check any boxes that apply:)
    ❑ Canvass door-to-door   ❑ Help process mailings   ❑ Install lawn signs
    ❑ Display a lawn sign   ❑ Work in a telephone bank
    ❑ Host a gathering of neighbors for Jeff to meet
I am enclosing a check (payable to **Support Jeff Golden**) for:
    ❑ $25   ❑ $50   ❑ $100   ❑ $500   ❑ Other $_____
            (Up to $50 per individual and $100 per couple is 100% tax refundable)
            ❑ *Suggestions? Comments? Please use the back of this card*
            Authorized by The Committee to Support Jeff Golden, 710 Cardley, Medford, OR 97504

FIGURE 1.2   Sample 3 by 5 Inch Donation Card

2

The Campaign Brochure

In this chapter
Campaign Theme and Message Development
Polling
Brochure Development
Pictures
Campaign Slogans
Logo
Layout

Campaign Theme and Message Development

Before you sit down to write a brochure, you must first develop a campaign theme and message. While political strategists use the words "theme" and "message" in different ways, sometimes interchangeably, for our purposes here, a "theme" covers the overarching issues that capture the spirit of the campaign, whereas a "message" is a single idea used to bring that theme to the voters.

By way of example, if you're working on a campaign to fund extracurricular activities for your school district that were eliminated because of budget cuts, your *theme* will likely include the individual programs to be reinstated, such as debate, sports, residency outdoor school (a camping trip designed to build community within school and faculty), and business clubs. Your *message* will center around the idea that it is no longer enough for students to have a 4.0 GPA if they want to get into a good college or land a better job; they must also be involved in after-school activities. Briefly, your message is "opportunity."

In the presidential campaign of 1994, Bill Clinton's theme included environmental protection, lower crime rates, education, and universal health care, among other things. Each of the issues of the overall campaign theme was conveyed to the American people through the message "It's the economy." For example: We need to

> "Leaders are people who step forward, who influence thinking and action. They emerge to meet the needs."
> —William Gore

protect our environment to ensure better jobs in the future; we need to provide better education to our children if we want a workforce that can compete in the world market; providing opportunities for everyone to get a college education means keeping America competitive; affordable health care allows a family to get ahead; high crime is destroying our communities and marginalizing business. Everything comes back to the message "It's the economy."

In Clinton's 1996 campaign, the message was "It's the little issues," or more concisely, "hope." Again the theme was similar to the 1994 campaign, but with the U.S. economy booming, Clinton's team changed the campaign focus and personalized it, something that was very effective and rarely done on a federal level. In that campaign, education translated into college IRAs, computers in the classrooms, and a million volunteers to ensure that every American child could read by the third grade. The environment became gifts to our grandchildren and places to recreate with our kids in the summer. Combating crime became distributing 50,000 cell phones to neighborhood crime watch groups. Health care became welfare reform and allowing new mothers to stay longer than twenty-four hours in the hospital. Clinton's assumption was that while people care about world peace, worry about the global economy, and dislike political repression in foreign lands, it is really the small issues that they feel are real. By delivering seemingly simple solutions to community and family issues, Clinton presented a clear message of hope.

Your message is how you communicate your theme to the public. It's a story you tell over and over, a story you can tell in a few seconds: "It's the economy"; "This is about opportunity"; "It's the small issues"; "It's hope." A well-crafted message moves the debate away from which candidate can be trusted in a general sense to whom the voters trust to do the job. A theme and message articulate that the candidate knows *what* job needs to be done. Voters will naturally make the connection that the candidate who knows what needs to be done will be the candidate more likely to do it.

In an issue-based campaign, a message should tell the voters *why* the job needs to be done. The message should reach them on an emotional level: hope, opportunity, safety, service, preserving our past, planning for the inevitable.

To create a theme and message your campaign team must assess the strengths and weaknesses of your candidate or ballot measure. Ask, and answer, who will vote for your candidate or ballot measure over your opposition and why. You must also look for the fatal flaws of your candidate or measure. The campaign message and theme will develop from this process and will become the foundation for your slogan, ads, and media responses. Once you have a message, do not get off it, and don't let your opponents pull you off.

> "Leaders can conceive and articulate goals that lift people out of their petty preoccupations and carry them above the conflicts that tear a society apart."
> —John W. Gardner

By taking apart your candidate or issue and listing the strengths and weaknesses, your campaign team is better able to shape the theme of the campaign and communicate that theme through your message. For example, if you are a woman who is energetic, feisty, and steadfast, this can translate into pluses and minuses. The pluses are that you're a fighter, have integrity, are honest, and will fight for your community. The minuses are that you could be perceived as pushy, shrill, dogmatic, or a single-issue candidate.

The charge of the campaign committee is to frame the negative into a positive, so that "pushy" becomes persistent or steadfast. Dogmatism becomes strength, which goes with honesty and integrity. All of this is communicated through your message, which must flow from who the candidate is. For example, if your community is being overrun by developers and the quality of life is being compromised by the inherent impact of growth, you couple your message of thoughtful, planned growth with your strengths of honesty, integrity, fighting for the community, and persistence. Again, your message is planned, thoughtful growth. Every question you answer comes back to this message, all under the umbrella of your theme.

Through this process you identify issues that create a relationship between your campaign and the voters. This process will also get you workers. For example, let's say your candidate has worked hard for clean air issues. That knowledge helps you establish a relationship between the County Clean Air Coalition and your candidate. As another example, people in a particular neighborhood are concerned about development, so your campaign issue includes creating a park in close proximity to their homes. You use this program to create a relationship and to get you workers within that neighborhood. This concept is important in direct mail, ads, brochure development, speaking engagements, debates, and campaign endorsements and is discussed further in later sections and chapters. Establish these relationships early, and when the time comes, they will help with volunteers and early money.

Very simply, you want a majority to see your side as right and the other side as wrong. This is the time to assess the strengths and weaknesses of your opponent, if you have one, or the opposition, if your campaign is about an issue. The brochure is basic to your campaign. You will walk it door to door, mail it to households, and hand it out at debates. People who receive it must get the message of your campaign; it will state in subtle and not so subtle ways why people should vote for your campaign cause. The brochure should also imply why they should *not* support your opponent. Obviously you will be giving your brochure to people inclined to vote for you or your measure, and the message of the campaign will reflect that voter propensity.

"I use not only all the brains I have, but all I can borrow."
—Woodrow Wilson

Polling

Benchmark Polls

> "Public sentiment is everything. With public sentiment, nothing can fail. Without it, nothing can succeed."
> —Abraham Lincoln

Conducting a benchmark poll may be the most efficient and accurate way to determine voter concerns prior to developing your message. While it is important to have elected officials who lead their constituency from a set of core values, as Rosalynn Carter said, "It is difficult to lead people where they do not want to go." Having a clear reading of voter concerns will help your campaign develop and direct a message where it will be best heard. Generally, a benchmark poll is done in advance of a campaign and can be invaluable in developing a campaign strategy, theme, and message.

While it is important to remember that a poll may help a candidate focus on issues important to the community, it can also be used for the opposite reason; that is, to know when to keep quiet and which issues to avoid.

I highly recommend hiring a professional to help here. However, if you have absolutely no money, a benchmark poll can be run by volunteers and with the help of a college professor who knows or teaches polling. Depending on the length of the poll, each caller can complete four to eight calls per hour. To obtain a list of registered voters, contact your county clerk and buy a random list of registered voters. The clerk's office will sell you a printout with the number of voters needed to achieve a 5 percent margin of error. In my county, approximately 25 to 30 percent of the list provided by the clerk's office already has phone numbers listed. Unless your list comes with all the phone numbers, be sure to set up a clerical team to complete this task. Do not expect your callers to look up phone numbers on top of polling.

Because polls must be either professionally conducted or supervised, they tend to be expensive. There are some ways to cut costs. First, offer to include other candidates in the poll if their campaigns will contribute to the cost. Second, some firms will come down in price if you provide the workers for the poll. Be aware that, depending on the length of your poll, this may be an enormous undertaking. However, because it can be done long before your kick-off, it is often possible to do a benchmark poll without adding too much extra stress to a campaign.

A benchmark poll can tell you

- What issues are important to the voter, by gender, age, and party affiliation
- The education, age, and gender of those supporting you or your opposition
- The income level of those supporting you

- Your name recognition, the recognition of your opponent, and whether that recognition is favorable or not
- The length of time those being polled have lived in your community
- Whom the voter would support if the campaign were held tomorrow
- What the voter does for a living
- If the voter intends to vote, is likely to vote, or is unlikely to vote

Be Creative

A lot of free information is available for the campaign that knows where to look. Many small communities conduct citizen surveys as a way to track resident concerns and assess job performance of city employees. This is part of the public record and available for the asking. You may also get similar information, minus job performance of the governing body, by going to a chamber of commerce.

Labor unions, women's rights organizations, environmental groups, and other such organizations may have recently conducted polls to track voter support of a particular issue, especially if that issue has been or soon will be placed before the voters. Within each of these groups, polls will break down support according to region, city, and sometimes even precinct.

Don't forget about the U.S. Census. Although the Census is conducted only once every ten years, it can be an effective way to track trends within your community, region, or state. For example, are the numbers of renters or homeowners increasing? What is happening to the population? Is it getting older, younger, better educated, richer, poorer?

Tracking Polls

Once a campaign is under way, tracking polls can be very useful to monitor candidate or issue support. Tracking polls are generally brief, cover only one or two questions, and are most helpful when conducted on a regular basis throughout the campaign. However, if you are running a small campaign on a low budget with an overextended volunteer base, a tracking poll may be out of the question.

An alternative would be to piggyback on a tracking poll being conducted for another candidate. This might cost your campaign a little money, but it would be far cheaper than if you were to go it alone. Often, when someone is running for state office, where partisan politics plays a more significant role than in local, nonpartisan

> "I've got to follow them; I am their leader."
> —Alexandre Ledru-Rollin

elections, political parties will conduct tracking polls for their candidates. Also, labor unions, teachers' associations, and political action committees (PACs) might be willing to conduct tracking polls for a candidate or issue their organization has endorsed.

> "When two people agree all the time, one of them is unnecessary."
> —William Wrigley

A tracking poll can be especially helpful in fine-tuning a campaign in a close election and shaping the spin to either increase your support or erode that of your opposition. For example, in the final days of a campaign you find that support by women is shifting away from your candidate. You may then go back to your benchmark poll and, using a high priority issue for women, generate ads or direct mail to win back this support.

A tracking poll may be used to

- Track candidate or issue support
- Fine-tune a campaign message
- Tell you if a particular campaign event or ad has left you or your opponent vulnerable
- Determine if negative campaigning on either your part or that of your opponent is helping or hurting (This is generally tracked in a quick response poll following an ad.)
- Indicate who is still undecided

Know the Law

Some states consider polls conducted by other affiliations on behalf of a candidate or issue to be a campaign expense and in-kind income. If so, know the law and account for this service on your Contributions and Expenditures form.

Brochure Development

While the campaign committee will help to develop the campaign message and theme, I usually have only one or two people work with me or the candidate on writing the brochure. Obviously you want a good writer who has a couple of free days. The writing takes only a few hours, followed by many rewrites. These rewrites will often go before the committee to check message and theme, and before I go to the printer my committee always reviews the final draft.

If you write your own campaign brochure, you must have someone read it critically when you finish writing it. The emphasis here is on *critically*. We all love our own words, and our friends are often loath to condemn them. You need someone you can trust, who has the political savvy to read your work, correct errors, and make suggestions.

Pictures

Prior to laying out a brochure, I visit a photographer. I have always been fortunate to work with local professionals willing to contribute to my campaigns with their talents. I have tried using friends with above-average equipment, but nothing compares to professional work. Amateurish photos hurt your campaign. If a professional will not volunteer his or her time, this is a good place to spend money. If the first sitting does not produce the right photo, be willing to invest in a second shoot. I also give a photo to the local papers (usually different shots but from the same sitting) so they will use my photo rather than one generated by their news team. After I'm elected, I continue this practice.

When you are campaigning for ballot measures, photos are much easier to come by. For example, if you are working on a school tax base, visit the yearbook class at the high school. They save photographs of all age groups, in all activities. If you need photos for a park program, try the YMCA. For historic photos of your city or county, try a local historian or historical society. Most photographers will let you use their photos if you credit them with bylines.

I use pictures as a way to break up the text and give the brochure a "feel." Most brochures for candidates contain at least a picture of the candidate. This is important to increase recognition. With that recognition comes familiarity, which is important psychologically for the voter. The candidate begins to feel like a friend and a celebrity all at once. You may also carefully select other photos to create an image of who this person is. There may be pictures of the candidate at work, with the family, at play (for example, at a softball game or fly fishing), with seniors, at a preschool or a public school, at a hospital, or at a park. Include whatever might both positively connect the candidate with his or her lifestyle and characterize what is important in the community.

If the brochure is about a measure, such as a school levy, show what will be accomplished with the passage of this measure through pictures as well as text.

Depending on your budget and the size of your brochure, you may just use the picture of the candidate. But if you use other pictures, be sure they add to or underscore the story you have selected for the text. Put thought into your selection of pictures. Try to show the diversity of your community in the photos: people of all ages and color, working class and professionals, men and women. If you are doing more than a studio shot of the candidate, be sure the candidate brings extra clothes. Brochures that show a candidate at a school, senior center, park, or with family are ostensibly intended to show the individual in his or her everyday life over a period of time.

> "Imagination is more important than knowledge."
> —Albert Einstein

If the candidate is wearing the same thing in each shot, it looks contrived and you miss an opportunity to create the feel you want.

Campaign Slogans

Years ago, slogans were printed next to a candidate's name on the ballot. At that time, with media playing a lesser role in politics, having a catchy slogan was critical for a win on election day. Slogans can still be very effective. However, they require a great deal of thought by the campaign committee. Do not invent a slogan just to have one. Know your campaign message and design a slogan that underscores and reinforces it. Sit with your committee, list the strengths of your candidate or measure, and brainstorm on a slogan. Once you think you have one, brainstorm on all the ways it could be used against you or hurt your cause. Work at this process until you come up with the right combination of words.

The slogan is a simple statement about why you should be elected or why the voters should vote for your measure. It should also imply why *not* to vote for your opponent or what a "no" vote may lead to in an issue-based campaign. Your slogan must not depart from your campaign message and should evoke a gut emotion. One very effective slogan used in an environmental race simply said, "Share the Water." Who can argue with the idea of sharing? It is a friendly thought and is encouraged throughout our lives. It also implies that the water is not being shared presently or may not be in the future.

I was on a campaign that used the slogan "Now Let's Choose Leadership." I was concerned that this slogan would sound patronizing. I was further concerned that those who had voted for the incumbent in previous elections would feel we were belittling them for past votes. It was especially problematic given that many misinterpreted our candidate's quiet nature as aloof and arrogant. This slogan tended to reinforce that perception.

Another problematic slogan was used by a Democrat running against a second-term incumbent for the Second Congressional District in Oregon. Since the district was formed nearly two decades ago, only Republicans—three to be exact—have been elected, and in overwhelming numbers. However, the incumbent had committed many campaign violations and was misbehaving both in public and in the House of Representatives in such a way that it looked as though this Democrat might walk into the spot.

The Democrat called on me and some other local politicos to talk strategy in our part of the district, and he also took that opportunity to share his brochure with us. Although it was a handsome brochure, it featured a poorly conceived slogan: "It's time we had a Congressman we can be proud of." While I understood that the brochure referenced the incumbent, who was in core meltdown, it overlooked the fact that for more than ten years, Second District Oregonians had voted in huge numbers for a congressman that they *were* proud of. You can't hope to attract voters to your side of the street by insulting them.

For a local restaurant tax to fund a wastewater treatment plant and open space program, our opposition used the slogan "Don't Swallow the Meals Tax" (see figure 2.1). I thought this was a really clever slogan and still do. It worked because it hit us on so many levels. People who swallow something are duped, and of course the tax was on food.

In one open space campaign, we used the slogan "Parks, Now and Forever." People who opposed the measure saw ours and used the slogan "Parks: Pay Now and Forever." This was a very clever counter-slogan; we should have chosen ours more carefully.

In the mid-1990s a group of Oregonians put together an initiative to overturn a previously voter-approved ballot measure allowing physician-assisted suicide. The new initiative was well financed, with billboards and lawn signs everywhere. In the upper right-hand corner of the signs was the previous measure's number (29) in a circle with a line through it. Next to that was the slogan "Fatally Flawed" and below the slogan was "Yes on 66."

This was clearly a professional, well-funded campaign with a very ambiguous slogan. Basically, it was stating that the previously passed ballot initiative (Measure 29) was "fatally flawed" (physician-assisted suicide) and that a "yes" vote on *this* measure would overturn that one. However, the way the sign was laid out, it appeared that Measure 66, not 29, was "fatally flawed."

During the campaign, when I was called by a local organizer to help defeat this initiative, I explained that all the campaign needed to do was adopt the same slogan: "Fatally Flawed." In that way every "Yes on 66" lawn sign, billboard, and commercial would become "No on 66." The voters will naturally associate a negative slogan with a negative vote. Whether they took my advice or came to it themselves, the "No on 66" campaign co-opted the same slogan as the "Yes on 66" campaign and with very little money it was defeated at the polls.

As a general rule, you don't want a negative slogan or idea associated with a "yes" vote (for example, "A Clearcut Solution" for a campaign measure to stop clear-cuts on privately held forest lands). It is preferable to have a negative slogan, such as the meals tax example given above, associated with a "no" vote and a positive slogan ("Share the Water") associated with a "yes" vote on a ballot measure or proposition (see, for example, figure 2.2). In the previous example, the "Yes on 66" campaign was expecting too much of the voter.

"Leaders have a significant role in creating the state of mind that is society."
—John W. Gardner

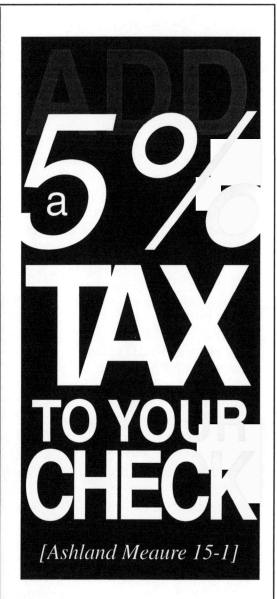

DON'T
SWALLOW
THE MEALS
TAX

[VOTE NO 15-1]

Measure 15-1, Ashland's proposed meals tax,
is a regressive tax because:

15-1 IS NOT A TOURIST TAX. THE BURDEN OF THE TAX
WILL BE PAID BY YOU, THE ASHLAND CONSUMER.

FOOD IS A BASIC NECESSITY. THIS TAX WILL SE-
VERELY IMPACT STUDENTS, THE ELDERLY, THE POOR,
AND OTHERS ON A FIXED INCOME.

IT IS NOT A LUXURY TAX. BECAUSE OF TODAY'S BUSY
SCHEDULES, AN AVERAGE OF 48c OF EVERY FOOD
DOLLAR IS SPENT ON PREPARED MEALS OUTSIDE THE
HOME.

IT WILL AUTHORIZE INCREASES UP TO 5% WITHOUT
FURTHER VOTE FROM THE PUBLIC.

IT IS CONFUSING, DIFFICULT TO MANAGE, AND COSTLY
TO IMPLEMENT.

IT IS SHORTSIGHTED. IF THE STATE LEGISLATURE
IMPOSES A STATEWIDE SALES TAX IT COULD NEGATE
ANY LOCAL SALES TAXES.

IT WILL PUT ASHLAND ON THE MAP AS THE ONLY CITY
IN AMERICA TO IMPOSE A MEALS TAX WITHOUT FIRST
HAVING AN OVERALL SALES TAX IN PLACE.

ADD
a 5%
TAX
TO YOUR
CHECK

[Ashland Meaure 15-1]

BROCHURE DESIGN BY ERIC BRADFORD WARREN

FIGURE 2.1 Don't Swallow the Meals Tax Brochure. Brochure layout: two-panel, front and back. Note that the front and top back of the brochure are visually striking, but the lower, dense, reversed type is hard to read. Also note that this brochure went to press with a typo on the front panel. Avoid this by having a number of people proofread the text.

YES ON 53 & 54

Parks
now and forever

On May 15, 1990, we'll be voting on a proposal to preserve 730 acres of parkland for the future. The plan reflects months of suggestions expressed in many public hearings and neighborhood meetings by a variety of concerned citizens.

1. WHY SHOULD WE CARE?

Ashland's special beauty lies in its setting, its use of open space and its pedestrian lifestyle. To preserve this beauty for our children, we must set aside area for parks and open space now.

2. HOW MUCH WILL IT COST ME?

Beyond extremely small indirect costs, the plan will cost each household $6 per year in the form of a .50 per month surcharge on utility bills.

Paid for by the People for Parks Committee, Fred Binnewies, Treasurer, PO Box 1, Ashland, OR 97520

FIGURE 2.2   Parks Brochure. Example of three panel brochure layout. The inside might include a map of the proposed area or text and pictures. With this particular design, the essential information is on the front panel. For those who look further, more in-depth information can be included throughout. If you choose, the front two questions can be changed for little additional printing cost. This way, your campaign can deliver specialized brochures to targeted precincts.

During my first run for mayor, I used the slogan "Building a Better Community." I chose this slogan because of city-wide concerns regarding growth and development. I wanted a positive slogan that suggested to people the subtle message that more was not necessarily better and that it was a community that needed to be built. In my second run I did not have a slogan because I was reusing some of my old lawn sign stock and my new signs were "busy" with graphics. The second sign did not need to say anything as the picture was the slogan.

Following are examples of slogans I have pulled from brochures in my files, some good, some bad. Using a slogan is optional, and it is better to omit it than have a bad one.

"The best . . . for the best"
"For Change, For Choice, For Us"
"A voice that will be heard"
"We all win with [name]"
"A leader for [name of the place]"
"A concerned candidate for all of [place]"
"Leadership in Action: [name]"
"A Strong Voice for [place]"
"With his experience . . . It makes sense"
"Vote for the Future . . . vote for [name]"
"[Name] is in touch . . . "
"Because nothing counts like results"
"Straightforward, Fair, Effective"
"Tough, committed, fighting for us"
"A New Voice! New Energy!"
"For a Change!"
"It's time to rotate the crops."
"A leader who makes a difference."
"At a time when experience and dedication are needed most."
"Taking care of [Place]."
"Experience money can't buy."
"This is about governing . . . and I've done it."
"People over politics."
"The Change Will do us Good."

In the past, when the economy was struggling and local government was simpler, voters seemed to place little value on experience. Consequently, candidates did not underscore experience in slogans. However, that no longer seems to be true. The days of "vote out all incumbents" are gone (at least for now). With government more complicated, no matter what the size of a city or county, people want leaders who have experience and will spend (and manage) their tax dollars wisely.

Logo

I regularly use the lawn sign image as the logo on my brochures and ads. I think it adds continuity to a campaign, conveying a subtle message that it is well organized and well thought out. If your race is a difficult one, such as a write-in, a logo can be more important. I cover the write-in candidate at the end of this chapter.

Layout

The layout of a brochure depends on how it is to be printed. Unless you know the business, you will need the help of a layout artist or graphic designer.

A good way to get ideas on layout is to go over past political campaign brochures. Often you can find the look you want and then copy that look. Some examples of different types of brochures are shown in figures 2.1 through 2.5, but your best resource will be the politically experienced graphic designer or layout artist.

Although many experienced campaigners believe brochure copy should be kept to a minimum, I worry about offending the astute voter with an empty brochure. I usually have quite a bit of information in my brochures and assume that if people do not want to read it, they don't have to. However, the text should be broken up with pictures and graphics. Unappealing brochures will be read by no one, even the most sophisticated voter. There are a number of ways to get your messages out within your brochure, such as a letter from the candidate, testimonials, or pictures, and it is best to bullet information items. Brochures are advertisements, so they must catch the eye. Once you have caught the attention of voters, they might appreciate a little more information.

Brochures can be done easily on a tight budget. A brochure may be laid out three-up on a single piece of paper. This way each piece will yield three brochures. With the cost of paper this is an incredible savings. Although each sheet of paper must be cut in thirds, cutting costs are less than the folding costs. Pictures add very little to the cost, and the visual relief is quite effective. Use them. I have even used card stock for this type of brochure. By using card stock, you have the advantage of being able to shove the brochure into doorjambs.

> "Genius is 1% inspiration and 99% perspiration."
> —Thomas Alva Edison

Obviously, the size of your brochure is in part determined by the size of the paper you use. Go to a print shop and check out colors and sizes. In a few campaigns on which I've worked, we used legal-sized paper folded in half. This size lends itself well to easy layout and visual impact.

As the size increases, paper costs may also increase; however, the layout gets easier. Decide both how much you need to say and how much you can afford to say. When the content and layout of the campaign brochure are mocked up, be sure to run it by your campaign committee for final approval.

Recently, I have been using 14 by 8 1/2 inch paper for a bi-fold or single-fold brochure. I have included examples of two bi-fold brochures that were used for money measures: one for a new county tax base (see figure 2.3) and the other for extracurricular programs for the Ashland schools (see figure 2.4). Each has examples of what to avoid in a brochure.

Although the county tax base brochure is pretty solid and the layout strong, there are a couple of problems that should have been corrected. First, the pictures are too small in relation to the text inside the brochure. A greater effort should have been made to reduce the text and tell the story more through the pictures. Second, the front of the brochure features two pictures (also too small) that should have been selected more carefully. While they're intended to show that government has changed (dramatically) since approval of the last tax base, they actually tell another story. The historic photo evokes more emotion and reflects back to a simpler, less chaotic time. The current photo, of an ugly new building, suggests that we would be better off not encouraging that kind of architecture with our tax dollars. While there was an opportunity to tell a story on the front of this brochure with the two pictures, and one was indeed told, the story was not that of supporting the county tax base.

Another example of a bi-fold 14 by 8 1/2 inch brochure was one we used for the Children's Cultural and Recreational Two-Year Levy (figure 2.4). It is probably the worst brochure I have ever been associated with and breaks just about every rule I outline in this chapter. In our defense, it was a complicated proposal that had to be presented to the voters—from beginning to end—in less than three weeks. It also did not help that the campaign committee had only two members with any campaign experience.

One year later, we came back to the voters with the Recreational Serial Levy again and used a single-fold 14 by 8 1/2 inch brochure (figure 2.5). Look at the difference between the two. In each we asked for the same amount of money and sold the same thing: opportunity. But the way the message was delivered in the single-fold brochure is both clearer and more compelling. Ironically, the second brochure doesn't provide as much information to the voters about *where* the money would be spent. This is great information to

1916
Jackson County had fewer than 25,000 residents when voters approved the tax base to pay for the services they wanted. Although a time of economic uncertainty, citizens agreed that the need was clear for an adequately funded county government.

Then. Sheriff patrol car in front of the County Courthouse, Jacksonville. (SOHS 863)

The County has changed in 80 years... but its funding hasn't.

1996
With 164,000 residents and population growing by 2,000 people a year, our county no longer can stretch its 1916 tax base to make today's ends meet. Years of serious cost-cutting, consolidation, and reduced services simply haven't been enough to keep pace with demand. After 80 years, it's time now to do something.

Now. Today's law enforcement needs require the County Sheriff to maintain a modern, well-equipped fleet of vehicles.

Inside are six _more_ good reasons to vote YES for the County tax base...

Our libraries.

Jackson County Library Services is more than books on shelves. It's a versatile gateway to a global network of resources affecting thousands of lives.

You'll find printed, digital, audio, and video information on how to find a job, repair a car, build a house, use a computer, cook a meal, write a book. Our County libraries provide modern reference materials to keep your business competitive, help your kids complete a school project, enable you to research a disease, or learn a new skill. There are more than 350,000 items to choose from in a county-wide system—the second-busiest in Oregon—all conveniently organized in a computerized catalog and available through any one of 15 community branches.

Our libraries serve everyone and anyone who needs the latest information or just a good book for a rainy afternoon. Supported entirely through county taxes, its current serial tax levy expires this June.

Authorized and paid for by Jackson '96, Tom Wilcox CPA, Treasurer, 1017 N. Riverside, Medford, OR 97501

Our health.

When one person falls ill, the entire community suffers. And pays. Studies prove every dollar spent on preventative community health care saves $15 in the cost of later care. Immunizations. Well-baby clinics. Mental health clinics. Crisis and suicide intervention. Counseling. All provided through our Jackson County Public Health agencies and partners.

The County ensures we have clean drinking water. County inspectors check restaurants for safe food and good hygiene. The County makes sure our pets are safe from rabies. The County keeps our air breathable by regulating woodsmoke emissions.

One way or another, we all depend on vital public health services provided through Jackson County. Many of them are paid for by federal timber dollars that are going away. The proposed tax base will stabilize public health funding at a level we all can live with.

(Printed on recycled paper.

Jackson
victims
operation
ticers
police d
Jacks
venile
your
comm
cour
depu
awar
kids
assist
tions
enfor

Jac
bation
titution program that makes young offenders pay back their victims with earned cash.

These and many similar County law enforcement services touch and protect every resident's life and property, no matter whether they live in or outside of a city. The proposed tax base replaces the current law enforcement serial tax levy.

dated into 13 to save on administration costs.

It's been a juggling act to keep parks open, but we may not be able to keep it up much longer. Without the stability of an updated tax base, our wonderful park system faces more cuts, closures, and consolidation.

household financial management for anyone who wants to participate. Rural residents get advice on how to best use their land.

It's a partnership that pays dividends to all of us. But unless there is financial stability for the county's share of this package, state and federal partners will pull out.

JACKSON '96
OUR FUTURE. OUR RESPONSIBILITY.
VOTE COUNTY.

It's a bargain.

How do you calculate the worth of a counselor who works with first-time juvenile offenders and their families to avoid a future of more serious trouble? How do you measure the value of clean water, safe streets, or help for families in crisis? Aren't they worth keeping?

As a community, we depend on these and other Jackson County services. And we owe it to ourselves to keep them vital. Because, in the final analysis, they're a real bargain.

These services can remain available to us for the price of a movie ticket—about $7, which is the average monthly increase in property tax proposed in the updated Jackson County tax base. Just 74¢ per $1,000 of assessed property value buys a stable future for basic health, safety, and social services we—and our children and neighbors and co-workers—depend on. No matter how you figure it, it's a bargain. For today and for our future. Vote County. Vote YES on Measure 15-42. It's worth it.

FIGURE 2.3 The County Has Changed Brochure. Example of a bi-fold brochure on 14 by 8 1/2 inch paper. Larger pictures with less text would make a better presentation.

Questions & Answers

WHAT IS THE CHILDREN'S CULTURAL & RECREATIONAL TAX LEVY –15.3?
The city charter allows the Parks & Recreation Department to propose a two year serial levy that would fund recreational and cultural activities usually provided by the school district. If approved by the voters, the city would collect the money and contract with the school district to provide the activities. The two year levy will restore funds to the Ashland School District budget to accomplish the return of some of the programs now designated for cuts. This is designed to provide interim financing only.

IF THE LEVY PASSES, WILL MY PROPERTY TAXES GO UP?
No. They will still continue downward, as mandated by Measure 5, but just not as much. Each of the next two years, they will drop by $1.53 per thousand, instead of $2.50 per thousand.

WHY HASN'T THE SCHOOL DISTRICT PLANNED AHEAD AND SET ASIDE FUNDS IN ANTICIPATION OF THESE CUTS?
The school district made the decision to use all monies available to continue the very programs we are now wanting to fund with the tax levy.

WILL THE LEVY SOLVE ALL OF OUR FUNDING PROBLEMS FOR THE SCHOOLS?
No. With a 2.9 million dollar shortfall this $800,000 is truly a temporary measure to bring back or keep in place a portion of the essentials, until the state comes up with replacement revenue that would make up the lost funding for the school district.

WHY ARE WE DOING THIS? ISN'T THE STATE SUPPOSED TO HANDLE IT?
The state failed to resolve the school funding crisis brought on by Measure 5. Ashlanders said, "Let's raise our own money and keep it in Ashland so we can save these programs and also regain some local control."

FUNNELING MONEY FOR EDUCATION THROUGH CITY GOVERNMENT SOUNDS UNUSUAL — IS THIS LEGAL?
Yes. Legislative Counsel has researched and confirmed it.

Questions & Answers

HOW WERE THE PROGRAMS TO BE REINSTATED SELECTED?
The list represents the best ideas of the whole community. It was developed by parents of Ashland students, the school board, the city Parks and Recreation Commission, the Booster Club, Ashland Community Coalition, city government officials and the Ashland Schools Foundation. The list was endorsed by school principals.

YOU HEAR A LOT ABOUT "GETTING BACK TO BASICS" AND "CUTTING FRILLS" IN EDUCATION — ISN'T THIS FUNDING DROP A GOOD STEP IN THAT DIRECTION?
No. We are trying to keep the basics: this levy directly protects co-curricular activities that public schools throughout the United States have offered for most of the 20th century; just check your own high school yearbook.

WILL CITY RESIDENTS END UP FOOTING THE BILL FOR THE 20% OF ASHLAND STUDENTS WHO LIVE IN THE COUNTY?
County students will have to pay to participate in these "co-curricular" programs.

WHY DOES IT SEEM LIKE SO MUCH IS GOING TO THE HIGH SCHOOL AND NOT MIDDLE OR ELEMENTARY SCHOOLS?
Remember this is a stop gap measure. If the students now attending high school do not have these programs, we jeopardize their opportunities for college entrance or securing skilled labor jobs. Hopefully, as funding becomes available, many of our excellent elementary and middle school programs will be reinstated.

WHAT HAPPENS IF THE PROPOSED STATE SALES TAX FOR SCHOOLS DOES PASS THIS FALL?
It will not be in time to save the cut programs for the 1993/94, 1994/95 school years. If broader funding sources become adequate again to fund the programs, this levy can be eliminated.

Authorized by United Ashland Committee. Linda and Chuck Butler, Treasurers. P.O. Box 1145, Ashland, OR 97520.

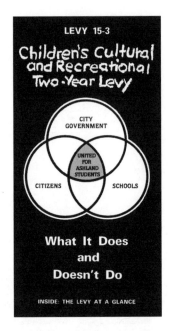

LEVY 15-3

Children's Cultural and Recreational Two-Year Levy

CITY GOVERNMENT

UNITED FOR ASHLAND STUDENTS

CITIZENS   SCHOOLS

What It Does and Doesn't Do

INSIDE: THE LEVY AT A GLANCE

RECREATIONAL AND CULTURAL PROGRAMS AFFECTED BY LEVY	WHAT LEVY DIRECTLY PAYS FOR	PROGRAMS BROUGHT BACK BECAUSE OF MONEY FREED UP BY LEVY	PROGRAMS CUT IF LEVY FAILS	PROGRAMS PARTIALLY FUNDED IF LEVY FAILS	NON SCHOOL RELATED PROGRAMS NEEDED TO COMPLY WITH STATE LAW	AFFECTS HIGH SCHOOL	AFFECTS MIDDLE SCHOOL	AFFECTS ELEMENTARY SCHOOLS	NUMBER OF STUDENTS AFFECTED
RESIDENT OUTDOOR SCHOOL (ROS)	•		•			•	•		280
LIBRARIES (½ of Budgeted Amount)	•			•		•	•	•	3,431
CO-CURRICULUM:									
SPEECH & DEBATE	•		•			•			
DECA (Marketing)	•		•			•			
FBLA (Business)	•		•			•			
VICA (Industrial)	•		•			•			400
YEARBOOK	•			•		•	•		
NEWSPAPER	•			•		•	•		
DRAMA	•		•			•	•		
K-12 MUSIC PERFORMANCES	•		•						
ORCHESTRA						•	•	•	
BANDS						•	•		700
CHOIR						•	•		
ATHLETICS:									
SOCCER	•		•			•			
CROSS-COUNTRY	•		•			•			
FOOTBALL	•			•		•	•		
VOLLEYBALL	•			•		•	•		
SWIMMING	•		•			•			
WRESTLING	•					•	•		
BASKETBALL	•			•		•	•		650
GOLF	•		•			•			
TRACK	•			•		•	•		
SOFTBALL	•			•		•			
BASEBALL	•			•		•			
TENNIS	•			•		•			
INTRAMURALS	•		•					•	
STUDENT AT RISK PROGRAMS:									
SUBSTANCE ABUSE COUNSELOR		•	•			•	•	•	
CHILD DEVELOPMENT SPECIALIST		•	•					•	860
YOUTH AT RISK SERVICES		•		•		•	•		
FOREIGN LANGUAGE	•			•		•			670
TEEN CENTER	N/A	N/A	N/A	N/A	•				
COMMUNITY CENTER ACTIVITIES	N/A	N/A	N/A	N/A	•				

FIGURE 2.4   Brochure of Children's Cultural and Recreational Two-Year Levy. Example of a bifold brochure. Although this was a very complicated serial levy presented to the Ashland voters, we made matters worse with this brochure. The levy was intended to bring back extracurricular activities eliminated by a state-wide property tax limitation measure. Our idea was to let people know exactly what it would bring back. It was too much information, presented too sterilely.

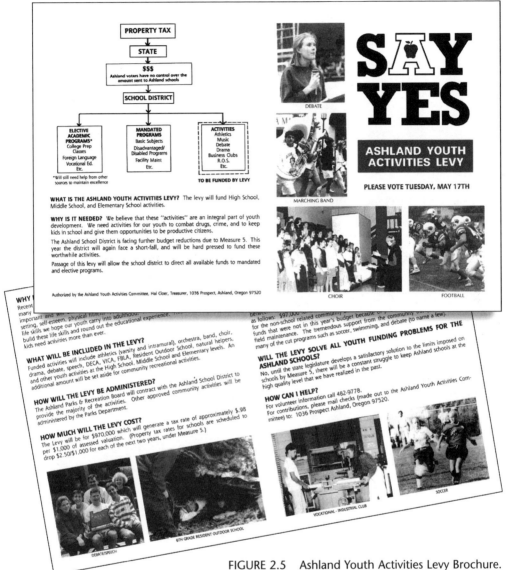

FIGURE 2.5 Ashland Youth Activities Levy Brochure. Example of a single-fold brochure also on 14 by 8 1/2 inch paper. This brochure has an open layout, uses pictures well, and clearly relays the message: opportunity.

have. In general, voters don't want to be a curriculum committee for the school district at the ballot box. Their preference is to know generally where the money would be spent (bricks versus programs), with technical decisions made through the elected school board, school administration, and a citizens' budget committee.

All things being equal, which levy would you be more inclined to support? Ashland voters agreed.

The Volunteer Organization

In this chapter
Methodology
Phone Banks
Scripts and Caller Responses
Clerical Workers
Time Allotments for Volunteer Tasks

No matter where you find your volunteers, you have to organize them and direct their efforts toward activities that will win you the election. Keeping track of your volunteers and assigning them responsibilities requires some sort of organized system. Although the following system can be adapted to a computer, the process I have set up here does not require one.

The methodology as presented in each of these activities really works. If you use it as outlined, you will almost never have no-shows. More to the point, you will be able to utilize your volunteers better and run a more effective campaign. Running an effective campaign means you have done all you can to organize it as efficiently as possible. If you do that, win or lose, you, your committee, and your volunteers can feel very good about what you have accomplished.

Methodology

Make a 3 by 5 inch card for everyone contacted by the campaign. (See figure 3.1.) Make a card even if it turns out that the person contacted does not support your candidate or cause. There had to be a reason the person was contacted in the first place, and after hundreds of calls, you'll forget and waste time by calling again. Keep the 3 by 5 inch cards you fill out for each person contacted together in one box, regardless of what that person says he or she is willing to do. Each 3 by 5 inch contact card is set up exactly the same.

It is important to keep track of donations because some states require additional information about donors (such as occupation and

> "These things are good in little measure and evil in large: yeast, salt and hesitation."
> —The Talmud

address) for anyone giving more than a certain amount of money. As a way to access workers who have volunteered for a specific task quickly, fold colored circle stickers over the top of each card, working from the upper right-hand corner toward the left. Place the sticker so that it looks like a half-circle on each side. You should be able to see the coding from the top of your index card box. You may also just color in half circles with marking pens, but this means that you will have to generate a new card if it turns out people can't do an activity they are coded for.

The color coding indicates which campaign activities, such as lawn sign placement, phone, canvass, or clerical work, the volunteer will work on. Be aware, however, that using more than four color codes can be a bit much on a 3 by 5 inch card. For my campaigns, I use a green circle for lawn sign help, blue for phones, red for canvass, and yellow for clerical. Feel free to alter the color scheme to fit your campaign. The color coding is a quick way to access who can do what because the colors are visible from the top of your index box and the cards can be easily pulled or flipped through to get names and phone numbers. This way you do not have to read each and every card to see what an individual is willing to do for the campaign. You will also be less inclined to sort according to activity, thus misplacing or scrambling cards. You will mark a card for every person the campaign contacts but will use color coding only for those who indicate they will work for the campaign. Therefore, there will be some cards in your box without color coding.

The "Notes" section on each card is important and helpful. This is where you can remind yourself of what volunteers have told you. If, for example, you have someone who is coded to canvass but cannot do it until October, that information should be noted on the card. Special needs or skills relevant to assigned activities are noted here as well (for example, "Won't canvass hills," "Don't call early A.M.," "Don't call after 8:00 P.M.," "Horrible on phones" "Has three staple guns"). I also use the Notes section if someone has been rude. I do not want to call that person back (or have a volunteer call), and the team needs to know why. After hundreds of phone calls you will not remember who said what if you don't have an accessible written record. Whatever the comments, the color coding remains the same. Figure 3.1 is an example of a contact card.

Organize Volunteer Activities

Once information is on the 3 by 5 inch cards, you're ready to set up volunteer activities. The following process works for activities such as phone banks, clerical work, money collection, canvassing, and lawn

Last Name, First Name	canvass (red)	lawn signs (green)	phone (blue)	clerical (yellow)

Occupation

$: Donation Amount & Dates (Receipt?)	Phone Home:
Partner's Name (Cross-reference if different)	Work: Fax:

Address _____

_____

_____

Notes _____

_____

_____

FIGURE 3.1   Example of 3 by 5 Inch Contact Card

		Activity: Canvass 10/14		
NAME	PHONE #	CB?	9:30AM–12:00	2:30–5:00PM

FIGURE 3.2   Example of 5 by 8 Inch Canvass Activity Card

sign placement or maintenance. To organize a campaign activity, use 5 by 8 inch ruled index cards set up as shown in figure 3.2.

Once the 5 by 8 inch cards have been prepared, proceed as follows:

1. Pull the names and phone numbers from the appropriate 3 by 5 inch index cards and transfer this information onto the 5 by 8 inch cards. (The 3 by 5 inch cards should never get far from their box.)
2. Have a list of alternative dates prepared so that you only have to call your potential volunteer once. If you are calling for an ongoing activity such as canvassing, have four or five dates and times. If one date doesn't work, another will. If none works, indicate that fact on your 3 by 5 inch card. The name you have called should remain on your 5 by 8 inch card with a line through it, to remind you that you called and the person could not do it. If you do not do this, believe me, you will forget and call again.
3. Call back every volunteer a couple of days before the activity is scheduled to begin. Record that call in the "CB?" column on the 5 by 8 inch card. My preference is to talk to my worker, so I leave messages only as a last resort. I never call to ask my workers if they are still going to canvass. Of course they are; they told me they would. I don't even call to remind them of the canvass. If they are very organized, they will resent the call. I call and remind my canvassers to bring a clipboard or ask if they mind doing hills or check to make sure that I gave them the correct meeting place or the correct time. Whatever it is, it's my fault or my screw-up, and I'm just checking to make sure I gave the information correctly. If they have forgotten, this reminds them. If they accidentally made other plans, this is my opportunity to reschedule. Potential no-shows, discovered by a phone call, are incredibly easy to reschedule.

Applying the Methodology

Every campaign consists of basic campaign activities, such as

- Running phone banks
- Canvassing the voters
- Developing a campaign brochure
- Designing ads or other media
- Organizing clerical support (including thank-you notes)
- Putting up lawn signs
- Raising money

Each of the these activities is volunteer intensive. You can apply the general techniques described above to find and keep track of volunteers. However, each activity requires specific techniques. This methodology will be applied throughout this handbook to organize each of the activities.

Phone Banks

Phone banks can be used throughout a campaign and are the most efficient way to retrieve information in a short period of time. They can be used to get a head count for a fund-raiser, to get lawn sign locations, to raise money, and to acquire more volunteers for the campaign. If you plan to do a get-out-the-vote effort on election day, you will have to identify (ID) voters who intend to vote for your candidate or cause. This can be done while canvassing, but it is easier and far more efficient to do it by phone.

When you are ready to organize a phone session, use the following procedure, which includes the steps followed above.

The 5 by 8 Inch Card Set-up

1. Go to the 3 by 5 inch card box and pull the names and numbers of phone bankers. It can be helpful if a friend calls from a separate list, such as The League of Women Voters, but check the lists you are calling so people are not called twice. Make sure someone will follow through on calling from home.
2. List the potential volunteer on your 5 by 8 inch card below the headings, as shown in figure 3.3. If you have more than one date and time available, you will have better luck placing the volunteer with a single call.
3. Sign people up for a particular date or time as you call them. If they cannot work, cross them out so you can still see their names. This way you will not forget and call again. Finally, remember to call them back one or two days prior to the phone bank. Put a check mark in your "CB?" column after you call.

> "Let us endeavor so to live that when we come to die even the undertaker will be sorry."
> —Mark Twain

The Volunteer Set-up

1. Assure people that they will be trained to work on the phone before actually doing so.
2. Assign a phone banker to work for only one hour and fifteen minutes (fifteen minutes for training and then one hour on the phone). Almost anyone will give up an hour or so for a

Activity: **PHONE BANK**						
[IF YOU HAVE MORE THAN ONE DATE, YOU CAN ADJUST AS FOLLOWS]						
NAME	PHONE #	CB?	(FIRST DATE)		(SECOND DATE)	
			1st Hour	2nd Hour	1st Hour	2nd Hour

FIGURE 3.3   Example of Phone Bank Activity Card

campaign he or she believes in, and if it turns out that the volunteer is bad on the phone, an hour is plenty. If I am desperate or conducting fast, really important calls, like a GOTV effort, I will put seasoned callers on the phone for up to two hours. Often, if the caller has worked for me at some time in the past, he or she will let me know if the full two hours will be too much. I then have others scheduled to replace individuals coming off the phones early.

3. Have two to three shifts each night. Individuals must arrive fifteen minutes before their shift for training. No one likes to go on the phone cold, so people rarely miss training when it's offered and expected.

4. Have volunteers begin to call after a fifteen-minute training session. The first twenty to thirty minutes that volunteers are on the phone, I circulate and answer questions. I do not get on the phone myself, especially in the first twenty minutes of a shift.

5. Have the next shift arrive fifteen minutes early for training, forty-five minutes into the hour of the previous shift's calls. This way, exactly one hour after the first shift starts, they get a tap on the shoulder from someone on the next shift, and they are off the phones.

6. Never tell people that you want them for a specific amount of time, then push them to stay longer. You will lose them as volunteers. When you ask someone to work for you, you have made a verbal contract for a specific job and a specific amount of time. Don't nudge.

7. Do a role play with your volunteers: Have one volunteer pretend to call another.

8. Do not expect your phone bank people to look up phone numbers. Use a clerical team of volunteers to do that ahead of time.

9. Always have prepared scripts in case a phoner needs one; however, the caller who ad libs will do best.

Phone Bank Training

The following is an example of what you might prepare for your volunteers who are phoning for the campaign.

Thank you for your help. The last days of a campaign are often called the longest because volunteers and candidates put in double duty to produce a win. Soon we will all be able to rest, but right now your work is critical in winning these two very important and very close elections.

Your job is to help us get-out-the-vote (GOTV). Each name you will be calling has been identified as a supporter of Judy Uherbelau.

At this point we do not want you to leave messages on answering machines. We will do that as the phone banks progress and the election draws nearer.

Should anyone you reach have a question about either Judy Uherbelau or Cate Hartzell, please refer them to the campaign offices:
  Judy Uherbelau   555–0000
  Cate Hartzell   555–0000

For those of you calling from the Absentee Voter List, please remind voters that they can turn in their ballots at any polling place in Jackson County up to 8 P.M. on election night (November 3).

I have included here a small instruction sheet for a Cate Hartzell write-in. Should the voter have any questions about the procedure for a write-in candidate, please refer to it.

Following is a sample script; feel free to adapt it or make your own.

> "Make no little plans; they have no magic to stir men's blood ... Make big plans, aim high in hope and work."
> —Daniel H. Burnham

"Hello, is *[the name of the ID'd voter]* there?

"Hi, I'm a volunteer helping to get out the vote for Judy Uherbelau and Cate Hartzell. I just want to remind you that Tuesday is election day and stress how important your vote is for both Judy and Cate to win. Polls indicate this will be a *very* close election.

"You know Cate Hartzell will not appear on your ballot. Do you have any questions about how to do a write-in vote for her?" *(Please refer to your card for the three-step instructions if they have any questions.)*

"Thanks for your support. Your vote will make all the difference for Judy and Cate."

"There is as
much greatness
of mind in ac-
knowledging a
good turn, as in
doing it."
—Seneca

Provide polling places for reference so the callers can answer voters' questions about where to vote; for example:

Precinct 1	Lincoln School, 320 Beach Street
Precinct 2	Ashland Community Center, 59 Winburn Way
Precinct 4	Briscoe School, 265 North Main Street
Precinct 6	Helman School, 705 Helman Street
Precinct 9	Ashland Sr. High School
Precinct 10	SOU, Student Union
Precinct 11	Ashland Middle School
Precinct 12,13,19	Bellview Grange, 1050 Tolman Creek Road

I use the following standard key list for callers to record responses:

B = busy
M = message machine (do not leave a message—we will on Monday eve.)
WV = will vote

Another example of what to tell callers is in Box 3.1.

What you ask for will vary according to the phone bank. For example, you could be calling for lawn sign locations, money, volunteer workers, a head count for an event, or voter ID (that is, the process of finding out if a voter supports your campaign or not). Think about your mission and prepare a short introduction for the caller. Sample scripts are included later in this chapter.

Phone Bank Locations

It can be difficult locating enough phones to run an effective phone session. I have found that realtors' offices work best because they usually have five or more lines in the same room. People love to have company when calling. I have also used law offices, although

Before You Pick Up the Phone—

1. *Be proud of what you are doing.* You are working for a cause you believe in. You are on the front line of a campaign.

2. *Think about what has motivated you to give up your time to work for the candidate or ballot measure.* People will ask how a candidate stands on a particular issue. While you cannot speak directly to that, you can share why *you* are working for this individual (or cause).

3. *Identify yourself only as a volunteer working for the campaign.* In general, you want the candidate's name to make it into the consciousness of the voter, not yours, unless, of course, you know the person.

4. *No matter what else happens, get <u>something</u> from the individual before you get off the phone.* "You can't canvass, ever? How about a lawn sign?" "You have a bad lawn sign location? Do you have a friend who might want one?" "Can we use your name on the endorsement ad?" "Would you make a contribution?" Whatever. You want that person in on the campaign with that single call or to know how he or she will be voting. (This is helpful information for the campaign.)

5. Thank you for taking the time to help in this important cause.

BOX 3.1   Example of Phone Bank Instructions

this is a little more touchy because of confidentiality concerns and the fact that callers can't see each other. Sometimes, campaign headquarters for a bigger race (such as president or governor) will let you use an office. You might also try labor union or insurance offices. Many businesses will support a cause or a candidate and open their doors for phone banks after hours if you simply ask.

Make no assumptions: On one campaign, a realtor who was working for the opposition let us use his phones because we were friends.

Scripts and Caller Responses

Wherever your phone bank is located, the important part of campaign phoning is to have an effective message. You should have scripts made up in advance for each campaign activity. While it is preferable to have people ad lib, they generally need a prepared script for the first couple of calls. It gets much easier after that. I also don't have anyone ask, "How are you doing tonight?" The reality is the volunteer doesn't care, and the person on the other end knows it. When I am calling for money and the calls are a bit longer and more involved, I usually ask the person who answers if he or she has

> "The whole is greater than the sum of its parts."
> —Buckminster Fuller

a moment to talk. However, with volunteer recruitment, the calls are so short that I just cut to the chase. Following are scripts for typical campaign phone sessions:

Lawn Sign Location

"Hello, I'm a volunteer working for the 'Cathy Shaw for Mayor' campaign. We're looking for lawn sign locations tonight. Will you be supporting Cathy in the general election? Great. Could we place a lawn sign? Let me verify your address. Someone will be coming by a month before the election to place it. We also have a crew who will be maintaining these signs; however, if it needs some attention, maybe you could help with it. Great. Thanks." [Hang up.]

Special Activity

"Hello, I'm a volunteer working for the 'Cathy Shaw for Mayor' campaign. Did you receive the invitation for the campaign dinner this Saturday? We are trying to get an idea of the number of supporters who will be attending the dinner for Cathy. The restaurant needs a pretty accurate head count. Will you be joining us?"

Canvassing

"Hello, I'm calling from the 'Cathy Shaw for Mayor' campaign. We're doing a last minute, get-out-the-vote door hanger. We are hoping to canvass the city in two hours and need about eighty-five volunteers to place door hangers at people's homes. There will be no door-knocking, just great exercise. Can you help?"

GOTV for Absentee and Mail-in Ballots

"Hello, I'm a volunteer working for the Judy Uherbelau campaign. We're down here working on phone banks tonight to turn out as many of her supporters as possible. As of a couple of days ago, your ballot had not yet been received at county elections. Is it possible you still have it at home?"

Voter ID

"Hello, I'm a volunteer working for the Judy Uherbelau campaign. As you may know, Judy is the Democratic candidate for state representative. Do you know if you'll be supporting Judy in her re-election bid this November? [yes, no, need more info]

Another . . .

"Hello, I'm a volunteer working for the 'Cathy Shaw for Mayor' campaign. Our notes indicate that you might be willing to canvass for the campaign. Is that correct?" "Great. I have a number of dates for some upcoming canvasses. Do you have your calendar handy?"

Undecided Response

With any of these scripts, if I call and discover that someone is undecided or leaning, I ask whether the individual would like more information from the candidate or campaign committee to help him or her decide. Finally, whatever a potential supporter might say, I ask my volunteers to make a note so that the campaign can follow up if need be.

Negative Response

Make a note for the campaign and get off the phone as quickly as possible.

Clerical Workers

The clerical team is an extremely important part of your campaign. Normally you think of people sitting around, stuffing envelopes, stamping, and labeling. While these tasks might make up the bulk of your clerical team's efforts, you should think of this function in broader terms.

Wherever I can break activities down into more manageable units, I do so. For example, on the day that lawn signs go up, you *cannot* expect your lawn sign team to arrive early in the morning, staple lawn signs, organize lists, and then head out for two hours of stake pounding. In reality each of those functions is very different and should be treated differently.

Your clerical team can come in days ahead of time to staple lawn signs or attach them to the stakes, depending on the type of sign you use. They can come in on still another day to help organize the lists, maps, and locations of where those signs are going.

Your clerical team is crucial in keeping your campaign tight and organized. Use them creatively wherever they can help with your workload or with the organization of an upcoming activity. Following are examples of how the clerical team can be used:

"It's not very difficult to persuade people to do what they already long to do."
—Aldous Huxley

- Staple lawn signs at the corners (if using poly tag)
- Attach lawn signs to stakes (if using corrugated)

- Look up phone numbers for an upcoming phone bank
- Assemble maps for a canvass
- Attach inserts in the brochures for a canvass
- Write thank-you notes for donations, lawn sign locations, or to volunteers
- Stuff, stamp, and address a mailing

To set up a campaign activity requiring clerical workers, proceed as follows:

1. Put "Name," "Phone #," "CB?" and the dates for your clerical work party across the top of lined 5 by 8 inch cards. (Time is much *less* flexible here than in most volunteer activities.) I usually have clerical parties that last two hours. As explained earlier in this chapter, list the clerical workers whose names you have retrieved from your 3 by 5 inch cards under the "Name" column. See the sample card in figure 3.4.
2. Try various groups if you need additional volunteers: senior groups that support you, The League of Women Voters, and your friends and neighbors. Given how much fun a clerical work party can be, it is usually pretty easy to turn out a crowd.
3. Make the clerical work party a social time in campaigns. For me the clerical work party is an opportunity to chat with friends that I sometimes get to spend time with only during a campaign. We share war stories about a canvass or some other topic while having coffee and cookies and doing a mindless task. These meetings are enjoyable and highly productive for the small effort involved.

   It is important for people to be comfortable while working and sitting for two or more hours, so be sure to do it where there is enough table space for each volunteer. Do not do clerical work in an already cluttered house. I also hate working on a soft, overstuffed couch or chair. Because of the age of my clerical workers and the general disintegration of our backs (young and old), I take the time to put together a comfortable work area.
4. Have some snacks around—coffee, tea, cookies, and the like—but not on the table where work is being conducted.
5. Have everything set up. Do not waste your volunteers' time.
6. Do one activity at a time: If the task is getting out a mailing or stapling lawn signs, do just that. When one task is done, usually ahead of schedule, don't bring out one more thing for people to do. Remember, as I said before, you have made a verbal contract with your workers. Once they are captive in

Activity: Clerical Work Party				
[IF YOU HAVE MORE THAN ONE DATE, YOU CAN ADJUST AS FOLLOWS]				
NAME	PHONE #	CB?	(First Date & Time)	(Second Date & Time)

FIGURE 3.4   Example of Clerical Work Party Activity Card

your home, to ask for more work past the designated time or task creates hard feelings. Workers who complete a task early and go home feel good about their participation and feel that they are helping in a well-organized effort.

7. Make sure that you have all the necessary materials at each station so people are not idle. Have extras of everything you need: staplers, sponges, stamps, envelopes, telephone books, rubber bands, or whatever else the task might require.

Time Allotments for Volunteer Tasks

Following are some general guidelines for what volunteers can do in a designated amount of time. The number of people you will need in the space of time you have available depends on the number of calls your campaign needs to make, the number of signs you need to put up, or how many homes you need to canvass.

> "Luck is the crossroads where preparation and opportunity meet."
> —Anonymous

Phone Banks

In general each volunteer can complete fifteen calls per hour. So, for example, if you have 4,000 calls to make by election day and only one phone bank location with six phones, you will need people on all six phones for three hours per night for fifteen nights. Obviously, if you have more phones or another phone bank location, the number of nights on which to call goes down.

For this or any task to be completed by a specific date, work your way backward from that date so that you have enough time to complete the task given your resources and contact goal.

> "The feeble tremble before opinion, the foolish defy it, the wise judge it, the skillful direct it."
> —Jeanne Roland

Canvassing

Because Oregon has vote by mail, our precincts are huge, with some having approximately 1,000 voters, or 400 to 500 homes. In general, precincts usually have about 400 registered voters with 120 to 200 houses. Using voter lists, you can get an accurate number of houses per precinct.

There are two types of canvassing for our purposes: a knock and simply a drop without talking.

Knock. Depending on how hilly and tightly compacted a neighborhood is, canvassers can cover anywhere from ten to fifteen houses per hour. That means that a precinct with 120 to 200 houses would require four canvassers working two to three hours each to cover the distance.

Drop. A literature drop can be done quite a bit faster than a knock canvass. With a drop, again depending on how steep the streets are and the proximity of homes, a canvasser can reach thirty to forty-five homes in one hour.

Clerical Tasks (Direct Mail)

Each volunteer can address about 100 envelopes per hour and stuff and stamp 200 per hour.

Putting Out Lawn Signs

Depending on the distance between homes, it takes approximately one team (a driver and a pounder) to put up twelve lawn signs in an hour, so, if you have 200 lawn signs to place, you will need sixteen people (eight teams) working two hours each.

4
Fund-raising

Your campaign theme and message are critical to a successful fund-raising effort. As indicated previously, the message is developed early so you can attract support from special interest groups promptly. This message and the relationships that develop result in endorsements and money. The endorsements will come from individuals, companies, political action committees, and formal organizations who feel your cause will further their efforts. Early endorsements equals early money equals early media buys.

I also look at early money as a way to communicate with the public. I want to show them that my cause or candidate has the support necessary to pull off a win. Then, throughout the campaign, I use major donors as another type of communication tool. For example, in Oregon, if individuals give more than $50 they must be listed individually, with their profession, on the Contributions and Expenditures form. I look for well-respected people who can carry votes with their name and then ask them to give in the $250 range, or some amount that will get them listed in a prominent way in the local paper. Obviously this amount is different for different races. A $250 contribution may be news for a city councilor or alderman in a small town but would not even register in a large city mayoral race

> "Apart from the ballot box, philanthropy presents the one opportunity the individual has to express his meaningful choice over the direction in which our society will progress."
> —George Kirstein

or congressional district race. Just remember, if you have a big name supporter, look for an amount that will get that name in the paper as a news story. Conversely, if I have a controversial organization or individual contributing a large amount, I will return the donation to avoid the association.

"Too often leaders are soft on issues and hard on people. We need to be hard on issues and soft on people."
—Charles Maclean, Philanthropy Now Consulting

In every campaign I have worked on, individual contributions tend to arrive at the end of the campaign. Supporters see the campaign in the paper and on television and hear it on the radio. They know that this takes money. What they do not know is that media time must be bought weeks and sometimes months in advance of when it will air or go into print. *Early money is critical to a successful campaign.* That is why many people take out personal loans to get a campaign rolling.

☞ Know the law: In some states you may not legally begin collecting money until you have filed with the county clerk, city recorder, or Secretary of State.

Campaign Budget

It is easy to do a cursory budget sheet based on the activities you intend to conduct throughout the campaign; all it takes is a few phone calls.

Figure 4.1 is an actual budget sheet from the last city council race I worked on. We were not given a choice to be in the voter pamphlet, which normally costs $300. This race covered a city of 19,000 people and 8,000 homes. There was no TV advertising in this campaign; however, should you decide to use TV, I discuss ways to save money for production and market penetration in Chapter 10, "Media."

This is a very typical campaign total for a city council or mayoral race in my town, although people have spent as little as $500 and as much as $9,000.

If you're wondering about how much you'll need, consider talking with those who have previously run for your office or another office in a comparable geographic district. Many candidates keep their campaign Contributions and Expenditures forms, and a little time spent with these records might give you an idea of where best to allocate your money. The following sections describe how you might go about determining a budget for each campaign activity.

Brochure

1. Find another brochure with a design and layout you like.
2. Take the brochure you like and either call or visit a graphic designer to get a price quotation for something comparable

SAMPLE CAMPAIGN BUDGET

(Five-week city council race, population 17,000, one newspaper, no TV advertising)

Campaign Activity	Cost
Brochure	
Layout and Design	$ 90.00
Printing (6,000)	$ 500.00
Ads	
Layout and Design	$ 125.00
Newspaper: 3 ads run three times each	
1st ad (2 × 8, 1st run @ $6.25/col. inch)	$ 100.00
1st ad (2nd run within 1 wk.: 25% discount)	$ 75.00
1st ad (3rd run within 1 wk.: 50% disc. + $31.50 to run in TV section)	$ 81.50
2nd ad (2 × 8 run 3× @ $6.25/col. inch)	$ 100.00
2nd ad (2nd run within 1 wk.: 25% discount)	$ 75.00
2nd ad (3rd run within 1 wk.: 50% discount + $31.50 for TV section)	$ 81.50
3rd ad (Endorsement) (3 × 13 @ $6.25/col. inch)	$ 243.75
3rd ad (2nd run within one wk.: 25% discount)	$ 182.81
3rd ad (3rd run within one wk.: 50% discount)	$ 121.87
Request for ad page placement	$ 87.01
Ad Total	$1148.44
Lawn Signs	
Design	$ 85.00
Printing (175 @ $3.10 each)	$ 543.50
Stakes (borrowed 25, purchased 150 @ $20/bundle of 50)	$ 60.00
Hardware	$ 25.97
Voter Lists from County for Absentee, GOTV	$ 25.00
Direct Mail: 1 piece: postcard	
Layout and Design	$ 35.00
Printing	$ 134.46
Postage (handled by mail house)	$ 638.38
Merge Sort Voter Lists from County (Democrats, Independents, Green Party, no absentees, one per household)	$ 26.90
Photocopying, Misc. Office Supplies	$ 60.00
Photo Session	$ 165.00
Total	$3662.65

FIGURE 4.1   Example of a Campaign Budget

that is camera ready. The designer will want to know how many photos you'll be using.

3. Determine which precincts you will target; using voter registration lists for those precincts, calculate how many brochures you'll need to print. Then call a printer or copy store and get a price quotation. Remember, you can always have more done down the road, so don't get carried away.

4. Call a photographer and ask how much a photo shoot will cost.

Lawn Signs

1. Repeat the steps laid out above. However, you must determine the number of signs you will need ahead of when you have them printed. I have worked on campaigns with as many as one lawn sign for every twenty homes and others where we have had as few as one for every sixty homes. It really depends on whether you can get the locations and whether you're running a strictly urban race or an urban/rural mix. Does the race warrant a great number of signs? One way to determine the number of signs you need is, once again, to call someone who ran for an office covering the same geographical area and ask how many signs were put up. While you're on the phone, ask for that person's list of lawn sign locations. Unlike brochures, short runs for signs can be expensive and take too long. So get enough printed the first time. Signs run around $4 to $5 each with stakes and the miscellaneous materials you will need for them.

2. Get the same number of stakes as signs, plus a few more. (Don't forget to call other campaigns to see if there are stakes to be borrowed.)

3. Price hardware, staple guns, and staples and list the cost of each. If you need to use staples and staple guns, be sure to call friends who are in construction and ask if you can borrow their staple guns. Better yet, ask them if they will help to put up the signs and bring the staple gun to use. *Label all borrowed tools.*

4. Buy lists of registered voters from the county if you have no locations, then call those living on arterials for possible locations. Ideally you would get locations from another campaign, but in my first race for mayor that wasn't an option. Volunteers went down the voter registration list cold calling those on arterials, a brutal but very effective technique.

In general, try to think of every little thing you will need to do to pull off a specific activity. After you have listed everything, take an hour or two to call around for some prices.

In a small community a pretty reliable ballpark figure for the amount of money you will need to raise is 50 cents per household in the voting district. If you have strong opposition, you will need more ($1 per household); if you have weak opposition, you'll need less. I am not talking voters in a district; I am talking households. The type and number of media buys will greatly influence this figure, because advertising is just about the only thing that can't be donated. For the same reason, the number of direct mail pieces you send will greatly influence the final budget figures. As population increases you may find some economy of scale and actually need less per household.

Everything you do in a political campaign requires money. While many of the people who work for you will also give you money, the bulk of it will come from those not directly involved as volunteers.

I never apologize or feel that I am begging when I ask for money for a candidate or measure. I assume that the potential contributor wants this person in office (or the benefits of the ballot measure) and is willing to back up that support with money to get the election won. When I ask for money, I think of it as providing an opportunity for the voter to get involved at another level than just at the voting booth. I also look at a request for money as less demanding than a request for an individual's time. How many times has someone called you to volunteer your time, and you thought how much you would prefer to give money instead? The reality is this: If you can find excellent candidates to volunteer their time to be in office implementing programs that you support, more power to them. Do all you can to help get them there.

In the state of Oregon, anyone who contributes to a political campaign may file for a state income tax refund of up to $50. If a husband and wife file a joint tax return, they can get a refund of $100. Sadly, only about 16 percent of citizens take advantage of the refund. The refund tends to level the playing field for grassroots campaigns. If your state has a similar program, find out about it and get this information to your potential donors.

Figure 4.2 is another example of a budget sheet you can use or modify for your purposes. Many local campaigns are too small and underfunded to have a campaign headquarters (other than in your home) or even staff. However, I included a staff section just in case you need it. Feel free to photocopy this page and modify it to fit your budget needs.

> "The highest use of capital is not to make more money, but to make money do more for the betterment of life."
> —Henry Ford

BUDGET FORM

CAMPAIGN ACTIVITY	AMOUNT	CAMPAIGN ACTIVITY	AMOUNT
Brochure		**Billboards or large lawn signs**	
Lay out and design		Rental space	
Photography		Design & lay out	
Printing		Printing	
Advertising		**Staff**	
Ad lay out		CPA or bookkeeping (contract)	
Photography		Attorney (contract)	
(I would run a separate budget sheet for		Campaign Manager, other staff	
print advertising and include the number of		salaries	
ads, the size of ads, and the cost of each		insurance, taxes	
with reductions as to the number of runs.			
Put the total for all here.)		**Television**	
Research		Production	
		Buys	
Direct Mail		*(Use the ad rep of each*	
(Do this for each piece)		*station to set up a schedule and*	
Lay out and design		*budget according to exposure you*	
Printing		*want. Put total here.)*	
Postage			
Lists and labels (or)		**Radio**	
Mail house (they handle labels, postage)		Production	
		Buys	
Polling			
Bench mark poll		**Office Supplies**	
Tracking poll		Postage, pens, software,	
		Telephone, fax	
GOTV		Staples, envelopes, etc.	
Voter ID lists			
Absentee lists		**Headquarters**	
		Rent, phones etc. (list it all)	
Lawn Signs			
Design & lay out		**Volunteer support**	
Printing		food, refreshments	
		staples, envelopes, etc.	
Misc. Printing			
Bumper stickers		**Fund-raising expenses**	
Flyers		Invitations, lay out, printing	
Body badges for volunteers		Postage	
Letterhead, envelopes		Decorations	
		Prizes	

FIGURE 4.2   Sample Budget Form

Direct Mail for Money

While direct mail can help create a relationship between your campaign and the voter, it is also an opportunity to raise money where those relationships are already established. Given that efficient direct mailing requires a mailing list of some already identifiable group of voters, I prefer to see which lists I can get and then formulate a letter or piece that will appeal to those voters. Remember, *your direct mail is only as good as the list to which it is sent.* Carefully match your appeal to people you are targeting.

In a direct mail piece, you might include a targeted letter, a campaign brochure, and a remittance envelope. Direct mail can be used simply to align your candidate with an issue such as a concern for jobs where unemployment is high, parks and playgrounds where there are none, or anti-growth in a neighborhood where a big development is planned. Be sure to color code your remittance envelopes with your direct mail pieces, so you know who is responding to what. That way you get some feedback on which letters were most effective, along with the money. I color code my envelopes by running a marking pen along the edges of a stack of envelopes.

Direct Mail Tips for Success

Opinions vary about how long a direct mail piece should be, the kind of paper it should be on, and what it should look like. While I have used direct mail to move voters toward a candidate or issue, I have used it far more for fund-raising. Following is a list of things I discovered when soliciting with direct mail. While they may be true in my area, some may not be applicable in yours.

1. You should use quality paper stock and printing. Keep graphics and fonts simple and clean. One candidate I worked for wanted a rolled look to his letterhead. It was to start dark at the top and get more faint as it reached the bottom of his name. The result looked like something went wrong with the printing job and we had to discard thousands of sheets of letterhead.
2. People in lower economic groups and those with less education respond in greater numbers to a longer "the house is on fire" solicitation. This group in general gives less money and votes less, so be sure you have targeted correctly before spending lots of money on a multi-page solicitation.
3. Wealthy, well-educated Republicans respond to letters that are no longer than three pages containing lots of "this is

> "I have only made this letter rather long because I have not had time to make it short."
> —Pascal, 1656

what I've done, this is what I will do" information. A single page will work fine for them.

4. Well-educated, affluent Democrats respond in greatest numbers to short, single-page letters explaining what community needs you will address and how their contributions will make a difference.

5. You should only solicit targeted lists (see below). Most people using direct mail to raise money will send to prospect lists (sometimes thousands of voters) to generate a "house list" from those who respond. The first mailing loses money and subsequent mailings to the house list make money. This works well for big campaigns, but local campaigns often cannot send to enough people to generate a large enough house list to make money on subsequent mailings.

6. If you have no targeted lists, spend the money and mail to as big a class of voters as possible to make money on subsequent mailings. For example, mail to every one in your political party.

7. Once people respond to the first mailing, solicit them again. For those responding the second time, solicit them again. After three letters, go back to your house list.

8. A direct mail piece followed up by a phone call from the campaign càn substantively increase your response rate.

9. Always include a remittance envelope and a P.S. The P.S. should not be a throw-away. This is often the only thing that is read in a fund-raising letter, so make it count. You may also want to include a donation card (see figure 1.2) to generate money and workers.

10. You should personalize the letter and envelope, if at all possible. The size and color of the envelope should not scream junk mail, such as 6 1/2 by 5 inch. Use a color other than white, such as powder blue, mauve, or light orange. Have volunteers hand address and use a stamp, even if it is a bulk stamp.

> "My practice is to go first to those who may be counted upon to be favorable, who know the cause and believe in it, and ask them to give as generously as possible. When they have done so, I go next to those who may be presumed to have a favorable opinion and to be disposed to listening, and secure their adherence."
>
> "Lastly, I go to those who know little of the matter or have no known predilection for it and influence them by presentation of the names of those who have already given."
> —Benjamin Franklin

Finding Targeted Mailing Lists

Throughout this manual are tips and suggestions for establishing relationships within special interest groups in your community or region. Direct mail is where that networking can really pay off. Think about who would be most interested in seeing you get elected or your measure passed. Will other candidates or office holders turn over their house lists to your campaign? Think about asking someone who previously ran for the office you seek, especially if there is an incumbent leaving. Who would sell you a list from their organization? Groups whose lists could generate money include

- Teachers, especially if you're working for a school or library bond measure or running for the school board
- Environmental organizations such as the Sierra Club, fly fishermen's organizations, League of Conservation Voters, Friends of the River, clean water groups, green way organizations, Critical Mass, or any organization that has a newsletter sent to a specific group of supporters
- Women's organizations such as Planned Parenthood, National Organization of Women, or Emily's List
- Your church
- Civic clubs, fire fighters, law enforcement personnel
- Historic preservation groups.

Determining the Amount of Money Needed

1. Decide how many mail pieces you intend to send throughout the campaign.
2. Look at some other direct mail pieces you like and get a cost estimate for layout and design.
3. Decide to whom you are mailing and then the number of households to receive the piece. For example, if you want to send a direct mail piece to your top five priority precincts, but only want to send it to members of the Green Party, Peace and Freedom Party, Independents, and Democrats, call the county clerk and get numbers of these party members in those precincts. Be sure to ask the clerk to pull out duplicate households. Often the clerk's office will download this information onto a disk for a nominal charge and you can deliver it to a bulk mail house where the merge-sort can happen. If you're mailing to the Sierra Club members list, ask how many are on the list and determine the amount you will need for the task.
4. Figure your printing and mailing costs for each piece based on your final number; 50 to 65 cents each is a good ballpark figure.
5. Multiply these numbers by the number of direct mail pieces you want to send and add a bit more. That will make up your direct mail budget line item.

> "Every experienced campaigner knows that money follows hard work. It is not the other way around."
> —Margaret Sanger

Special Events

Special events are campaign-sponsored activities intended to raise money and support for the campaign, such as a coffee at a supporter's house or a campaign-organized luncheon, dinner, or picnic. Although I have done many special events for campaigns, compared to the candidate calling supporters directly, they raise very little money and take untold amounts of campaign time. The people who attend are usually supporters who have already given and have every intention of voting for your candidate or cause.

With all that said, it is important to stress that fund-raisers are not only about raising money. Special events are also for public visibility and education, for involving volunteers so they are more committed to the campaign and candidate, and for promoting "friend-raising" by strengthening bonds volunteers and guests have with the candidate. I have had great success with a few events.

When approached as an opportunity to advertise the candidate and cement relationships, special events can be worth the commitment of resources necessary. But don't underestimate the commitment involved. You need to be cautious about the strain special events put on the campaign committee, volunteers, and the candidate. If someone other than the campaign committee is sponsoring the event, as is often the case with a coffee, you need to be ready to help that event be a success.

Ensure a Good Turnout

The one thing you must avoid if you schedule a special event is a poor turnout. If it looks like a fund-raising event will have marginal attendance, I invite all my volunteers to attend for free. Not only can I thank them with a free meal, but numbers are more important than money when holding a special event in political circles. Whatever the attendance, you need to be certain that the people who do attend don't have a bad experience. If for some reason people can't find the location or can't find parking or feel uncomfortable in the situation, they are likely to blame you.

A common special event problem is someone's name being accidentally omitted from a guest list. You can turn this potentially very embarrassing situation into an opportunity by giving this person special attention. I was once involved in a dinner for a candidate with a special guest speaker. It was a Monday night downtown at one of the nicer restaurants. We had called all of the people receiving invitations ahead of time and had an exact prepaid head count. On the night of the dinner, someone not on the list showed up. The woman checking people in at the door was scouring the list looking for this supporter's name.

I happened to notice what was going on and could see the embarrassment on the guest's face as those behind waited and those in front looked back. I told the receptionist I had probably forgotten to put his name on the list. I then gave him my seat and leaned over and thanked him for his ongoing support. The important thing is to remedy an uncomfortable situation as quickly and gracefully as possible.

You never want to lose a supporter over a fund-raising meal. It costs the campaign almost nothing to keep this individual on board. You must try to anticipate and avoid anything that might humiliate a person and leave a bad impression about a campaign. Take care of your supporters.

Holding a Special Event

A good rule of thumb for planning special events for fund-raising is that you need one week of preparation for every ten people you plan to attend. The preparation takes place in four stages:

1. You must define the purpose or purposes the event is to accomplish.
2. You must plan the event.
3. You must promote the event.
4. You must conduct the event.

Tips for handling each of these stages are discussed below.

1. Determine the Purpose and Type of Event.   Be clear about the purpose of the event. Is it to attract donors, raise money, raise support, thank volunteers and supporters, or just to get the word out on the measure or the candidate? Special events can, of course, have more than one purpose, but you need to focus on one purpose before you can pick the event. Focus on the main purpose when choosing the type of event; then see whether other purposes might be accomplished as well.

Dinner Parties

I have had great luck hosting dinners as fund-raising events. I contact a supportive restaurant and ask whether the owner will donate the dinner at cost in the restaurant. I then sell it to the guests at retail. Generally the restaurant can't afford the whole affair, so I go to another eatery and ask whether the owner will donate the dessert, and another for a donation of the coffee, wine, and so forth. You can ask a local group to volunteer their talents for the music to make the occasion special. Restaurants are often closed on Mondays, making it a perfect night for your fund-raiser.

> "Where there is no vision, the people perish."
> —Book of Proverbs, 29:18

I have also had great luck with intimate affairs at people's homes. This is different from a coffee and usually involves a well-known person providing a lavishly catered meal for a well-known candidate at a pretty hefty price. I try, in this scenario, to be selective about whom I invite, although usually the price will select who will attend, and the invitees know that. We have brought in as much as $6,000 in our small area at this type of dinner.

Coffees

I have found that coffees sponsored by a supporter can be a good special event. I will add, however, that they can also be a miserable failure. To avoid this they must, like all special events, be closely supervised. Because the campaign is not the sponsor, the critical factor is who hosts the coffee for you. If the sponsor is a local leader, such as a county commissioner, state representative, mayor, president of the college or university, highly regarded business leader, philanthropist, or anyone with a following, there will be a good turnout.

> "Never think you need to apologize for asking someone to give to a worthy object, any more than as though you were giving him an opportunity to participate in a high-grade investment."
> —John D. Rockefeller, Jr.

Most people do not like to go to political fund-raisers such as coffees, so the drawing card should be the combination of the candidate and the host of the coffee. Regardless of who holds the event, the campaign should oversee the invitations and conduct the follow-up phone calls to ensure good attendance. A host who invites sixty people only to have three show up may feel humiliated because he or she let you down. Or the host may feel the candidate is responsible for the poor turnout. Either way, the candidate and the campaign manager have been deprived of one more night at home or time that could have been spent raising money by phone, preparing for a debate, or getting volunteers for a canvass.

Nothing is worse for the candidate than going to a poorly attended coffee, especially if you're already worried about winning. It is awful for the three supporters who do show up. Lending campaign support to ensure a successful coffee is time well spent.

If it is at all possible, have the candidate call the people invited to the coffee, or at least some of them. This will ensure a donation if they are going, and if they can't make it, it is your opportunity to ask for money or support.

Following is an example of what the candidate should say when calling:

> "Hello, Sam? Cathy Shaw. Say, I just got a list of all the people invited to Shirley's coffee, and when I saw your name, I had to take a moment to call and tell you how much I am looking forward to you being there. It should be a lot of fun. Bring some tough questions for me, will you? Great, see you there."

Using coffees effectively will bring you money, workers, and lawn sign locations. So if you are going to host them, pay attention to the details and make each one as successful as possible.

Auctions and Yard Sales

Another good fund-raiser is an auction. You and your campaign team can go to businesses or supporters and get a wide variety of donations. For example, you get four different video places to donate one children's movie and then put them all together for one auction item. Your campaign volunteers can donate baked goods for the auction. It may work to have the candidate or the spouse be the auctioneer. I have used a popular local person who can really work the crowd. Be creative and you can have a fun event that actually brings in money. A good auction will bring in a minimum of $5,000 in a small community.

If an auction is too much, how about a yard sale? If you're going to plan one, make it an event. Get a huge yard and lots of donations, old and new. Advertise the great stuff well in advance. Yard sales can be very good fund-raising events because almost no money is spent to set one up. An effective one will, however, take a lot of campaign committee and volunteer time to set up, run, and clean up after. Because a big yard sale can be grueling, be careful not to schedule one during other labor-intensive activities such as canvassing. A good yard sale can bring in $2,000. Because most of the money comes in the first day, I strongly recommend you advertise it as one day only. Should you decide to do two days, cut the second day short so it ends by noon or 1:00 P.M. Be sure to buy some pizza from the proceeds of the yard sale for your volunteers to eat for lunch.

Involve Attendees

One event I held in a small community was a dessert bake-off. I called specific supporters in that area and asked that they bring their very best desserts. I charged an entry fee for all but the bakers. The campaign provided the coffee (donated), and I involved other locals as the judges. I made up ribbons with different awards such as "Dessert Most Likely to Keep a Marriage Together," and each dessert won a prize. Because it was held in a small community, all who attended knew each other. Everyone had a great time, and other than the rental of the building, there were no costs to the campaign.

> "I've learned to use the word impossible with the greatest caution."
> —Wernher von Braun

General Considerations

Whatever the type of event, a big consideration is the location. Is it big enough? Too big? How about the atmosphere? For indoor events, *never* use a huge hall or room, unless you are expecting a huge crowd. When selecting locations, I look for places where rooms can be closed off in case of poor attendance. No matter how many people come, I want the event to look like it is well attended and successful. You want people to have the impression that just the number invited and expected came. In selecting a restaurant for a dinner, try to find one that has a medium-sized room with another adjoining it that can be used or closed off as needed.

When choosing the type of event to have, consider your budget. Then figure roughly what it will cost the campaign and what income it is likely to generate. You also need to estimate the commitment necessary from the candidate, the campaign team, and your volunteers. Don't forget to consider the economic climate in the community. A $50-a-plate dinner in a town where the last factory just closed might not be a very good idea, even if it would make you money. When considering an event, always ask: Does this make sense? Does it fit? Does it feel right?

2. Plan the Event. Planning an event is an extension of choosing the event. All the considerations that informed your choice of the event must now be put into an action plan. In other words, it is time to sort out the details. Some events will require licenses or permits from local government. They can be a factor in deciding to hold an event, but once it is decided, someone has to make sure the permit is obtained. Similarly, the location, which was a factor in deciding on the type of event, must now be secured. The theme of the event, whether a human services luncheon, environmentalist dinner, or a school auction, now influences the details of the event.

To run a successful special event, it is critical that you know who your audience is and how to reach it. Are you planning a library support dinner? If so, you need to get a mailing list from supportive groups.

Once you know whom you want to reach, you must decide how to reach them. Printed invitations with a phone call follow-up might work well for a formal dinner. If, however, the event is a yard sale, just advertise it in the paper or place flyers around town. Whatever the means, people must be assigned to accomplish it. Invitations must be printed. Flyers must be designed, printed, and distributed. Ads have to be written and delivered. All this takes time and people, and you will need to plan accordingly.

A good way to make sure the details are taken care of is to put the event on a time line map or flowchart like the one for the entire campaign (see Chapter 13), only smaller. Placing the event on a time line and scheduling in all the tasks will require leadership: Some *one* person needs to be in charge. That person needs to have volunteers assigned to all aspects of the event. Like the campaign itself, successful special events are the product of organization. If you assign the leadership of a special event to one person, provide ample volunteer help, develop a time line, and plan a budget, you will have a successful event.

Although budgets are an extra step, making one will not only help you get a handle on expenses but also remind you of things that need to be done. For example, listing the cost of the room expense may remind you to check the date of the event to see what else is going on in the community at that time. If you're hosting that dinner to support your town library, you don't want to find out right after you printed the invitations and rented the hall that it is on the same night as the homecoming game for your high school. Paying for the ads for your auction may remind you to see whether the hospital auction is on the same weekend. Following is a list of the things that could be included on a budget that also may remind you of tasks that need to be accomplished:

- Site rental
- Drinks
- Printing
- Mailings
- Professionals
- Advertisements
- Insurance
- Use permits
- Clean-up
- Thank-you mailing

- Food
- Supplies
- Entertainment
- Parking
- Decorations
- Fees
- Liquor licenses
- Awards, door prizes
- Rental (sound system, tables, chairs)

In planning your event, remember that, although someone in your organization is in charge, when it comes time to actually pull it off, you may need to help, not only with volunteers, but with training. Training and staffing requirements must be met before the actual set-up begins.

In addition to having trained helpers available, you must plan for the supplies you will need. Often supplies must be ordered well ahead of the event. For example, decorations may require lead time. These are the kinds of things that go on your special event time line. Remember that things such as decorations that will cost you money are also in your special event budget. If you keep going back to the budget and to your expense list, it will remind you of things you might have forgotten.

When planning an event, keep in mind that some things won't show up on your budget or time line but may nonetheless be critical. For example, legal issues such as not being able to hold political events in public buildings must be considered. On the more mundane, but not less critical, level, be sure to have duplicates of essential items. If a slide projector is necessary for an event, it is wise to have two projectors or at least two bulbs. How about extension cords or an extra microphone? While you're thinking about duplicates, how about dupli-

> "Fatigue makes cowards of us all."
> —Vince Lombardi

cate lists of all the important phone numbers of the people you are depending on, such as the vendors, caterers, entertainers, staff, and volunteers? Maybe you will want to get a cellular phone for the event. Don't forget to acknowledge all sponsors and your volunteers.

3. Promote the Event.   To promote a special event properly, you must have a target audience in mind. Consider the income level and age of your target audience. Once you have that audience in mind, you must find some way to reach them. Your first job is to figure out where you are going to get lists of the people in your target audience. If you have a narrow group in mind, such as teachers, doctors, or human services advocates, you can often get mailing lists from the special interest groups these people belong to or support. If your audience is broader, as it would be for a neighborhood bake sale, you can take the list from a general source such as a precinct list from your county.

Once you know whom you are trying to contact, you must decide how best to do it. Some options are

- Invitations
- Flyers
- Radio and TV
- Press releases
- Posters
- Newsletters
- Handbills
- Calendars
- Word of mouth

Whatever the vehicle you use to get your message out, the content and design must be attractive, professional, and clear. Include the date, place, time (beginning and end), cost, and map or clear directions for getting there. You need to include how much of the charge for the event is tax refundable. For example, if the cost of the meal is $10 and you're charging $25, then $15 is tax deductible or refundable. Instead of putting the math in the ad, simply put a footnote at the bottom of the ad stating what amount of the price is deductible.

4. Conduct the Event.   When it is time to conduct a well-planned and -promoted special event, the most important thing you can do to ensure success is to set up early. Everything should be ready forty-five minutes to an hour ahead of time. As the organizer, you need to keep focused and calm. Your volunteers will take their cue from you, and that message must be calm efficiency. It is a nice touch to have a packet for volunteer organizers with their names on it. Include the overall plan, as well as the individuals responsible for each of the volunteer activities.

Once people start to arrive, your focus should be on hospitality. How you greet people and work with them will set the tone of the event. Allow adequate time for the candidate to circulate. Do not schedule or allow the candidate to "help" with the operation of the event. The candidate should not be doing things other than meeting the supporters. Name tags will help the candidate when greeting the guests. Be sure to have attendees place the name tag on their right breast side. This way when the candidate goes to shake hands the name tag moves closer to his or her line of sight and can be read more discreetly.

Remember to thank everyone, even the people who sold you things. Everyone involved—volunteer, guest, or vendor—is forming an impression of the candidate and the campaign. You need to do everything you can to make a positive impression. That means a good clean-up, even if you have rented the facility, so make sure there are volunteers who will stay to clean up. Never, as an organizer, leave people to clean up alone. Stay until it is done.

Candidate Calls to Raise Money

Direct contact by the candidate remains the most effective, quickest, and cheapest way to raise money. It is critical to the success of a campaign. Remember, as the candidate, you are willing to do a job and volunteer your time at a task that few want to do. If people support your programs and ideas, they must show that support by contributing to your campaign and thereby helping you get your name out. Do not sound apologetic. You are doing the community a favor.

As a campaign manager, I often call for moderate money and leave the calls for big money to my candidate. However, when I have been the candidate, I have made all the calls. It is very difficult for people to turn the candidate down, and I have found it to be time well spent. Set up some time each day to make the calls. It is helpful if the calls can be made from a prepared list that has phone numbers and suggests the amount to ask and the name to use.

Calling for Money for Ballot Measures

When fund-raising for ballot measures, it is sometimes easier to set up a goal for a specific item such as a full-page ad or TV buys. Let people know what you are trying to buy and how much it will cost so they can contribute accordingly.

If you are going to use a phone bank for fund-raising, use just a few people who are committed and identified in the community

> "A great leader is seen as servant first, and that simply is the key to his greatness."
> —Robert K. Greenleaf

with the measure. Following is the procedure for calling to ask for contributions.

1. Take your 5 by 8 inch card, as described in Chapter 3, and label it "Fund-raising." Print "Name," "Phone #," "CB?" and "Amount Pledged" across the top (see figure 4.3).
2. List the people you want to call and their phone numbers.
3. Let people you call know what they are buying. For example, I might tell people that I am trying to raise $1,500 for a last-minute ad campaign and ask what they can give toward it.
4. Print amounts pledged under the "Amount" column.
5. Tell potential donors that you are "X" dollars away from your goal; people prefer to sign onto something that's going to fly.
6. Have the campaign decide whether contributors will send the check to you or the treasurer. In a pledge situation such as this, I have done it both ways, although I like it better when they send the check to me directly. In this way I can keep track of who sent their pledges and make follow-up phone calls.
7. Make quick reminder calls in cases where the check is not received by the campaign within a week. Note the call in the "CB?" column.

Your fund-raising will go much more smoothly, particularly in a small town or county, if you never spend more money than you have and never *look* as though you are spending more money than you have. Voters do not look favorably on candidates who cannot live within their fund-raising abilities.

One thing I do to be sure this does not happen is to set up business accounts everywhere. Newspapers require that campaign advertising be paid before the ad runs, but printers, typesetters, small newspapers, and other vendors will allow you to run an account and pay with one check at the end of the campaign. While the money is technically spent, it does not show up as such when you are filing your Contributions and Expenditures report. Setting up accounts around town means printing fewer checks, which can also save you money. I usually get by on a small election with bank-issued dummy checks alone.

The Campaign Finance Committee

A campaign finance committee can be a crucial component of a successful fund-raising effort. If you are running for a congressional

Activity: Fund-raising			
NAME	PHONE #	CB?	AMOUNT PLEDGED

FIGURE 4.3   Example of a 5 by 8 inch Fund-raising Activity Card

seat that covers a fairly large area, you may want more than one finance committee, but within a city or county, one should do.

Whether working on a large campaign or a small one, the set-up
is the same. Begin by sending a direct mail solicitation to people
who have either supported your candidate in the past with money,
supported candidates like your candidate, or supported issues that
your candidate supports, especially if they are different from issues
supported by your opponent. For an issue-based campaign, send the
letter to people who have given to causes or organizations that best
reflect the ideals of your ballot measure or proposition.

The work and scope of the tasks of the fund-raising effort should
be at a low enough level to be managed by a small group of volunteers (the finance committee plus workers they recruit using the
campaigner cards shown in figure 4.5) and completed within a
short time frame, usually no more than three weeks. This committee works independently of the candidate's efforts to raise money
and does not include major donors. Major donors are called only by
the candidate, the candidate's spouse, or someone close, like another family member.

Carefully select the people to head up your finance committee;
look for workers rather than well-known people. However, a combination of big names and workers is best. These people will generate
the volunteers needed to complete the fund-raising goal using the
campaigner card.

You need a real "cheerleader" to head up this committee, someone who has no other campaign tasks during the time of this fund-

"Lives based on having are less free than lives based either on doing or being."
—William James

raising effort. It must be a person who has a reputation for getting things done. You do not want your campaign to have to use precious time to clean up after a mess has been made.

I evenly divide finance committee members into groups of three or four and have each team select a name. For example, one could be called the Animals, another the Vegetables, and another the Minerals. These teams compete with each other for prizes that are awarded based on the dollars each team brings in. The prizes are usually nothing big but tend to be fun, like coffee from a local coffee house (thanks a 'latte). In the end, for the team that raises the most money, I will have bigger prizes, such as donated pottery or artwork. Each of the teams should have a team captain who calls team members on a regular basis and keeps everyone competitive and happy in a friendly way. These team captains report back to the person heading up the effort.

Campaign Finance Committee Packets

The finance committee packet (see figure 4.4) is designed to be used with the campaign finance committee. As you prepare packets for your finance committee, include each of the tiered sheets shown in figures 4.8A–H, modified to fit your needs. To give these sheets substance for presentation, print them on a heavy-weight paper and alternate in a two color scheme. Avoid loud or garish colors.

In addition to the tiered sheets you will need to prepare campaigner cards (figure 4.5), donor cards (figure 4.6), and a sheet that reads "Friends I Will Call" (figure 4.9). You will find the "Friends I Will Call" sheet for photocopying in Appendix 1.

The campaigner cards are to be given to each of your hand-picked finance committee members. Each of these members, in turn, will use this card to enlist two more individuals who will work on the fundraising effort. This method of recruitment increases the finance committee's reach three-fold and often will bring new faces to a campaign. Campaigner cards can be printed on regular-weight paper.

The donor cards are for potential supporters who will be called and asked to give. You will need as many donor cards as people who have been mailed the direct mail letter minus the number who already responded to your appeal. (Donor cards *must* be printed on card stock.)

Once the original finance committee members have enlisted their additional workers, mail a letter to the full committee welcoming them on board, thanking them in advance for their commitment to work on the campaign, and reminding them of the first meeting (see figure 4.7). Include with this letter the "Friends I Will Call" sheet and a copy of the "Telephone Campaign Overview" (figure 4.8B).

"The first thing you naturally do is teach the person to feel that the undertaking is manifestly important and nearly impossible. ... That draws out the kind of drives that make people strong, that puts you in pursuit intellectually."
—Edwin H. Land, founder, Polaroid Corp.

LETTER SENT TO SUPPORTERS

CASE FOR SUPPORT

TELEPHONE CAMPAIGN OVERVIEW

"THE ASK" ... STEPS FOR SUCCESS

HOW TO MAKE A SUCCESSFUL CALL

ANSWERS TO COMMONLY ASKED QUESTIONS

ANSWERING MACHINES

1. If you don't know the supporter and it is your first contact attempt, hang up. If you know the supporter well enough to

CAMPAIGNER RESPONSIBILITIES

	Date	
1. Personally make a financial commitment to the campaign.		Below the date heading you will place when each of these activities will take palce.
2. Attend Kick-off at [location] to pick up Donor Cards and participate in training.	Thurs. Sept. 5th 6:30-8:30	A general rule of thumb is that the campaign should run no longer than three weeks and the call in pizza party happens halfway into the process
3. Personally assist in the solicitation of contributions	Sept 5-26	
4. Turn in completed donor cards to the campaign.	on-going	
5. There will be a Call Night/Pizza Party for campaigners to get together to make their calls as a group. Campaigners are encouraged to attend.	Tuesday Sept 17th 6:30-8:30 PM Thursday Sept 26th 6:30-7:30 PM	
6. Turn in last of completed Donor Cards at Victory Party.		

FIGURE 4.4   Example of Campaign Finance Committee Packet

ELLE DANIELS FOR MAYOR
BUILDING A BETTER COMMUNITY
CAMPAIGNER CARD

Finance Committee Member _____

1st Campaigner's Name _____ Phone _____

Address _____ City _____ Zip _____

2nd Campaigner's Name _____ Phone _____

Address _____ City _____ Zip _____

FIGURE 4.5   Example of Campaigner Card (print three to a sheet of paper and cut to size)

70

FRONT:

DANIELS FOR MAYOR
PO BOX 1
ASHLAND, OREGON 97520
555-5555

Place donor label here. Include:
  Name (include partner or spouse)
Address
Phone number
And giving history if you have it.

Amount Pledged_____

Payable: [ ]   Send envelope and information sheet   Turn Down [ ]

[ ]   Pay half now, half later   Contact/Attempts:_____

[ ]   Other arrangements   _____

_____

[ ] Visa [ ] Mastercard #_____Expiration Date _____

BACK:

Campaigner: *Please fill out card, front and back, and return with your weekly reports.*

New address (street or box, city, zip)   _____

_____

New phone number (area code and number)   _____

Out of town; expected return date   _____

Contact later; date to contact   _____

Wrong phone number; present number unknown _____

If turndown, reason given   _____

Comments   _____

FIGURE 4.6   Example of Donor Card (front and back). These are printed on card stock.

Dear Bonnie,

Thank you for volunteering as a campaigner for the Daniels for Mayor campaign. This fund-raising effort promises to reach an all-time high in dollars raised and fun to be had.

Please pull out your calendar and write the following dates and times down.

ALL EVENTS ARE LOCATED AT CAMPAIGN HEADQUARTERS
LOCATED AT 525 BEACH STREET

CAMPAIGN KICK-OFF   THURSDAY   SEPT. 15 6:30-8:30PM
CALL NIGHT PIZZA PARTY   MONDAY   SEPT. 27 6:30-8:30PM
TURN IN PLEDGE SHEETS   ON GOING THROUGHOUT MONTH
VICTORY PARTY...LAST OF
PLEDGE CARDS TURNED IN   THURSDAY   OCT. 6 6:30-7:30PM

Now that you have these important dates written down, take a second to look over the enclosed information. I have included a campaign overview to let you know just where we are going with all of this and a "Friends I Will Call" sheet.

Please pay special attention to the "Friends I Will Call" sheet. This important list will accomplish two things. It will help you think of friends and acquaintances you could call who may be interested in supporting Elle Daniels for Mayor. It will also allow us to cross-reference those individuals with the list being called to eliminate the chance of call duplications. Please send it to me as quickly as possible or bring it to the campaign kick-off.

If you have any questions please feel free to contact me at work (number) or home (number).

Thank you again,

FIGURE 4.7   Sample Letter Welcoming Finance Committee Member to the Campaign

CAMPAIGNER RESPONSIBILITIES

Date —————

(Below the date heading, print when each of these activities will take place. A general rule of thumb is that the campaign should run no longer than three weeks, and the call-in pizza party happens halfway into the process.)

1. Personally make a financial commitment to the campaign.

2. Attend kick-off at (*location*) to pick up donor cards and participate in training.

   Thurs. Sept 15 6:30–8:30 P.M.

3. Personally assist in the solicitation of contributions.

   Sept. 5–Oct. 6

4. Turn in completed donor cards to the campaign.

   ongoing

5. There will be a call night pizza party for campaigners to get together to make their calls as a group. Campaigners are encouraged to attend.

   Tuesday Sept. 27 6:30–8:30 P.M.

6. Turn in last of completed donor cards at victory party.

   Thursday Oct. 6 6:30–7:30 P.M.

FIGURE 4.8A   Sample Text for Campaigner Responsibilities Sheet

TELEPHONE CAMPAIGN OVERVIEW

- The finance committee kick-off is (*place, date, time*). EVERYONE is asked to attend. This is where you will pick up your donor cards (approximately thirty-five), get more detailed information and training about the campaign, and meet your team members.

- The donor cards will have names of those individuals who have a history of giving to this campaign or similar causes. During the three-week fund drive, campaigners will call these supporters at their convenience.

- There will be three teams consisting of approximately six campaigners and one team captain.

- Teams compete with one another for a variety of awards and prizes.

- Cards are turned in to the captains or the campaign as they are completed. This is done either directly to your team captain or to the campaign office.

- There will be a call night pizza party on (*day and date*) for the finance committee to get together to make their calls as a group. Callers are encouraged to attend.

- A party is scheduled for (*day and date*). All remaining cards must be turned in on this evening. The winning teams will be announced and honored. We will all be winners at this point and so will the campaign.

- Fun *is* a requirement for this campaign, so plan on having a good time for a very good cause.

IMPORTANT INFORMATION

All donor cards **must** be returned (even if they haven't been called).
Please do not give donor cards to supporters.

THANKS FOR YOUR TIME AND SUPPORT!!!!

FIGURE 4.8B   Sample Text for Telephone Campaign Overview Sheet

CASE FOR SUPPORT

This page is where you most clearly outline what your candidate (or issue-based campaign) stands for. It may be an opportunity to outline the differences between the candidates or to simply make your case without regard to the opposition.

Depending on whom you are soliciting, this sheet may change to accommodate a different focus or emphasis. For example, if you are targeting a Sierra Club mailing list with a letter and follow-up phone call, you may want these notes to include the candidate's stands on environmental issues or past votes if the candidate previously held an office. If you are calling members of a teacher's union, you may want to include the candidate's stands on school issues and libraries. For the chamber of commerce membership or Rotary Club list, you might focus on the candidate's strengths in business issues. And so on.

It will keep your caller more focused if you match this "white paper" with the potential donor's interests. You can best determine those interests by knowing the origin of the mailing list.

If you are simply calling a list of general supporters, have a number of important community issues itemized here and your candidate's stands on them. If you're working for an incumbent, list accomplishments while in office.

FIGURE 4.8C   Case for Support Sheet

LETTER SENT TO SUPPORTERS

ELLE DANIELS FOR MAYOR
BUILDING A BETTER COMMUNITY

Your logo, message should be part of your letterhead

COMMITTEE
TO
SUPPORT
ELLE DANIELS
FOR MAYOR

It is sometimes effective to list your big-name people on your letterhead. If you are working in a county, you may choose to list support by city. Remember, these are not necessarily the same names that form the campaign committee.

Work with your committee to draft the body of your letter. You may include:

1. Who you are and your background/roots
2. Why you want the office you seek
3. Ways to impress upon your supporters that the undertaking is manifestly important and nearly impossible (this brings out the best in people)
4. No more than two or three issues that will *really* matter to your readers
5. Include a "Donation Card" (Figure 1.2)

Remember:
- Campaigns are about emotion.
- The letter should be kept to one page if possible.
- Include a remittance envelope.

P. S.   A "P.S." is sometimes the only thing that gets read. It is *very* important.

KNOW THE LAW: Don't forget your disclaimer: Paid for by or Authorized by… committee name and treasurer, whatever wording is required by election law. Make it microscopic.

FIGURE 4.8D   Letter Sent to Donors

ANSWERING MACHINES

1. If you don't know the supporter and it is your first contact attempt, hang up. If you know the supporter well enough to get a callback, leave your name and number on the tape (and, if you think it's a good idea, the reason for your call).

2. If you don't know the supporter well and it's your second or third taped greeting, rather than give up, leave your name, volunteer status, reason for the call, and phone number:

   Example:

   Hi, this is _____ *calling at* _____ *o'clock on* (day of the week).
   I'm volunteering for (name of campaign) *in hopes that you would consider a gift to help support* (place short message here: it could be the candidate's name and office or it could be something that the candidate stands for that will resonate with this particular donor. For example: management of forest land or fly fishing or choice issues or libraries. This must be worked out ahead of time with your volunteer caller and/or noted on the donor card).

   I've tried to reach you a number of times by phone and although I __am__ giving up reaching you in person, I'm __not__ giving up on the idea that you'll support (name of candidate and office sought). *I'll ask* (name of candidate) *to send you another return envelope. We would be __so__ grateful if you would use it to support* (again, place an issue here that will resonate with or appeal to interests over intellect. For example, you might say, "to support better management of our forest resources through [candidate's name]").

   This is an extraordinarily close race with a lot at stake. And we can only win with help from people like you. If you have any questions, please give me a call at _____.

3. On the donor card write that another blank return envelope needs to be sent to the supporter and get it back to the campaign as soon as possible. A nice touch is to include a short handwritten, signed note, such as, "Sorry I missed you."

4. If leaving a message does not fit your style, perhaps you could send the potential supporter a note and enclose it with an envelope from your folder. Please note on the donor card that you have done so.

GOOD LUCK!!!!

FIGURE 4.8E   Sample Text for Answering Machines Sheet

ANSWERS TO COMMONLY ASKED QUESTIONS

Example questions:

Didn't I already give to this candidate (campaign)?

Previous gift information, when available, should be on the donor card or printouts, depending on which you are using. It's okay to give the information to the donor, but volunteer it only when you have a purpose. For example, donors gave $50 to a similar candidate or cause and you want them to increase their gift.

I give money to my PAC at work and they're already supporting this candidate.

"That's great. However, if we can show that the bulk of our money comes from individuals, such as you, rather than PACs, it encourages others to contribute also. While PAC money will help, we depend upon direct support from individuals to pull off a win in November."

I don't know much about either of these candidates. How are they different?

Have two or three key issues that clearly show the difference between your candidate and the opponent and place that here. These key issues should be appropriate for the donor list you are soliciting.

How does this candidate stand on _____ ?

Think of two or three issues that might come up in a phone solicitation. This is the place to touch upon a couple of key issues that might be of concern to the community. However, volunteers should use caution in discussing campaign issues in too much detail. For the caller to have more background your "Case for Support" sheet should cover the issues in greater depth.

Who else supports this candidate?

Include a short endorsement list here of organizations and well-known citizens that support the candidate. Prepare here! For example, if you're calling realtors, don't mention an anti-growth group to the potential supporter. Instead, your list might include members of the chamber of commerce, the Rotary Club, or your downtown association. Again, fit the endorsement with the people being called.

FIGURE 4.8F   Sample Text for Answers to Commonly Asked Questions Sheet

HOW TO MAKE A SUCCESSFUL CALL

BEFORE YOU PICK UP THE PHONE:

1. Be proud of yourself for working on the front lines of a campaign. Many talk a good game, but you act.

2. <u>Feel camaraderie with the person you're calling.</u> In nearly every case, the person has previously given to an organization supporting our efforts, directly to our candidate, or to another candidate who embraces similar ideals as those of our campaign.

3. <u>Remember what motivates you about</u> (*the candidate or ballot measure*) and why you agreed to pitch in with the campaign.

4. <u>Decide how much you will ask for.</u> If you know the person and their giving capabilities, don't be afraid to be bold. Otherwise you might say that people are giving on an average of $50 but that any amount would be welcome and put to good use. I often just let the people tell me what they want to give. ("What should I put you down for?" Offering increments of $25, $50, $100 works well.) <u>It is important to get an amount.</u>

MAKING CONTACT WITH THE DONOR:

5. Identify yourself by name and as a volunteer, and <u>ask for the donor by his or her first name.</u>

6. <u>If a couple is identified on the donor card and you don't know which one cares about the campaign,</u> an effective approach is to give your name and say you're a <u>volunteer</u> working for (*name of campaign*) as part of a fund-raising effort to get (*name*) elected. Then ask whether it is x or y or both who support the candidate. Then ask to speak with that person. Say you'll call back if the person is not then available.

7. Show the donor that you are sensitive to the possibility that your call might come as an intrusion. For instance: ***Do you have a minute to talk now?*** If the answer is "no," ask when it would be convenient to call back. Note the callback time on the donor card and then follow through. If the answer is "yes," you're on your way!

8. <u>Refer to the letter sent out by our campaign.</u> Included in your packet is a "Case for Support" paper that will help guide you.

FIGURE 4.8G   Sample Text for How to Make a Successful Call Sheet

"THE ASK" ... STEPS FOR SUCCESS

1. Strategies for "The Ask":

   The campaign should include some issues that are important to the donor. For example, if the donor's name came from a NOW list and choice is an important component in the campaign, use this information. Use the information about where the donor's name came from to build a relationship. Whether the source is the chamber of commerce, a school union, an environmental group, a women's activist organization, or even the town you live in, use this information.

   Find ways to connect with the potential donor. For example: In a county-wide race you may live in the same town as the prospective donor and recognize the last name as a parent with children going to school with your children. *Hi, I'm a volunteer out working for* (name) *tonight. As a parent with the Jacksonville School District, I'm supporting* (name) *because of her leadership within our community schools. Tonight we're raising money to send* (name) *to the Board of Commissioners and we're hoping you will join our effort. Would you consider a pledge of $50 toward the campaign?*

   A very effective technique is to tell the donors how much you are trying to raise for a specific campaign function. For example: *Hi, I'm a volunteer helping* (name of campaign). *We're trying to raise $12,000 for some TV spots that have to be bought now for the November election. Would you be willing to make a pledge or send a gift to support our efforts?* If they say yes, ask what you can put them down for. If they say no or are curt with you, ask if they would rather be pulled from the mailing list.

2. Once you have made the request for money, let the donor respond. Do not distract the donor with nervous small talk. Just be silent. Remember: after the ask, the first one to speak loses. If the donor declines the ambitious amount you've suggested, ask if the donor would prefer to break the gift down by half and give twice. If that doesn't work, fall back to a more modest amount.

3. If the donor indicates that a pledge probably will be made but hasn't decided how much, suggest that the campaign can send another envelope as a reminder, and the donor can send whatever amount he or she feels comfortable with.

4. Finally, verify the address on the donor card and ask if the donor has any objections to being acknowledged in an endorsement ad. Please note the response on the donor card and use the cards to record any other information that has even the slightest chance of being useful, such as issues that the voter cares about, or if he or she wants to work for the campaign or would like a lawn sign.

5. Thank everyone, including turndowns, for their time.

FIGURE 4.8H   Sample Text for "The Ask" ... Steps for Success Sheet

80

FRIENDS I WILL CALL
(Business-Social)

Caller's Name_____

Name		Phone
Address		
City	Zip	Pledge

Name		Phone
Address		
City	Zip	Pledge

Name		Phone
Address		
City	Zip	Pledge

Name		Phone
Address		
City	Zip	Pledge

Name		Phone
Address		
City	Zip	Pledge

Name		Phone
Address		
City	Zip	Pledge

Name		Phone
Address		
City	Zip	Pledge

Name		Phone
Address		
City	Zip	Pledge

IMPORTANT: PLEASE BRING THIS LIST TO THE CAMPAIGN KICK-OFF SO WE CAN CHECK FOR DUPLICATIONS.

FIGURE 4.9   Friends I Will Call Sheet

The "Friends I Will Call" sheet is great because finance committee members will list the friends or co-workers they believe to be supportive of the cause. Obviously this does two things: It increases your donor base and gets friends to call friends. This form should be filled out and returned to the campaign prior to the kick-off party. However, because many end up arriving on the night of the kick-off, be sure to have a couple of campaign workers handy to check these lists against your existing donor cards and the other names on the "Friends I Will Call" sheets. This is important to eliminate duplications. People who hate being called once for a solicitation can get downright nasty on the second or third call in a single evening. Once donor card duplications have been pulled and duplications within each of the lists eliminated, return the "Friends I Will Call" list to the volunteer so he or she may make the calls during the fund-raising campaign.

Prepare a finance committee packet for each caller (see figures 4.4 and 4.8A–H). Each packet includes eight pieces of paper in different lengths so that it creates a tiered effect. Also include paper and envelopes. These are used by the callers for a quick thank-you note. They should write these notes between calls. Personally, I hate writing thank-you notes, but I know no one who hates receiving them. By doing this task along the way, callers can personalize the message while the conversation is still fresh in their minds. An example is provided in figure 4.10.

This personal and efficient touch works. I use nice paper, cut in half, with a small envelope that measures 4 1/2 by 5 1/2 inches. If you have time, the campaign can draft a thank-you note and print it out on the half sheets so the caller need only sign it. I usually include some prepared thank-you notes as well as blank paper. Callers attach a thank-you note to the donor card with paper clips and I have a clerical team address, stamp, and mail it.

In my finance committee packets I include a great deal of information about the candidate or issue-based campaign. Why? Because I have found that callers are more successful at raising money if they have plenty of information. Obviously, they do not have to read it if they choose not to, but those who do seem to be more at ease in the task. However, here as with canvassing, I discourage volunteers from answering specific questions about a candidate's stands on issues. The volunteer can best answer specific questions by saying: "You should ask *[the candidate]* directly. I will tell you, though, I am working tonight to raise money because I really like how hard *[the candidate]* has worked for better schools (or the environment, or tax relief, and so forth)."

"It does not matter so much where we are ... as the direction which we are moving."
—Goethe

It's a nice touch to personalize each of the finance committee packets by putting the caller's name on the front. Even just a

Dear Peter,

Just a quick note to let you know how great it
was to talk to you tonight and to thank you for
your generous pledge.
    Without the support from people like you we
would not be able to pull off a win this
November.
    Oh, I hope that your son did well on his
Spanish test.

Thanks again,
Joan

FIGURE 4.10   Sample Thank-you Note from Campaign Finance Committee Member
to Campaign Donor

printed label tells the volunteer that he or she is important and
counted upon.

On kick-off night, when each committee member receives a
packet and stack of donor cards, the candidate and campaign manager should be present. Callers are to make the calls within a three-
week period, usually from home. It is a good idea to set up a phone
bank party halfway through the period and to provide refresh-
ments. This really gives callers a shot in the arm, and most will complete their calls at this time. I have found that people prefer to call
in the company of others and therefore save many of their calls for
this night. Make it a fun evening.

It is important to remember that the people being solicited in this
manner are not major donors. Again, major donors should be contacted by the candidate, his or her spouse, or someone close to the
candidate.

Potential Sources for Names

Following are individuals and organizations that may be able to
generate lists of people for solicitation by the campaign.

candidate	finance chair	friends of the
campaign staff	finance committee	campaign
clubs	business associates	issue groups
churches	college classmates	the party
candidate's spouse	contributors to other	professional
and relatives	campaigns	organizations

In Summary

1. Carefully select the people to head up your finance committee; get workers before well-known people. "Names" *and* workers are best.
2. Give each member a campaigner card and ask each to select two or three people to help with the calls and to serve as part of the finance committee.
3. Set up competing teams to raise money.
4. Set a goal and divide it by the number of teams.
5. Get lists to the callers and help team members generate their own names. Check for duplicates.
6. Have the head of the finance committee act as a cheerleader and help the teams meet their goals.

Fund-raising Tips

Be aware that campaigns are about emotion, not intellect.

Talk to the people, not about the mechanics of the campaign. A campaign and candidate don't have needs, the community has needs and problems to address. The candidate or campaign should represent opportunity, solutions, answers, and ability to meet those needs.

Be visionary; present a vision. Address opportunity. People need to feel that investing in a campaign will make life better, both now and in the future. They should feel that your winning will strengthen the community. Make your case larger than the office you seek or the program you hope to fund.

Invite donors to invest in leadership, solutions, vision. Through a candidate or a campaign, people are making an investment in their community. Generally, people contribute to a campaign or candidate because they believe that they will get something in return. Describe to the donor, the voter, the citizen what he or she will get through this election. Address issues that are in front of voters.

Look for early money. "He who gives early gives twice" (Cervantes). It is said that money flows in a river. Do not look at fund-raising as though there is just so much money and no

> "Men take only their needs into consideration, never their abilities."
> —Napoleon

more. This is not a well. There is plenty of money if you can demonstrate that the gift will be used wisely. This applies to candidates and campaigns as well as schools, libraries, parks, and other ballot measures for money.

Remember that you are marketing a candidate or campaign measure, not selling it. You're offering something that the voter wants: opportunity, vision, solutions, parks, better schools, less traffic, lower crime, clean air. Look at your campaign as the vehicle for the voters to get what they want. Charles Revson, founder of Revlon, said, "In the factory, we make cosmetics. In the stores, we sell hope."

Never think of fund-raising as begging. If you're a candidate, you're putting yourself out there, at no small sacrifice, to do a job that people want done. If you're working for a ballot measure, you're creating opportunities for a community to realize a vision.

Remember that there's a difference between an underdog and a loser. People want to help an underdog but usually will not financially support a loser. Being an underdog suggests that people are investing in the American Dream. Investing in a loser suggests giving to a deficit or something that will never pay off.

Stay on your message. Your message should always be at the center of every appeal. Incorporate it into "the ask" while keeping the targeted donor's profile and interests as the focus.

Be organized. Because people equate organization with winning, by showing a strong organizational core you are more likely to get people to give.

Think community. Community campaigns are the most successful. A community campaign presents issues that people understand. It presents solutions, involves volunteers, and encourages investment in the future.

Know who you are before others find out. "People will not follow a leader looking for a path" (old Chinese proverb).

Most important, don't be afraid to ask for money. This is the primary means of funding your campaign.

Fund-raising Ideas That Take Less Than One Month of Preparation

1. Personal solicitation.
2. "Friends I Will Call" list.
3. Dinner at a restaurant. Ask the owner to open the restaurant on an evening when it is normally closed. Ask also if the owner will prepare a set menu for a certain number of people at cost. Get wine donated by a local winery, dessert donated by a bakery, coffee from a coffee house, music from local talent, and

so forth. Get a guest speaker and send invitations. Don't forget to follow this up with a phone bank to ensure a great turnout.

4. "Sponsored by . . ." Dinner or brunch at a house of someone well known. This is a variation on a theme of a coffee, but whereas coffees are usually free, a dinner is sponsored by someone and has an admission fee.

5. Theme dinner. These are great fun. First, and most important, you need an incredible friend who is willing to open his or her home and do the preparation of food with other friends. A theme dinner usually will focus around a period (turn of the century), author or set of authors, an important leader, and so forth. For example, you might have an evening focusing on Jane Austen. One friend would research her life and prepare some text that could be read throughout (or between) courses of the meal. Others would prepare a meal that features the types of foods eaten at that time period.

   Another type of theme dinner can center around many authors. In this case, your really great friend would prepare favorite dishes of certain authors or dishes featured in books, such as *Like Water for Chocolate*. We have done this with high school girls and boys acting as the servants (dressed in black and white). You will also need different people to read appropriate passages from books that pertain to the courses being served. Because these dinners are a real treat—almost time travel—and lots of work, charge plenty. Make sure you sell enough tickets to make it worth your while before heading out to shop for groceries and cooking for days.

6. Small auctions. These are surprisingly easy to conduct. You need volunteers who are willing to approach businesses and friends to get donations for a candidate. Combine donations to make more attractive prizes. For example, many people have a children's video that no longer gets watched. By combining five to seven of these you have a pretty substantial item for an auction. Other ideas: a pair of shoes from a local shoe store, someone who is willing to give tennis lessons or golf lessons, a historian who will give a tour of your historic district, a ride in a private plane.

7. Softball tournament. This requires lots of work and makes very little money but is great fun and a perfect project for that guy who wants to help but doesn't quite fit in anywhere else.

8. Birthday party for the candidate. The price of admission should equal the candidate's age.

9. Raffle. This requires someone to be completely on top of the event, someone who can really track where the tickets are. You need a big prize and some lesser prizes plus a bunch of people

> "We make a living by what we get, but we make a life by what we give."
> —Winston Churchill

to sell tickets. Again, you can combine donated items or services to create a big prize such as dinner for two, two theater tickets, after theater dessert, a night cap at a popular bar.

10. A donated weekend getaway. Have someone donate a weekend at a cabin at the lake or in the woods. Do you know anyone with a condo in Hawaii? If a travel agent supports you, he or she might be willing to forgo the commission and help with a really cheap fare that wouldn't be a nightmare for the campaign to pick up. Be creative.

11. An afternoon with . . . Have a local celebrity or author put together a reading or entertainment for a targeted audience. How about just asking the governor to pop in as he or she is moving through town? Have some great donated pastries and assorted hot beverages on hand.

12. Tasting and toasting. This is a kind of theme coffee with admission charged. It is just what it sounds like: wine tasting with finger food and a couple of big names.

"Hey, Big Spender"

Chances are, if you've read this far, you don't have millions of dollars to throw at your campaign. My guess is you don't even have thousands. So what happens when you head up a ballot measure or pull a petition against big money? Don't worry, there's hope. While big spenders get a lot of press, they don't always win. In fact, a study by the Center for Responsive Politics reported that in the 1996 congressional races only 19 of the 149 candidates who spent more than $100,000 of their own money won: that's less than 13 percent.

While a deep pocket does not always buy a win on election day, it can buy name recognition. So, if you're running a campaign against someone with unlimited resources you need a tight message, a lot of volunteers, a well-organized campaign, and an edge. In this manual there are a number of tips to help you compete with big money. However, if you know you will be outspent, pay close attention to developing a powerful message and communicating it in effective ways that resonate with the voters.

With a booming economy and the complexities of government more in focus for the voter, experience is playing a larger role in electing and re-electing candidates. While "I don't know" can initially sound romantic and even charming at the beginning of a campaign, it can wear thin as time goes on. Although there are exceptions, candidates who are vague about issues eventually will come across to voters as lacking substance whether they have lots of personal wealth or not.

In 1998, Gray Davis won a successful bid for governor of California by first defeating a big money candidate, Al Checchi, in the primary, and then another millionaire, Dan Lungren, in the general. Using the campaign slogan "Experience Money Can't Buy," he effectively attacked the wealth of each of his opponents while focusing on his own government experience.

Similarly, in the 1998 Nebraska gubernatorial primary, Mike Johanns, who was hugely outspent by his two opponents, used another effective slogan, "This is about governing . . . and I've done it," which focused on the candidate's experience while implying a shortcoming of the opposition.

By contrast, an under-financed Republican, Bill Redmond of New Mexico, was elected to Congress in 1996 in a heavily registered Democratic district by focusing not on his experience but rather on the ethically questionable activities of his opponent. And his campaign used one other very effective trick. Facing a strong Green Party candidate, Carol Miller, the Redmond campaign sent a direct mail piece to Democrats urging them to vote for her, thereby splitting the Democratic turnout.

In all these campaigns, message, a disciplined organization, volunteers, and communication won in not just difficult but, in the New Mexico example, seemingly impossible races, all while being outspent. While Redmond and, to a certain extent, Davis incorporated negative campaigning, in the Nebraska election Mike Johanns never went negative.

In my town, we effectively fought and won a campaign for a prepared food and beverage tax to pay for an open space program and wastewater treatment plant upgrades against local restaurateurs and the Oregon Food and Beverage Industry. Although we were outspent five to one, we had an effective message that resonated with the voters and hundreds of volunteers to deliver that message.

There are a number of reasons that money does not always translate into wins:

1. Many voters feel that money is not entitlement to hold a public office and that a candidate must have substance, a clear stand on issues, and experience.
2. There is a perception that a candidate who works hard to get into office will work hard once in office. If the candidate is buying everything for support, he or she does not always appear to be working as hard as the candidate who does not.
3. Clear communication will beat money every time. The voter knows that if a candidate can clearly communicate during an election there's a good chance he or she will be a good communicator in office.

"Nobody roots for Goliath."
—Wilt Chamberlain

4. Because there is a perception that candidates with great personal wealth do not need financial support, they have a more difficult time raising money from both large and small donors.

5. Money is a way to communicate with the voters. It tells them who supports a candidate and, in essence, why.

6. There is a perception that candidates with great personal wealth do not need as much volunteer help; they can pay for strategists, pollsters, campaign managers, and direct mail. Therefore, they have more trouble recruiting community volunteers and have fewer volunteers to pull in their friends and family for support.

7. There is fundamental voter suspicion when outside money tries to buy an election. This is most apparent in small communities that take on money measures that poke at large political action groups using unlimited resources to influence the outcome of an election. I have also seen allegations of outside-money influence used to defeat state-wide ballot measures.

Even though you set a budget based on what you thought you needed or could raise, as momentum builds, raise more money and think smart about whom you can persuade to contribute. A campaign should be a fluid activity.

So, what if you have lots of money and want to get elected or pass your ballot measure? Following are some tips for those who have plenty of money to spend.

1. Remember, the messenger is the message. If you're working to defeat a ballot measure, carefully choose who will deliver your message to the voters. In the 1998 California general election, the Indian gambling proposition had the out-of-state Las Vegas casinos fighting it while the proponents used Native Americans to promote it. Guess who won. During a recent tort reform ballot measure, lawyers used victims of drunk drivers rather than themselves in ads. Carefully consider the baggage that your messenger may have and use one who evokes an emotion or a positive feeling with the voters.

2. Hit the campaign trail. Don't spend all your time with the high end of society. Get out and meet the public, kiss babies, shake hands, go to malls, get your face or issue out there. Do the walking and talking.

3. Distance yourself from any legislation or policies that look like they will benefit your business, either directly or indi-

rectly. A good politician will embrace issues that are good for the community, especially for the long run. That may not be good for your business in the immediate future, but it will be good for you as a candidate and office holder.

4. Be informed about the issues, have a tight message, and communicate it well to the public. Get your campaign organized and don't apologize for your money.

5. Spend your resources as though you don't have a lot. Use lawn signs, newspaper ads, radio, and direct mail. Even though you can afford it and it's easier, you should avoid communicating with the voters only through TV ads.

6. Don't run as a businessperson, run as a leader in your community. Talking about your business success can be misconstrued by the voter. Instead, relate your business experience to serving in office. While people love to say government should be run like a business, that's not exactly true; streets make no money, sewer and water services make no money. Government is not about making a profit, it's about service to the community: it's business with a heart. Characterize the differences so voters know that you understand what they are.

7. Don't parade your wealth to the voters by saying how much you will spend to win. You never want to appear as though you're buying votes. It's far more important to the voters that you earn them.

8. Always appear to be one with the average person. This is most important. Integrate this idea as part of your core. Too often, those who are very wealthy project an image of being out of touch with the common person.

"Time is the most valuable thing one can spend."
—Theophrastus (300 BC)

5

Lawn Signs

In this chapter
Logo and General Information
Location, Location, Location
Preparing for the First Day
Big Signs
Maintenance of Signs
Lawn Sign Removal

Lawn sign placement and maintenance is a great opportunity to involve people who are not interested in interfacing with the public (or people you feel might make an unfavorable impression). Although it is a huge time and money commitment for a campaign, with enough volunteers a well-run lawn sign campaign is an excellent way for a voter to feel involved in a campaign while elevating candidate name recognition or increasing awareness of a ballot issue. Lawn signs can also demonstrate support for a candidate or issue within a community. However, that is really all they do. Given the expense and hassle of lawn signs plus the demands on your volunteer base, you should carefully consider whether to use them. In a small community, if your opponent is using them, you almost have to as well.

In my town, lawn signs cannot be placed more than thirty days prior to an election. I therefore have everything prepared for the big day when all the signs suddenly appear.

There are two schools of thought about lawn sign placement. One is not to worry if you do not have a lot of locations at first because the number you end up with is what counts. This argument holds that what is important is the appearance of *building momentum*. The other school of thought is that BOOM! here comes the candidate. Suddenly the name is out, and everyone supports that person. I am of the latter school. I work like crazy to get as many locations as possible for the big day. I do this obviously to make a big visual impact, but also because I only have to organize the signs going up once. I know that there will always be additional requests as the campaign goes on, but not so

> "Few things are harder to put up with than the annoyance of a good example."
> —Mark Twain

many that one or two people can't handle them easily. I always have volunteers whose sole job in the campaign is to put up lawn signs as people call and ask for them or as canvassers secure the new locations.

It is important to have everything ready and organized for the teams. Also note that it is especially important that people work in pairs in this activity: one to drive the car or truck and the other to hop out and pound.

Logo and General Information

For the purposes of this handbook, a logo is your name or ballot measure and a message printed in a memorable way. Sometimes the name will be printed with a star and streamers behind it, or a wavy American flag, or stars and stripes. I had one that was quite blocky with the name in different colored bars. I did another one that was fairly complicated, with a backdrop of the city, trees, clouds, anchovies, the works. Because I have no imagination and even less talent in these areas, I take this task to a professional. The going rate for developing a logo in my area is $100. Because you will be looking at your logo for months, invest a little time in its development. The logo represents time and money well spent.

Lawn signs, like all advertising, must easily identify your cause or candidate. You need to develop your own "look." Once you have a logo, try to use it on all campaign literature and advertising. If you or your campaign team do not have the skills, you will have to use a graphic design artist or a typesetter to design your name logo.

Regardless of who does your signs and logo, it is a good idea to visit a lawn sign printer. Such printers usually save at least one of each of the signs that they have printed. This way you can shop for ideas in style and color combinations without any out-of-pocket expenses. When you're designing your sign, keep in mind that two colors cost a lot more than one, but they're worth it. To save some money, you can get a two- (or even three-) color look by doing almost a solid color over the stock while leaving the lettering with no color. This produces white lettering on what looks like colored stock. Then use half tones (a mix of the white sign and the solid color showing through) for a design or part of the lettering. The result is very classy.

Weatherproof Stock

Even if money is a big problem, *do not cut costs on your stock*. Get good paper stock that is weatherproof; poly tag or corrugated works well. The corrugated stock is nice because it is printed on both sides of the same sign, thus eliminating the need to staple signs back-to-back. Stapled signs often come apart and need repair. Also, corrugated can be attached to the stake prior to pounding it in the ground. (Be sure to use screws and washers.)

If you are using poly tag, remember to bring in your clerical team to staple the signs back-to-back. This needs to be done prior to placing the signs in yards. *Do not attach poly tag signs to the stakes prior to pounding the stakes into the ground. THEY WILL FALL OFF!*

Have the signs and the stakes bound together in groups of twenty-five. If you have the signs and stakes already counted, you need only assign the area and direct the team to take the appropriate number of bundles of stakes and signs.

Remember, anything that is not weatherproof will curl with the first strong dew or rain, and your campaign "look" will be one of litter. Political lawn signs are a touchy subject in some communities. Keep lawn signs neat and together at all times. If you're sloppy about quality, placement, or maintenance, lawn signs may do more harm than good. But if you place them right, they make your campaign look well organized and well staffed.

Stakes for lawn signs are expensive. To save money, I ask other campaigns to give me their stakes after elections. I then bundle the stakes in sets of twenty-five and redistribute them to campaigns I support. Call around to those who have run and lost or are not running again and collect stakes. This works especially well if you are running a single campaign in the fall and someone you know lost in the primary election. If you have no luck, try to get a secondary wood products company or nursery to donate them. Still no luck? Ask supporters in the construction industry to make you some. Still no luck? Swallow hard and buy them. You can count on your lawn signs plus stakes costing $4–$5 each, depending on the size and number of colors. Budget accordingly and place them carefully. Plan on buying 3 to 4 foot stakes.

Obviously, the size of your lawn sign can affect the cost of printing and especially stock. Lawn signs come in all sizes, so while you're visiting the printer to look at other political signs, check out size as well. A typical size is 18 by 24 inches; however, I've seen some very effective signs that were only 9 by 24 inches. The latter size works quite well if your candidate has a long name that fits comfortably in that space. In the first Clinton-Gore race, the local team used signs that were 20 by 30 inches. The stock was so heavy that the signs continually fell off the stake. The local team eventually had to come back in and place each sign on two stakes. They still looked bad, so the team came back in and added a stick across the top of the stakes and then attached each sign on three sides. I would not recommend something that large.

"Taxation with representation ain't so hot, either."
—Gerald Barzan

If you are endorsed by fire fighters or some other well-organized group, they may have the ability to print lawn signs, with some limitations, such as number of colors or size. Check out such groups; it could save you money.

Recently, a new kind of lawn sign has hit my area. These signs are like plastic sleeves that fit over large croquet wickets. I priced them for one campaign I worked on and found them to be more expensive than the conventional lawn sign. However, they are easy to transport, the wickets are practically indestructible, and the sign itself does not need to be stapled or attached with hardware to stakes. All the advance work to prepare the signs for placement is eliminated, and the wickets push and pull in and out of the ground very easily. No need to carry mallets or staple guns or look for soft ground.

> "Eliminate risk and you eliminate innovation. . . don't eliminate risk; knowingly take it on."
> —Vaughn Keller

Halloween

If you are running a fall campaign, you should be prepared to send all of your lawn sign workforce back out the day after Halloween, which is just a few days before the fall general election date in November. You want your campaign to look great right up to the end. Extra effort and foresight are not lost on the electorate, nor are the opposite traits. To get any benefit from lawn signs, you need to attract the attention of voters.

I know this may sound obvious, but be sure the signs are put up perpendicular to the street. The point of lawn signs is for people to see them from a distance as they drive by. Your "look" and how you present it will determine the success of your signs. In a mayoral race some years ago, an outsider ran a really great lawn sign campaign. One of the most distinguishing marks of his campaign was small, undersized lawn signs that he used in place of the normal-sized signs. Neighborhoods began having competitions to see who had the most signs up. Some houses would have ten of these signs on the front lawn. In some areas, neighbors would try to get their entire block to be covered with the "cute" little lawn signs. Meanwhile, the opponent ran a very traditional campaign using only billboards and, needless to say, lost. Don't hesitate to be creative and bold. You never know what will work. Bold, however, does not mean elaborate. Simple signs with a simple theme are the least offensive and easiest to read at high speeds.

Location, Location, Location

Getting good locations to display your signs is the second half of using lawn signs effectively. One way to find good locations is to contact previous campaigns. Often people who have run for office in previous elections will have records of where their lawn signs were placed. Try to get such lists and call them first. This works best when you share political ideology with a former candidate.

Another way is to get a "walking list" (list of addressees within a particular voting district) for your district from the county clerk. Using a map and this list, note the arterial streets. You can then set up a phone bank to call people living on the favored arterial and ask whether they will allow you to place a lawn sign on their property. This really works.

If the walking lists from the county do not have many phone numbers, set up a clerical team to come in and look up phone numbers ahead of the phone bank. The idea of having a system for organizing volunteers is that you can quickly bring groups of people to bear on problems. Organization allows you to accomplish tasks without overloading your workers.

When possible, try to avoid placing your signs where many lawn signs have already been placed. Give high priority to placement of signs in yards of people registered in the opposite party or where there are lawn signs of people running in another race in the opposite party. This gives voters the impression that you are supported by a wide cross-section of your community.

Preparing for the First Day

Setting up for placing lawn signs follows the same process as the other campaign activities I have talked about. After getting locations and making sure that the posters and stakes are ready to go, you now need to organize the team that will put up the signs.

Begin by placing all of your lawn sign locations on 3 by 5 inch cards (see figure 5.1). Once the cards are filled out, organize them by addresses that are close to each other. Use maps or people who know the neighborhood. If you cannot find a street on the map, call the home for a location. What you are after is some kind of logical walking or driving pattern that will allow your placement team to save time and motion. I use groupings of no more than twenty to thirty locations. Each route will take about two hours.

After you have the 3 by 5 inch location cards organized, place the cards for each grouping in sandwich bags along with a map with the target area highlighted. Set these plastic bags aside for your placement crews.

Placement crews work in twos. If you are using poly tag, the crew needs a staple gun (to attach the sign to the stake), a stapler (in case the sign comes apart at the corners), and a mallet to pound the stake into the ground. If they are placing corrugated signs, they will need only a mallet and maybe a metal pole to use for making a pilot hole. In either case, it is a good idea to bring along extra signs or

> "He who gets a name for rising early can stay in bed till noon."
> —Irish proverb

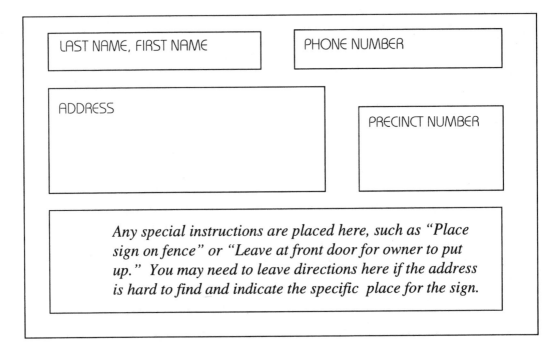

FIGURE 5.1   Example of 3 by 5 Inch Lawn Sign Card

repair kits (washers, screws, electric screwdrivers, staple guns, staples, stakes, mallets) in case a sign breaks. If you are using something other than either of these types of signs, just remember, send extras of everything.

Assigning crews is simply a matter of handing them a sandwich bag with the locations on 3 by 5 inch cards plus a map highlighted with their area and the appropriate number of signs and stakes. Ask as many volunteers as possible to bring tools or borrow enough ahead of time from friends. Be sure everything borrowed by the campaign is labeled and returned promptly.

It is also critical that the volunteer brings back the plastic bag with the 3 by 5 inch cards. You will need your cards for the maintenance crews to repair signs after Halloween and for sign pick-up at the end of the election.

I am a firm believer that poorly constructed, poorly designed lawn signs hurt your campaign more than they help. If you are going to use lawn signs, they are far too expensive and too labor intensive to cut corners on design and production. If you can't raise the money to do them right, don't use them.

With that said, there may be times when you deviate from this rule for strategic reasons. In one campaign, due to lack of funds, we printed only one-third the normal number of lawn signs. Although they were carefully placed to maximize visibility, they soon began to disappear. People were calling wanting signs; others were calling requesting replacements. We knew it was a close race and our diminishing number of signs made it look as though support was waning.

Using the same color as on our signs, I hand-painted more in my barn on the back of old lawn sign stock. In the middle of the night I placed them throughout the city. I did not want these to be next to each other, but rather to lend the impression that the homeowner had taken the initiative to paint a sign. I wanted the look to be one of individual, rebellious support for our side and angry opposition to the money fighting our effort.

Big Signs

Large signs placed along highways can be very effective advertising. I have worked on campaigns where large signs have been painted by hand and others where they were commercially printed. Naturally, such signs are not cheap. My preference is to have volunteers paint them for free, but that is a lot to ask of anyone because it is so time consuming. I would add here that this can be a touchy issue if the hand-painted signs look amateurish and you feel placement would be detrimental to the campaign. However they are produced, location is the primary concern when using large signs.

Large sign locations can sometimes be found by calling realtors who have parcels listed along highways and in cities. Ranchers, farmers, or owners of large vacant lots who support you will occasionally allow signs on the corners of their land. If you're running a local campaign during a general election, talk to state or even national campaigns about possible large sign locations near theirs.

The volunteer crew putting up large signs must be carefully selected. They should have some construction experience so the structure can withstand wind and the weight of the sign. They will need more than a hammer and nails to put up a large sign. Supply them with or ask them to bring post-hole diggers, shovels, hammers, nails, and additional wood for supports or bracing. This is a big production.

Maintenance of Signs

Large or small, campaign signs must be maintained once they are up. Depending on the circumstances, you may use the same crew that placed the signs to maintain them throughout the campaign, or you may use a completely different crew. The maintenance crew must travel with a mallet, staple gun, extra signs, stakes, stapler, and so forth in their cars at all times. Ostensibly, maintenance crews are ready to repair any ailing sign they see in their normal daily travels. However, from time to time there may be a need for the crews to travel their assigned placement routes for a more systematic check of the signs.

"Whatever is worth doing at all, is worth doing well."
—Earl of Chesterfield

As I indicated before, you will need to keep your maps and sandwich bags of 3 by 5 inch lawn sign location cards for your maintenance crews, for post-Halloween repairs and for sign removal after the election. As well as hanging on to the cards, I keep all lawn sign locations in my computer. That way I can print sections of the lawn sign list as I need them to give to the maintenance people. Before I computerized, in addition to my 3 by 5 inch cards, I kept the locations handwritten on paper according to area. I then photocopied these lists for maintenance people. If you do not have an organized maintenance crew, you will need these lists only for the day after Halloween or after a severe storm.

Besides maintenance, there will be the chore of putting up new signs as people call in requesting them or as canvassers return with requests for lawn signs. If there aren't too many, you can assign new locations to the appropriate maintenance crew or have special volunteers to do this chore on an ongoing basis.

In one campaign with which I was involved, there was a street where every night all of the lawn signs disappeared. The man who put the signs in that area was also in charge of maintenance and just happened to drive this street to and from work each day. After the signs disappeared and were replaced a couple of times, the volunteer decided to take them down on his way home from work and then each morning on the way to work put them back up. You can't buy that kind of loyalty.

It is best to get requested signs up as soon as possible. However, if there are too many requests, it may be necessary to organize another day for placement. If you do this, be sure to include all of your current locations so that signs can be repaired or replaced if missing.

Lawn Sign Removal

Your crews should be ready to remove all of your lawn signs the day after the election. If they are left up longer, homeowners begin to take signs in and even throw them away, and you won't have them for your next election. At a minimum, you will want to retrieve the stakes or wickets for future campaigns. Because you have to get them down eventually, you might as well look organized and responsible by getting them as quickly as possible.

I like to set up a crew for the day after the election. Again, I work volunteers in pairs and give these crews maps and the 3 by 5 inch cards containing the addresses. When they return, you must remember to get your cards and maps back for the next election. This is also a great time to get together a volunteer thank-you party to disassemble your lawn signs, put them away for the next election, and bundle your stakes in sets of twenty-five with duct tape.

6

Precinct Analysis

The Sinners, the Saints, and the Saveables

In this chapter

If you intend to canvass or run a get-out-the-vote (GOTV) effort, you must do a voter precinct analysis. You will need a precinct analysis to determine where best to invest your money, time, and especially your canvassing efforts. Unlike some campaign activities, precinct analysis is something that can be done months ahead of the election. Take advantage of this and get it out of the way. If you have money, you may hire a voter contact service to do it for you. If not, read this chapter carefully. Twice.

Precinct analysis is based on the premise that people who think and vote alike live near each other. Precinct analysis looks for voting trends, specifically precinct-by-precinct voting trends, to give the campaign a geographic location of your core supporters. It will tell you where to find high support and low voter turnout for similar candidates or causes in past elections so that your canvassing efforts will activate likely support. This is crucial. You want to invest most of your effort in those high-support, low-turnout areas to get out your vote.

> "Aim at the souls that can be saved."
> —Bill Meulemans

In every race, there are two kinds of voters: those with their minds made up and those who are either undecided or don't care. For our purposes we divide the first category into two groups, the sinners and the saints, and focus on the remaining group as the saveables.

The Sinners. These are the voters that will not cast a vote your way regardless of what you say or do. You *never* want to give them a reason to get out to vote and, therefore, you don't canvass them and hope they will forget to turn out on election day.

The Saints. Those who will vote for you rather than your opponent almost no matter what. If these voters turn out in record numbers, they need little attention in the campaign. If you spend time and money here, you are preaching to the choir. However, this is a group that needs attention in your GOTV activities.

The Saveables. This is that vast group of voters who are undecided or pay little or no attention to politics. These include swing voters, who do not strictly follow party lines and will often respond to a candidate or issue based on emotion rather than issues or facts. These are the people who say they voted for a candidate because: "I liked him," "she's honest," "I could understand him," "she cares about us." For this group it is form over content. In 1984, polls indicated that more voters supported Walter Mondale's stands on issues than Ronald Reagan's, yet they elected Reagan in a landslide.

> "If you would persuade, you must appeal to interest, rather than intellect."
> —Benjamin Franklin

This categorization is not intended to sound cynical. While the sinners and the saints may feel smug that they support an ideology, I can't tell you what it's like to canvass homes and have the voters say they want no literature because they always vote party. The saveables, while less attached to their political core and ideology, are saying: "What good does it do to have a smart or experienced candidate if he or she cannot communicate and inspire?" If you have a candidate who embraces a strong ideology that moves your saints to work, and he or she inspires, it's a killer combination.

Through precinct analysis, you can determine where the saveables live, then by further study of education, age, and past voting history you can determine the likely numbers of those who will *actually* get out and vote. While a precinct analysis will give you important information for canvassing purposes, you must also find the likely voters and contact them, through either canvassing, direct mail, phoning, or all three, in hopes that they will support your campaign issue or candidate.

Directing your money and efforts toward likely voters is important. For example, in my city we have a university and the students living in that precinct vote in a very predictable way, *when they vote*. However, this precinct has the dubious distinction of having the worst voter turnout in the state of Oregon. No matter how hard we try, they will not vote. So save your time and money: Don't go to voters who will not vote, regardless of how strongly they may support your candidate or issue in theory. Later in this chapter I explain ways to couple your precinct analysis with methods to determine the likely voter.

By conducting your precinct analysis early and by studying who is most likely to vote, based on issues and past elections, you gain information to shape your campaign theme and message. Obviously, if your message is focused on the large group of voters who are either undecided or disengaged and you know where they live, you have a better chance of activating them and pulling them over to your cause.

The Full-blown Analysis

The precinct analysis is a little different for a primary than for a general election. In a primary, candidates of the same party square off, so the analysis is composed of past voting records for candidates of that particular party. For the general, you are comparing past voting trends of all parties voting if the election is for a candidate. If it is for a ballot measure, you are comparing voting histories for similar ballot measures or propositions. In either case, the materials you need to do a precinct analysis are the same. You need the county printouts of the identified elections and a number of copies of the forms found in this chapter. Typically, depending on the size of the area you are analyzing, you will need one to five copies of the Election Data Form (see Appendix 1, Form 1), one copy of the Precinct Targeting Worksheet (Appendix 1, Form 2) and the Precinct Priorities Worksheet (Appendix 1, Form 3), and three copies of the Targeting Priorities and Strategy Worksheet (Appendix 1, Form 4).

Start your precinct analysis by researching past local elections that were similar to the one you are working on. Be as specific as you can about elections. For example, was the election:

- A school board election with a liberal running against a conservative?
- A county commission race between two conservative Democrats?
- A county commission race between two liberal Republicans?
- A liberal Republican running against a conservative Democrat?
- A primary election between a man and a woman?
- An incumbent running against an outsider in a general election?
- School tax levies?
- Bond levies for construction of swimming pools?
- County-wide tax base?

> "More than any other time in history, mankind faces a crossroads. One path leads to despair and utter hopelessness, the other, to total extinction. Let us pray we have the wisdom to choose correctly."
> —Woody Allen

Whatever the combination of your particular candidates or ballot measures, find a recent past election with a similar combination.

Once you have identified the appropriate past election(s), go to the county election office and request a printout of the particular race or races that you've identified. Bring home the printouts and set aside a couple of hours to work with the precinct analysis forms. First, you need to make enough copies of the Election Data Form to cover the number of precincts involved in the election. Each copy of the Election Data Form will hold twenty-two precincts. Be sure to retain the original of the Election Data Form for future use. Fill it out according to the example shown in figure 6.1.

"Democracy is the worst form of government except for all the others that have been tried."
—Winston Churchill

Election Data Form

Your analysis begins by going through the printout to get the information necessary to complete the Election Data Form. You will notice that the county printout includes more information than you need. Ignore the information that does not pertain to the race or races you have identified for analysis. Go to the candidate or issue of interest on the printout and transfer that information to the Election Data Form.

On Scratch Paper

Next, on a separate piece of paper, arrange the precincts in order of support (see figure 6.2). Transfer the precinct numbers to a copy of the Precinct Targeting Worksheet (see figure 6.3). Retain the original form for future use.

Precinct Targeting Worksheet

To fill out the Precinct Targeting Worksheet, you need to decide what constitutes high support for the issue or candidate you have selected as a model for your race. It might be a win of 60 percent or of only 52 percent. This can be a tough call. What you are looking for is the best support, comparatively speaking, for that particular election.

The best support may not necessarily be overwhelming support. I once worked on a campaign effort to defend an office holder against a recall attempt. The only other recall of a county commissioner in our area had occurred ten years earlier. Because this previously recalled county commissioner had a similar ideology to that of my office holder, I did a precinct analysis based on the outcome of that election. Once I got the abstracts, I could see that the analysis would be very difficult. Not only had the precincts changed with the census,

ELECTION DATA FORM

Candidate *Elle Daniels* County *Grant*
Election Date *Primary, 1980* Page *1* of *1* Pages

*T/O = Turnout   U/V = Undervote

Pre-cinct	Reg. voters	Reg. Dems.		Dem. T/O	Reg. Reps.		Reg. T/O		Nelson (D)		Com-stock (R)		Daniels (R)		Dem. U/V	Rep. U/V
01	1,366	710	52%	64%	529	39%	65%		55%		19%		66%	2nd	45%	14%
02	820	452	55%	69%	296	36%	72%		51%		19%		64%	4th	49%	17%
03	772	456	59%	54%	228	30%	56%		56%		30%		57%		44%	11%
04	698	380	54%	59%	247	35%	64%		57%		22%		69%	1st	43%	8%
05	900	494	55%	64%	313	35%	65%		58%		26%		56%		42%	18%
06	871	529	61%	57%	244	28%	59%		57%		21%		56%		43%	23%
07	497	313	63%	38%	125	25%	43%		57%		31%		59%		43%	9%
08	770	332	43%	65%	384	50%	72%		64%	1st	26%		65%	3rd	36%	10%
09	930	494	53%	57%	341	37%	62%		63%	2nd	39%	4th	53%		37%	8%
10	606	301	50%	65%	240	40%	62%		60%	5th	30%		59%		40%	11%
11	1,219	600	49%	59%	478	39%	68%		49%		44%	1st	46%		51%	10%
12	1,139	568	50%	61%	432	38%	67%		50%		22%		64%	5th	50%	14%
13	107	49	46%	53%	30	28%	70%		62%	4th	14%		52%		38%	33%
14	121	39	32%	69%	61	50%	54%		59%		42%	2nd	36%		41%	21%
15	368	234	64%	61%	92	25%	77%		52%		39%	5th	51%		48%	10%
16	225	146	65%	48%	60	27%	72%		51%		42%	3rd	37%		49%	21%
17	836	467	56%	60%	287	34%	61%		54%		32%		49%		46%	19%
18	499	316	63%	51%	148	30%	61%		58%		35%		51%		42%	14%
19	729	380	52%	57%	254	35%	60%		58%		38%		40%		42%	22%
20	982	590	60%	57%	287	29%	60%		63%	3rd	29%		58%		37%	13%
21	1,041	519	50%	58%	420	40%	66%		59%		34%		53%		41%	12%
22	283	127	45%	50%	134	47%	63%		52%		38%		52%		48%	11%

FIGURE 6.1   Example of Election Data Form Filled Out

Declining Order of Support

Daniels Support			Republican Turnout		
04	69%		15	77%	
01	66%		02	72%	
08	65%	(5)	08	72%	(5)
02	64%		16	72%	
12	64%		13	70%	
07	59%		11	68%	
10	59%		12	67%	
20	58%		21	66%	
03	57%		01	65%	
05	56%	(10)	05	65%	(11)
06	56%		04	64%	
09	53%		22	63%	
21	53%		19	62%	
13	52%		10	62%	
22	52%		17	61%	
			18	61%	
15	51%				
18	51%		19	60%	
17	49%	(7)	20	60%	
11	46%		06	59%	(6)
19	40%		03	56%	
16	37%		14	54%	
14	36%		07	43%	

FIGURE 6.2   Example of Tabulating Precincts in Order of Support

but the commissioner had been voted out about two to one. Find-ing *any* precincts with a win for the commissioner, much less "high" support, was next to impossible. Therefore, I adjusted the curve so that precincts where the official *kept* her office or was only *narrowly* recalled were considered "high" support. Medium support was adjusted also. For purposes of this analysis, the medium-sup-port areas consisted of precincts where she had been recalled, but not in overwhelming numbers. Low-support areas were those precincts where she was recalled in huge numbers.

In a similar manner, you may adjust what you would consider high-, medium-, or low-support areas. In other words, you are breaking out the precincts where the issue or candidate that is rep-resentative of your issue or candidate has done well, fairly well, or poorly. On the Precinct Targeting Worksheet (Form 2) on the left-

PRECINCT TARGETING WORKSHEET

* High Support   ** High Turnout

H/S* Support	H/T** Turnout
⟨04⟩	15
01	02
08	08
02	16
12	13
M/S	**M/T**
07	11
10	12
20	21
03	01
05	05
06	⟨04⟩
09	22
21	09
13	10
22	17
	18
L/S	**L/T**
15	19
18	20
17	06
11	03
19	14
16	07
14	

FIGURE 6.3   Example of Precinct Targeting Worksheet Filled Out

hand side, list the precincts you have selected according to the appropriate category of support.

Now that you know where your support is likely to come from, you must identify precincts with high, moderate, and low voter *turnout*, that is, the percentage of registered voters who actually voted. To determine this, I divide the difference between the highest precinct turnout and the lowest into thirds. For example, if the lowest precinct turnout in the election was 25 percent and the highest was 75 percent, my high-, moderate-, and low-turnout categories would be: high turnout, 60 percent and higher; moderate turnout, 45 percent to 59 percent; and low turnout, 44 percent and lower. List the results of your voter turnout analysis on the right-hand side of the Precinct Targeting Worksheet by category, just as you did for support.

Precinct Priorities Worksheet

You are making this step-by-step analysis to know where best to spend money and time. Once you have support and turnout broken out on the Precinct Targeting Worksheet, go to the Precinct Priorities Worksheet, Form 3 (see figure 6.4). As with the others, make a copy of the form and retain the original.

The Precinct Priorities Worksheet is where you will be listing the precincts from highest to lowest priority for canvassing or getting out the vote. This is accomplished by matching high support and low turnout precincts from the Precinct Targeting Worksheet to establish your priority list. For example, all precincts that fall in both high support *and* low turnout categories on the Precinct Targeting Worksheet are placed in the first, or highest priority, box of the Precinct Priorities Worksheet. Those with low support and high turnout are the lowest priority. Other precincts will fall in between on support or turnout and will end in boxes 2 through 8 of the Precinct Priorities Worksheet.

Targeting Priorities and Strategy Worksheet

Make three copies of the Targeting Priorities and Strategy Worksheet (see figure 6.5). Take the first one and list all the high priority precincts on that form. List the moderate priority precincts on the second sheet. On the third sheet, list your lowest priority precincts. You can now assign your canvass or GOTV teams where they will do the most good. High priority gets done first, then moderate priority. Leave low priority alone.

Although the saints may not need as much attention as the saveables, it is important that you ground your high-support areas or consolidate this base. Do not take the saints for granted. This may not be

PRECINCT PRIORITIES WORKSHEET

(1) H/S + L/T = High Priority	(6) M/S + H/T = Medium Priority 13
(2) H/S + M/T = High Priority (04) 01 12	(7) L/S + L/T = Low Priority 19 14
(3) M/S + L/T = High Priority 07 20 03 06	(8) L/S + M/T = Low Priority 18 17 11
(4) M/S + M/T = Medium Priority 10 05 09 21 22	(9) L/S + H/T = Low Priority 15 16
(5) H/S + H/T = Medium Priority 08 02	

FIGURE 6.4   Example of Precinct Priorities Worksheet Filled Out

an area where a candidate spends a lot of time, but it may be a good place to do a drop piece or have volunteers canvass once.

You may be tempted to look over the lowest priority precincts and pull those on the cusp for a possible canvass, but I usually avoid these precincts. Although these are not necessarily the sinners, they tend to vote for the opposition. Low-priority precincts are just that: low prior-

TARGETING PRIORITIES AND STRATEGY FORM

Rep.   Daniels   Rep.   Rep.

	Prio-rity	Pre-cinct	Reg. voters	Party density	Support	T/O	U/V	Precinct location	Campaign strategy
	2	04	698	35%	69%	64%	8%	*Hills*	*Athletic canvassers*
	2	01	1,366	39%	66%	65%	14%		
HIGH (7)	2	12	1,139	38%	64%	67%	14%		*Senior canvassers*
	3	07	497	25%	59%	43%	9%		
	3	20	982	29%	58%	60%	13%		
	3	03	772	30%	57%	56%	11%		
	3	06	871	28%	56%	59%	23%		*Candidate canvasses*
MEDIUM (8)	4	10	301	40%	59%	62%	11%		*(etc.)*
	4	05	900	35%	56%	65%	18%		
	4	09	930	37%	53%	62%	8%		
	4	21	1,041	40%	53%	66%	12%		
	4	22	283	47%	52%	63%	11%		
	5	08	770	50%	65%	72%	10%		
	5	02	820	36%	64%	72%	17%		
	6	13	107	28%	52%	70%	33%		
	7	19	729	35%	40%	60%	22%		
	7	14	121	50%	36%	54%	21%		
LOW (7)	8	18	499	30%	51%	61%	14%		
	8	17	836	34%	49%	61%	19%		
	8	11	1,219	39%	46%	68%	10%		
	9	15	368	25%	51%	77%	10%		
	9	16	225	48%	37%	72%	21%		

FIGURE 6.5   Example of Targeting Priorities and Strategy Form Filled Out

ity. Similarly, where you have high support and high turnout already, you have to ask yourself what canvassing that precinct is likely to accomplish. These are the saints. With limited money, time, and volunteers, do you want to spend time where you already have the vote?

I once worked for a candidate who did not believe in precinct analysis. I had conducted an in-depth precinct analysis of a number of elections where there were candidates seeking office who embraced a political ideology similar to that of my candidate. I also reviewed initiatives that covered issues similar to ones with which my candidate was closely aligned. It was clear from the analysis that a handful of precincts would not support this candidate, and I told him which ones they were. These precincts were off limits because they came in as both low support and low turnout.

Notwithstanding the warning, toward the end of the campaign (with all the high priority and medium priority precincts done), the candidate decided to burn up some restless energy by covering these low-priority precincts. His feeling was that if *he* personally went to the door, people would be swayed. My concern was that these low turnout precincts would turn out in higher than usual numbers and would not vote the way we needed. The candidate disagreed and went ahead with canvassing low-priority precincts.

The low-support precincts, not surprisingly, turned out to be difficult canvasses. People were rude, and mishaps occurred. The candidate came back demoralized but decided to press on.

Following the election I did a precinct analysis, which showed that the low-priority precincts had turned out in huge numbers and voted two to one against my candidate. Given that we lost by only a few hundred votes, the election might have swung our way had some of these people stayed home.

Ballot Measure Form

To conduct a precinct analysis for a ballot measure, follow the example in figure 6.6. As with any other precinct analysis, you must find an election that was similar to the one you are working on. Don't worry about party affiliation; perform the same tasks that you did for the candidate precinct analysis.

Finding the Saints Among the Sinners

Within each precinct there are a certain number of voters who will never jump party lines (base party vote), there are some who will move to follow a specific candidate (swing vote), and there are some who will switch party ranks within the same election (switch hitters).

> "Everything should be made as simple as possible, but not simpler."
> —Albert Einstein

BALLOT MEASURE FORM

Precinct	Reg. voters	Turnout	Count yes	Count no	Turnout %	% Yes	% No	UV
1	707	552	263	202	78	48	37	
2	680	507	252	188	75	50	37	
3	705	566	305	196	80	54	35	
4	714	501	270	184	70	54	37	
5	639	473	240	189	74	51	40	
6	813	622	296	229	77	48	37	
7	696	487	216	200	70	44	41	
8	858	593	251	248	69	42	25	
9	915	606	291	218	66	48	36	
10	660	403	136	149	61	34	37	
11	752	507	226	208	67	45	41	
12	642	454	233	161	71	51	35	
13	693	531	239	242	77	45	46	
14	715	550	287	210	77	52	38	
15	633	509	277	188	80	54	37	
16	538	423	230	139	79	54	33	
17	734	575	301	218	78	52	38	
18	922	668	316	286	72	47	43	
19	728	506	240	224	70	47	44	
20	1,061	744	321	350	70	43	47	
21	150	101	44	50	67	44	50	
22	676	449	171	239	66	38	53	

FIGURE 6.6   Example of Ballot Measure Form Filled Out

Base Party Vote

This is a useful and very easy number to calculate. What it tells you is the minimum votes a candidate of your party can hope to get, the worst case scenario, if you will. To determine this number:

1. Go to the county clerk and ask for the election results where a candidate of your party was pounded. Because you're going to translate these numbers precinct by precinct, it really doesn't matter if the poor outcome for your party covers exactly the same voting district.

2. List the percentage of votes that the candidate received, precinct by precinct.
3. Multiply this number by the most current registration figure the county has.
4. Multiply this number by the expected voter turnout.

To determine the expected voter turnout, find a similar past election in the same season, for example, in May on an off year or May in a presidential primary or a special election or a general off year. Find the same season (spring, summer, or fall) and the similar election (off year, on year, or special). Using this, make an educated guess about your turnout. (See 4 below.) Figure 6.7 is a sample form for determining base party support. Thirteen actual local precincts are listed.

This will give you the number of people who will vote for your party no matter what.

1. List all the precincts in the area where you are running (column A).
2. List for each of the precincts the percentage of votes the individual in your party received (column B). Remember that this is a race where your party's candidate lost big.
3. List, precinct by precinct, the voter registration (column C).
4. List the percentage you expect to turn out in column D. (You determined turnout by the number of people who voted in a similar previous election at the same time of year.)
5. Finally, multiply the percentage of the expected turnout times the current registration and then that number times the percentage of votes that the same party candidate got in the previous election, (D x C) x B. This number represents those who vote party irrespective of the candidate.

Party Turnout

Another useful task is to determine the strength of party turnout. This will give you the average number of people in a party that will generally support a candidate of the same party. While this information is most helpful for partisan races, I also use it for ballot measures. For example, in my area, Republicans are more inclined than Democrats to vote against school funding, tax bases, building improvements, and library operation and maintenance levies. On the other hand, they are more inclined to vote for sheriff patrols, jail upgrades, and criminal justice services. Knowing the average of party turnout can help mold your campaign efforts.

To estimate party turnout for your election, look at three or more partisan races that had little controversy or big issues pushing one

> "A citizen of America will cross the ocean to fight for democracy, but won't cross the street to vote in a national election."
> —Bill Vaughan

SAMPLE FORM DETERMINING BASE PARTY SUPPORT

A	B	C	D	E (D × C) × B
Precinct number	Percentage of votes same party candidate	Current voter registration	Percentage expected turnout	Number of voters who won't leave the party
58	35	655	67	153
59	37	916	73	247
60	38	707	72	193
61	37	676	76	191
62	42	424	66	118
64	45	822	74	274
65	46	693	72	230
66	43	703	67	202
67	37	756	62	173
68	41	740	72	218
69	38	949	70	252
70	36	723	65	169
71	35	1038	71	258
TOTAL		9,802		2,678

FIGURE 6.7   Sample Form for Determining Base Party Support

party to vote over another. Basically, choose three very average elections, then,

1. List the percentage of the party turnout for each precinct for all three races and figure the average of each.
2. Multiply this number by the current registered voters.
3. Multiply this number by the predicted voter turnout.

Figure 6.8 is a sample form for determining average party turnout.

Swing Voters

If your precinct analysis is being done for a partisan race in a general election, you need to find the swing voters. Swing voters are those who are registered in one party but will vote for someone from another party. They are sometimes called "smart voters" because they vote according to issues and information rather than party. However, among them are also voters who are swayed by emotion and their impressions of the two candidates rather than focusing on issues embraced by these candidates. Your job is to find

SAMPLE FORM FOR DETERMINING
AVERAGE PARTY TURNOUT (REPUBLICAN)

Precinct number	Party turnout 1st election	Party turnout 2nd election	Party turnout 3rd election	Average party turnout (B + C + D/3)	Current Republican registration	Average # Republican turnout (E × F)
A	B	C	D	E	F	G
58	43%	63%	35%	47%	267	125
59	61%	54%	37%	51%	295	150
60	46%	55%	38%	46%	232	106
61	64%	62%	37%	54%	345	186
62	50%	53%	42%	48%	78	37
64	42%	69%	45%	52%	209	109
65	54%	60%	46%	53%	351	186

FIGURE 6.8   Sample Form for Determining Average Party Turnout

these people and persuade them that they should jump party ranks and vote for your candidate.

To find swing voters, create a form based on figure 6.9 and go back to the county election department.

1. Find an election in which a Democrat did very well and then find another election in which the opposite happened.
2. List in column A the precinct numbers.
3. List in column B the results of the election in which the Democrat had a big win and in column C the results for the election in which the Democrat suffered a big loss. For example, let's say the 1998 Democratic candidate for governor won county-wide by a three to one margin, whereas the 1996 Democratic congressional candidate lost by better than two to one. Going through the precincts, one by one, you would list the percentage of the best outcome and then the percentage of the worst outcome for D. Let's say, in precinct 1, the support for the 1998 race ran 62 percent, whereas in the congressional race the candidate support came in at only 47 percent. By subtracting the second from the first (62 percent – 47 percent), you end up with the percentage of voters who could potentially swing in precinct number 1 (15 percent).
4. Take the full count of registered voters for a given precinct and multiply that by the difference of the high and low support for the same precinct.
5. Multiply what you believe the turnout will be by the answer you got for number 4. This will tell you the number of peo-

"80% of life is just showing up."
—Woody Allen

SAMPLE FORM FOR DETERMINING SWING VOTERS

Precinct number	High Democrat win by percent	Low Democrat win by percent	Percent of swing (B − C)	Projected turnout	Current voter registration	Number of voters who could swing (D × E × F)
A	B	C	D	E	F	G

FIGURE 6.9   Sample Form for Determining Swing Voters

ple who could swing from party to party in a given precinct in a given election. It is the same for both Ds and Rs. (*Note:* Do not use an election in which there was a third party candidate.)

Switch Hitters

A variation of a swing voter is someone within a party who will divide his or her vote and switch parties within a given ballot; that is, vote for a Republican in one race and a Democrat in another. These voters are sometimes called "switch hitters."

To determine the number of switch hitters, you must again look at voting history. Find an election in which a candidate for one party did well while another within the same party did poorly. Again, list the percentages and subtract one from the other. Multiply the difference by the total current registration and then again by the expected voter turnout. This will give you the number of voters, precinct by precinct, who will not vote straight party ticket. This is helpful information in elections where a strong candidate from another party, who appears elsewhere on the ballot, is sure to bring out his or her party support.

Undervote

Another thing to look for in precinct analysis is the undervote. The undervote represents voters who go to the polls or return an absentee ballot but skip voting for a particular candidate or issue on their card. Undervotes may result from a candidate running unopposed, or because the voter didn't like any of the choices, or because the voter knows nothing about an issue or candidate and decides to leave the decision to those who do. The reasons for high undervotes are of interest in shaping a campaign. For example, if your candidate, running unopposed in the primary, has a high undervote (45 to 60 percent) in a high-priority precinct, it may be a good idea to put the candidate in for a canvass. At the very least, do something to consolidate your base.

I once worked for a candidate who ran uncontested in the primary. I came on board with his campaign only in the general election because I had been involved in a different campaign during the primary. This candidate had decided that because he was running unopposed in the primary he would not spend money during that election. He was betting he could make the campaign happen in the general alone.

After the primary I did an analysis of the primary vote for both my candidate and the general election opponent. The analysis revealed that the opposing candidate, who also was uncontested but ran a modest primary campaign, had a relatively small undervote. My candidate, with no primary campaign at all, had undervotes as high as 60 percent. The high undervote may have been the result of the perception that the voters thought the candidate was aloof and somehow thought he was too good to campaign. Being invisible during the primary only fed this belief. We corrected this with canvassing prior to the general election, but it is important to run a primary election campaign regardless of the opposition. You can make use of an opportunity to present the candidate to the voters as a sincere person who genuinely wants their votes.

The Quick and Dirty Precinct Analysis

If you do not have the time for an in-depth precinct analysis, there is a "quick and dirty" way to do one. This method will not give you the kind of information that the full analysis will, but if you are doing just a single city or school district, it works pretty well. As with the full-blown version, you must research similar elections to find a voting pattern. Once you have identified the races you are interested in, call the county and ask for the summary sheets or the abstracts for those elections. Summary sheets are usually compiled by the county for all elections and list only the votes for and against and the turnout by precinct. Most counties will fax these sheets to you. If not, ask for copies and pick them up at the courthouse.

To do your analysis, take a yellow highlighter and go through the summary looking for precincts that voted "correctly" (likely to support your cause) but had a low voter turnout. These precincts are

"Our goal is progress, not perfection."
—Williams & Williams

your number one priority. Once you have your high-priority precincts, look for precincts that show support with a medium or high turnout. These will be on your moderate list. If you see precincts where you are likely to lose big, just avoid them.

If you have access to a data spreadsheet program you can save a great deal of time at the adding machine or calculator if you do the following.

For the Ballot Measure Form, create a spreadsheet with at least nine columns. List from left to right:

Precinct Number
Location
Yes
No
Registered Voters
Turnout
Percent Turnout
Percent Yes
Percent No

From the county records data, input the first four columns and then have the computer calculate the last three in the following way:

- For percentage of turnout, divide turnout by registered voters.
- For percentage of yes, divide yes votes by turnout.
- For percentage of no, divide no votes by turnout.

For the Election Data Form do the same, except adjust columns for that form and have the computer calculate the percent columns in the following manner:

- Percentage of Democrats: Divide registered Democrats by registered voters.
- Percentage of Republicans: Divide registered Republicans by registered voters.
- Percentage of party turnout: Divide turnout by the respective party registration number.
- Percentage of support: Divide individual candidate support by the respective party turnout.

When Precinct Analysis Isn't Enough

The kind of precinct analysis outlined above is a great tool for guiding campaign resources geographically. Often, in fact, most of the time, campaigns are so strapped for money, especially if the candidate is deemed a long shot, that campaigns must be very focused and very organized very quickly. If you're a Democrat and certain areas represent solid support and solid turnout (your saints), you will need to make a huge assumption that they will vote for you. If they don't, you'll lose anyway, and that will be that. You must feel that you can count on them with no money or time expended on their vote.

By contrast, there will also be those who support the Republican ticket consistently in election after election. The areas where these voters live should be avoided to keep from activating them to vote and to save volunteer time and campaign money. As an aside, I recently went to an event where the wife of a candidate for county commissioner came up to me to talk about her husband's loss in the November election. As a Democrat he had won Ashland by better than two to one, "and with almost no effort" she said. However, in reference to a two to one loss in the county's third largest city, she said, "and we canvassed every neighborhood there." As I had never known that city to support a Democrat for a county commission seat, I asked her why they canvassed there. She said, "Because we were such a cute couple." True story.

It doesn't matter how swell you think you are, if you spend time, money, or energy in areas where you know you will lose, that means you are not spending time, money, and energy in areas where you need to win. Work smart: Write off the sinners, trust the saints, and persuade the saveables.

You can determine how many votes you need to win by doing the following:

1. First, determine what the voter turnout will be, precinct by precinct, for the election you are running as outlined above.
2. Then take the precincts that constitute your saints and add up the votes for your candidate and the votes for the opposition based on your projected numbers for voter turnout. (Refer to your Precinct Priorities Worksheet, Form 3, figure 6.4.) The precincts of the saints are all those with high-support precincts, regardless of turnout. (*Note:* Those with high support/low turnout and high support/medium turnout are a canvassing and GOTV priority, not a voter persuasion priority.)
3. Next, take the precincts that constitute the sinners and again add up the votes for your candidate and for the opposition (Refer to your Precinct Priorities Worksheet; the sinners are those who are low support/low turnout, low support/medium turnout, and low support/high turnout.)
4. Finally, again referring to Form 3, list the precincts with medium support, their registration numbers, and their projected turnout.

> "An elected official is one who gets 51% of the vote cast by 40% of the 60% of voters who registered."
> —Dan Bennett

SAMPLE FORM FOR DETERMINING THE VOTES YOU NEED TO WIN

Precinct number A	Total registered voters B	Projected turnout (%) C	Projected turnout (#) (B × C) D	Percent swing vote (calculate above) E	Votes up for grabs (D × E) F	Percent your support G	Number your support (D − F) × G H	Percent opposition support I	Number opposition support (D − F) × I J	Votes you need to win (J − H) + F/2 plus 1 K	Votes left F − K L
1	681	65%	443	15%	66	45%	169	48%	180	11 + 66/2 = 38 + 1 = 39	27
						Total			Total		

FIGURE 6.10 Sample Form for Determining the Votes You Need to Win

Figure 6.10 is a sample form for making these calculations. In this form, Precinct 1 (column A) has 681 registered voters (column B).

- The campaign has projected a 65 percent voter turnout (column C) *based on past election performance.*
- The projected turnout is calculated by multiplying the projected turnout percentage (column C) by the total registered voters (column B). That leaves a projected turnout of 443 voters.
- The campaign also calculated that Precinct 1 had a 15 percent swing voter potential. (To calculate swing voters, use the form in figure 6.9. Remember, the swing voter percentage is the difference between an election with a very poor showing for a candidate in your party and an election with a very high showing for a candidate in your party, precinct by precinct.)
- To calculate the number of votes your candidate and the opposition will get you must:

  1. First calculate the number of people who will actually vote (multiply total registered voters by the percentage of turnout: B x C = D). This result goes in column D.
  2. Next calculate the actual *number* of swing voters per precinct (D x E) to get the possible votes that are up for grabs: the result is 66 votes (column F).
  3. Then subtract the swing voters from the number that will actually vote (columns D – F). This will give you the actual number of votes that will be divided between you and your opponent based on past voting history percentage.
  4. Next multiply this number by the percentage who will support your candidate (column G) based on past support of a similar candidate for that precinct. That will give you 169 votes (column H) in precinct 1 that will probably go to your candidate or issue ([D – F] x G).
  5. Repeat the previous step to calculate the number who will support the opposition, except that for this number you will multiply the percentage of votes the opposition normally would get (48 percent, column I) by the expected turnout minus the potential swing voters (D – F). That means your opposition will probably pull in 180 votes in precinct 1 ([D – F] x I). Obviously, the difference between the votes you will get (169) and the votes your opponent will get (180) is how many more votes your opponent will receive in this precinct than you will (11 votes).

> "You've got to be very careful if you don't know where you are going, because you might not get there."
> —Yogi Berra

6. Now figure out how many of the swing voters you need to make up the difference and win by at least one vote. Add the difference (11) to the swing votes (66) and divide by 2 (because there are two of you). The result is 38. But you need to win by at least one vote, so add one vote to the 38. You need 39 votes of the 66 swing votes to win. The difference between the 39 you need and the 66 swing votes that are up for grabs is 27 votes (column L). Even if your opponent took all 27, you would still win precinct 1 by one vote.

7. Continue this process with every precinct and add up the number of votes you need from the swing voters in all precincts to win the election.

8. Add this to the total votes that you think you will get; the result is how many total votes you need to win.

At this point you may be inclined to give up or say, "I'll come back to this when I have more time." If I could give you one word of advice, it would be to stick with the process I outlined above. You need to know where to concentrate your campaign resources and volunteer energy if you want to win. Find your swing voters, find where they live, and determine how many of them you need to vote for you.

Finding the Likely Voter

Age, Education, Absentees, and Voting History

Nationwide, age, education, absentee registration, and voting history are some of the best clues to finding the likely voter. For example, according to a 1993 Simmons Market Research Bureau of George Washington University study, those who graduated from college were 33 percent more likely to vote than the average adult and those with a graduate degree were 41 percent more likely to vote. Identifying these voters early and persuading them to support your candidate or measure are critical to a win because they *will* or *are likely to* vote.

Although absentee voters are discussed in more detail in Chapter 8, your campaign should work them long before the GOTV effort with a separate and focused campaign. Why? Because those requesting an absentee ballot are more likely to vote than any other group. While the percentage requesting an absentee ballot may vary from state to state and region to region, their turnout doesn't. And often the absentee voter can represent a huge part of the overall turnout. In the past, before people could register absentee permanently, those requesting absentee ballots typically ran about 25 percent of all the registered voters in Oregon. Now, in some areas they account for 50–60 percent of the voter turnout. In the 1998 general election, 74 percent of those requesting an absentee ballot returned that ballot.

Age is an excellent guiding factor for determining voter turnout. According to election statistics posted by the Federal Election Commission on its Web site (www.fec.gov), since 1972, when eighteen-year-olds were given the right to vote and 50 percent of them did, that age group has been in steady decline. By comparison, those in the forty-five to sixty-four and sixty-five and up age groups have had a very consistent voting history, hovering close to 60 percent turnout for twenty-five years. What is helpful in shaping the message and direction of a campaign is to look at both the voting history of your district (who will actually vote) and party registration.

The breakdown of nationwide voter registration shown in table 6.1 presents a relatively even split of Democrats and Republicans among all age groups, with the exception being the over sixty voters. However, when weighing the voter turnout according to age, party disparity is more pronounced.

In 1998, the Field Institute of California conducted a survey of California voters. According to the director of the Field Poll, Mark DiCamillo, "Voting rates are directly correlated to age. The older and more educated you are, the more likely you are to vote." This was borne out in the 1998 November election in California, where people over sixty represented only 19 percent of the population but a whopping 30 percent of the voters. By contrast, those in the eighteen to twenty-nine age group made up 29 percent of the population but only 13 percent of the voters.

While the eighteen to twenty-nine age group may be evenly divided in party registration, their lack of interest in voting adds significant weight to the additional 10 percent party registration held by the GOP for those sixty and older. Of further interest is that of those sixty and older, 75 percent are registered to vote, whereas only 51 percent of the eighteen to twenty-nine age group is registered to vote. (This information comes from the Federal Election Commission Web site, www.fec.gov.)

Just to demonstrate the voting power of the sixty-plus age group in this scenario, if all these percentages held for the 1996 election, in which 10 million California voters actually voted, the sixty-something crowd would weigh in with a million more votes than the eighteen to twenty-nine age group. So if you're spending your campaign time and money wooing the eighteen- to twenty-nine year-old age group around the college and ignoring the retirement village by the golf course, better think again.

Of course, there are exceptions to this generalization. The most dramatic occurred in the 1998 general election in Minnesota, where

> "Phyllis Schlafly speaks for all American women who oppose equal rights for themselves."
> —Andy Rooney

TABLE 6.1   Voting Tendencies by Party Registration and Age in 1998

1998	Nationwide		California	
Age	Percent Democrat	Percent Republican	Percent of voting population	Percent likely to vote 11/98
18–29	48	48	29	13
30–44	49	49	24	20
45–59	50	46	28	37
60 & older	44	54	19	30

SOURCE: Federal Election Commission Web site (www.fec.gov).

laws allowing same-day registration contributed to a record number of twenty-something voters turning out to support gubernatorial candidate Jesse Ventura. Ventura ultimately carried every age group under sixty.

Turnout can also be predicted by education and income levels as well as voting history. Because education and income tend to go hand in hand, look for statistics in either area. This information can be determined through either professional firms specializing in data collection or the U.S. Census. If your campaign had enough volunteers you could actually poll the swing precincts to determine this information. However, if you're going to the trouble to call voters, you could actually skip income questions, which some might find invasive, and instead ask questions that would determine voting history.

In this scenario, you would ask not only if the voter intended to vote in the upcoming election, but also how many times he or she actually voted in past elections. This information is also available through your county clerk or elections office.

Gender and Ethnic Gaps

The Gender Gap.   Although there have been more women eligible to vote than men for many years, it wasn't until 1976 that women actually registered nationally in greater numbers than men and not until 1984 that they began to turn out in larger numbers. By 1996 over 7 million more women voted in the presidential election than men. (This information is available at www.fec.gov.) For our purposes, it is important to look not only at who votes but also how they vote when they do.

In 1994 Public Opinion Strategies conducted a survey that found that white men were inclined to support GOP congressional candidates over Democrats by 51 to 23 percent. A later study by the National Election Studies out of the University of California–Irvine found similar numbers indicating that 53 percent of white men identified with the GOP, 37 percent identified with Democrats, and 10 percent identified with Independents. This same study showed that white women preferred Democrats over Republicans by 48 percent to 42 percent and that black women revealed an even greater contrast, with 88 percent favoring Democrats, 7 percent favoring Republicans, and 5 percent favoring Independents. While the 1998 gender gap did not materialize to the degree it was predicted for the general election, there is no doubt that it played a role.

In that election, the low Republican turnout (that is, older white men) added strength to those turning out to vote Democrat. Remember, a win isn't just based on who votes for you but also who does not vote for your opposition. Precinct analysis and looking at voting trends allow you to activate those who will vote your way, persuade those who are inclined to vote your way, and either ignore or discourage those who will support the opposition. By ignoring the sinners you hope they will forget to vote. By discouraging them (disseminating negative information about their candidate) you hope they will be too disgusted to vote.

The Ethnic Gap. The black, Hispanic, and Asian votes can have an impact on the outcome of an election. For example, in San Francisco the 1997 football stadium funding win was largely due to the number of minorities getting out to vote in predominantly ethnic areas. Whites living in the upper income sections of the city opposed the measure but were ultimately overwhelmed by minorities hoping for improvements in a marginal neighborhood. Minorities living outside the affected neighborhood indicated they had supported the stadium in hopes that their neighborhood would be next.

Also, in 1997 the San Francisco Asian vote had a large impact on a freeway retrofit. The Hispanic vote in California, Texas, and Florida also played a large part in the general election of 1998. Table 6.2 shows minority vote by party registration in the 1998 election.

In the November general election in 1998, Hispanics and blacks cast 15 percent of the votes, an increase of 3 percent from 1994. Table 6.3 shows the minority voter turnout in 1994.

Depending on the demographics of your area, your campaign needs to be aware of the gender and ethnic gap voting potential. Determine the influence of these issues for shaping message, persuasion, and GOTV.

Table 6.4 shows how the gender and ethnic gaps affected the 1996 presidential race.

> "Illegal aliens have always been a problem in the United States. Ask any Indian."
> —Robert Orben

TABLE 6.2   Minority Vote by Party Registration

	Percent Republican	Percent Democrat
White	55	42
Black	11	88
Hispanic	35	59
Asian	42	54

SOURCE: "How They Voted Nationwide in November of 1998," *Newsweek*, November 16, 1998, 42.

TABLE 6.3   Minority Turnout

	Percent Registered	Percent Voted
White	67.7	56
Black	63.5	50.6
Hispanic	35.7	26.7

SOURCE: 1994 Registration Totals and Turnout, Federal Election Commission Web Site (www.fec.gov).

TABLE 6.4   Women and Minority Vote in 1996 Presidential Election

	Clinton (percent)	Dole (percent)	Perot (percent)	Percent of All Voters
Men	44	44	10	48
Women	54	38	7	52
Black	83	12	4	10
White	43	46	9	83
Democrat	84	10	5	40
Republican	13	80	6	34
Independent	43	35	17	26

SOURCE: How the Gender & Ethnic Gap Affected the 1996 Presidential Race, Federal Election Commission Web site (www.fec.gov).

7

Canvassing

In general, to get a vote, you must ask for it anywhere from three to eight times. You can ask in ads in the newspaper, on TV, over the radio, via direct mail, on lawn signs, or by canvassing. In small communities, canvassing is a great way to get a feel for your constituency and their concerns, and it can also be among the most elevating and gratifying experiences in a campaign.

However, canvassing is not about changing minds. It is about changing voter turnout. You can do that by going door to door in the high-support/low- (or medium-) turnout areas, thereby reminding supporters that you need their votes to win. *Canvassing is about activating supporters; that is, reminding them to vote.*

Do not think you will go into a neighborhood, drop off a piece of campaign literature, and have someone read it, hit herself on the forehead, and say, "My God, I have been a fool! *This* is the candidate for me." It doesn't work that way. Canvassing does not change minds. Nine out of ten people don't even read the material. Your hope is that they will place it somewhere in their home and remember the name or ballot measure while voting. Don't get me wrong; there will be a few who thoughtfully read and digest the material and even change their minds, but they are the minority. When you canvass, you are simply *activating* people already sympathetic to your cause or candidate.

I have never worked in a campaign where I did not canvass. Canvassing is an effective and inexpensive way to get your message to the voters. It can also be a great way to get a feel for your chances of winning. In my second bid for mayor, the lawn signs for the opposition lined the main street through town, and my chances looked

> "A great many people think they are thinking when they are merely rearranging their prejudices."
> —William James

bleak. However, after I started canvassing, I realized how handily we would win, and I felt much more relaxed in all my campaign activities because of this. Canvassing will give you this information, and it will help you get additional lawn sign locations in key spots.

If canvassing is done right, you will also get valuable feedback on voter concerns so that you can shape and mold advertising and debate emphases to meet those concerns. For example, in Ashland's very controversial open space campaign, a woman who should have been fully behind our cause and who, in fact, had agreed to a lawn sign, told a canvasser that she was unsure about her vote because of all the controversy and the number of lawn signs for the opposition. (*Note:* A good canvasser will get this information back to you.) I already knew that the opposition had placed lawn signs exclusively on the main street through town. I hoped that it just *looked* worse than it was. However, with this feedback it was clear we had trouble.

With less than a week left before the election, I got together with my ad person to create a flyer in response to these concerns. In our flyer we identified exactly who the opposition was, as well as the money and reasons behind their opposition. The flyer reviewed issues that had come out during the campaign but that needed restating and reinforcing. Three days before the election, about ninety people canvassed the city with this one-page flyer that cost next to nothing to produce. Given that we won by only 150 votes, I'm convinced it was the single biggest reason why we won that campaign.

Canvassing is a time-consuming, resource intensive way to activate sympathetic voters and bring your message to the people. Nevertheless, there are few, if any, campaign activities that will give a bigger return on investment.

With that said, it is important to note that canvassing is not for everyone. Sadly, some cities are too risky for the traditional canvass. Please be careful and know the area you are going into. Never send someone to canvass alone or go alone yourself and never enter a house, if for no other reason than that your partner will not be able to find you.

Map Packets

Before volunteers or the candidate can canvass the electorate, you must first determine where your high support/low turnout and high support/medium turnout is through a precinct analysis so you will know where to expend your efforts. Then you must prepare maps of those areas for your canvassers. After these tasks have been completed, the canvassing activity itself begins. Although I always do the precinct analysis and map preparation myself, I like to break my city in half and have two canvass coordinators. If you are in a bigger city, you may want to break it down even further. If you are in a county, keep breaking it down so that your coordinators can oversee manageable units of people and space.

Setting up canvass map packets is a critical element to a successful canvass. Do not wait to do this with the canvassers when they first arrive. Map packets should be organized and ready when volunteers walk in the door. Remember the rule about not overburdening your volunteers. Set up all activities so your volunteers can see that this is an efficient, well-organized effort.

Setting up map packets for canvassing begins by going to the county clerk and getting a precinct map booklet for your county. This booklet consists of large photocopies of the county with the precincts outlined in bold and precinct numbers written on top of each of the voter precincts. If you are running a city election or a school board election, you will not need the entire book of county maps, so make copies of what you do need. Then put the county book away for future use. I have also worked on campaigns where we have used maps from real estate offices, regular road maps (not great for this purpose), and maps from the chamber of commerce. Check around if your county clerk doesn't have what you want. Figure 7.1 is an example of a canvassing map. Figure 7.2 is an example of a canvassing map packet.

Typical voter precincts have anywhere from 300 to 600 voters or 200 to 400 homes. If your canvass is a knock you can count on canvassers covering anywhere from fifteen to twenty-five homes in an hour and thirty to fifty an hour for a straight literature drop. All of this is dependent upon how spread out or densely concentrated the homes are. Generally, I use six people working in pairs for about two hours each to complete a precinct canvass. Larger or more difficult precincts I give to eight people for a two-hour shift. If it's your campaign, you should know your precincts better than anyone. If you don't, hop in the car and take a little drive.

To accommodate a six-person team canvassing in pairs, you need to break precincts into thirds. If you're using eight canvassers, divide them into fourths. Precincts are often separated from one another down the middle of a street, which, for canvassing purposes, is a little silly. When dividing precincts for canvassing teams you generally want one team to take both sides of a street. Also, it will sometimes be more efficient to include a section from two precincts. You know your area best. As long as the territory assigned is equal to about one-third of a precinct, things should work out fine even if you mix some precincts together.

On the canvass maps for the pairs, highlight in yellow the part of the precinct that you want the canvassers to hit. Be sure to line up

"If you're on the right track, you can get run over if you just sit there."
—Will Rodgers

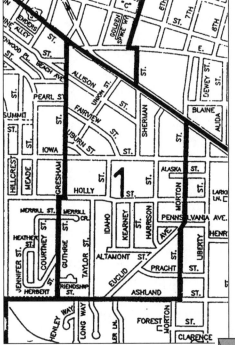

FIGURE 7.1   Example of Canvassing Map

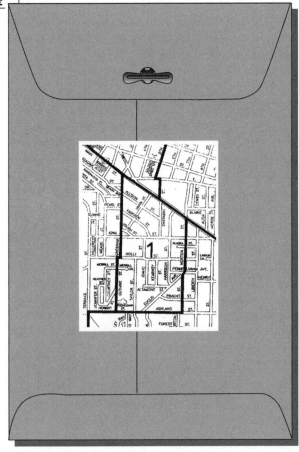

FIGURE 7.2   Example of Canvassing
Map Packet

your team maps on a window, or at least side by side, to check that streets haven't been missed or double-colored on different packets. Canvassing houses twice is wasteful of volunteer time and annoying to both your volunteers and the voters. It's bound to happen, but do your best to minimize it.

You will need two highlighted maps for each pair of canvassers. Everyone needs a map to work with; no exceptions. I don't care how well someone claims to know the area. Have canvassers mark off the blocks they complete on their map. This information helps you keep track of both the canvass and canvassers.

To get your canvassing teams ready to hit the streets, you will need many large manila envelopes, about six per precinct. I have one whole drawer in my office where I collect used envelopes to reuse for campaigns. If you tell your friends that you need some, you'll likely have more than you can use in a very short time. If push comes to shove, buy a box. You may also reuse manila envelopes during a campaign. For example, once an area has been canvassed, pull the map from the front of the envelope and tape another map in its place.

Take each of your pairs of color-coded maps and attach one map to the outside of a manila envelope. Remember, you will have two packets that are identical because people work in pairs, and these *must* stay together. Sometimes I will fold the duplicate manila envelope with the map on it and stuff it inside its partner manila envelope, or I staple them together. If they get separated, you are bound to have two different teams pick up the same packet and canvass the same area two times, so pay attention to this detail.

Place the materials necessary for the type of canvass you are conducting into each envelope. If you are doing a get-out-the-vote (GOTV) or using walking lists to contact particular people, this is the packet in which you place those materials. Put all of the lists inside one envelope and the matching envelope inside with them. The canvassers will separate out the walking lists when they divide up how they want to work. You may either place a bunch of brochures into the packet or leave them loose in a box by the door for the volunteers to pick up on their way out. Volunteers should take additional brochures so they do not run out before they have finished their areas. Having map packets keeps brochures looking pretty fresh by the time they reach the door step, and it will also protect them in bad weather.

I often tape a 3 by 5 inch card on the back of the envelope. That way, if someone canvasses the home of a strong supporter, the canvasser can write that information on the card and it will get back to the campaign in a form that's easy to use (see figure 7.3). For example, supporters may tell the canvasser that they want a lawn sign or

> "Ninety percent of the politicians give the other ten percent a bad reputation."
> —Henry Kissinger

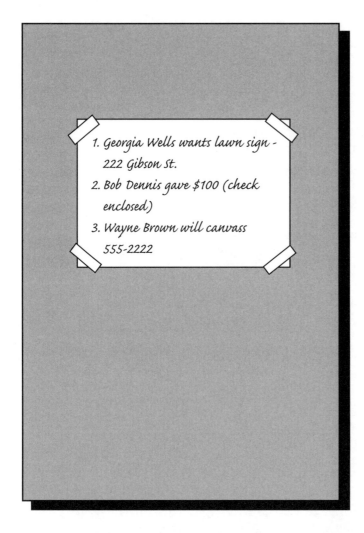

1. Georgia Wells wants lawn sign - 222 Gibson St.
2. Bob Dennis gave $100 (check enclosed)
3. Wayne Brown will canvass 555-2222

FIGURE 7.3   Example of 3 by 5 Inch Note Card Attached to Back Side of Canvass Packet

would like to be in an endorsement ad or to contribute money if the candidate calls. The canvasser can write this down on the card. When a canvasser returns, just pull off the card and process it. If you do not have time to tape a card to every canvasser's envelope, it works nearly as well to have the canvasser just write down the information directly on the envelope. This method, however, requires that you make sure to transfer that information before the envelope goes out again.

Make sure you have enough pens so each canvasser has one. I remind people to bring pens when I call back about the canvass, but there are those who forget.

Sometimes I staple a personalized message for neighbors in a particular precinct to the brochure. If you do this, you must stuff these brochures inside the canvassing packet. Otherwise, canvassers will get confused and grab the wrong brochures. This is an inexpensive way to get a direct-mail testimonial to the doors of potential supporters and well worth the effort to have it ready for the canvassers. I encourage my canvassers to write "Sorry I missed you" on the front of the brochure for people not at home. I prefer this note be in red, blue, or green ink so that it will stand out on the brochure.

Consider posting a large map of your city or county on a wall where you can mark off areas as they are canvassed. Color code the wall map according to high, medium, or low canvass priority. As volunteers complete streets, mark them off in different colored inks. In this way volunteers get to see their collective work and feel part of a well-run campaign.

To summarize the steps outlined above:

1. Get precinct maps from the county clerk and make plenty of photocopies of the areas you want to canvass.
2. Break each precinct down into thirds or into halves, depending on size.
3. Make duplicates of each portion of the precinct and keep them together for people canvassing in pairs.
4. Highlight the portion of the precinct that each pair of volunteers is to canvass and attach precinct maps to the outside of a large manila envelope.
5. Tape a 3 by 5 inch card to the manila envelope for volunteers to write down notes from households offering lawn sign locations, volunteers, or money.
6. Staple specialized notes for specific precincts to brochures and place them inside the appropriate manila envelope. Have plenty of brochures available for volunteers to grab on their way out the door with their packets.
7. Provide pens or pencils inside each of the packets.
8. Have volunteers mark areas that they canvassed on the maps on their manila envelopes. Keep track of your progress on a large wall map by coloring in streets as they are completed.
9. Send out crews to finish up partially completed precincts as indicated on returned maps.
10. Remove and reuse the manila envelopes of completed map pockets.

> "This country will not be a good place for any of us to live in unless we make it a good place for all of us to live in."
> —Theodore Roosevelt

Note: I make duplicates of all my highlighted maps. That way I have a complete set to prepare map packets for future campaigns. Don't give in and use your originals when you're in a hurry, or you'll be sorry the next time you need them.

Organizing the Volunteer Force

Have your volunteers arrive fifteen minutes early if they have not canvassed for you before. The moment they walk in, ask them to read the brochure to familiarize themselves with the contents. Generally, I put out a plate of cookies or brownies or some little thing to eat, plus juice and water. I have coffee on hand if someone asks for it, but I do not set it out because people will have to go to the bathroom the minute they get out the door (and generally they will go back home to do that). Coffee or not, urge people to use the bathroom *before* they head out to canvass.

When training canvassers, I tell them never to talk about the issues. That is for the candidate or the campaign team. No canvasser, I don't care how closely related to the campaign, can possibly know how a candidate stands on all the issues. So what do canvassers say when asked a question at the door? They can say, "That is a good question. Why don't you give *[the candidate]* a call and ask him or her?" Never offer to have the candidate call to answer a question. He or she will get little else done, and a voter who truly wants to know will take a moment to pick up the phone.

The only thing canvassers can truthfully say is why *they* are out working for the candidate. It might be because of the candidate's stand on the environment, development, timber, air quality, transportation, children's issues, taxes, jobs, libraries, public safety, or human resources. Every person who works for you will have a reason for volunteering. Urge your volunteers to think what that reason is before they head out to walk. This directive should be part of your pre-canvassing spiel. Be sure to include things like: "What would motivate you to get out and canvass on a beautiful Saturday when you would probably rather be home with your family?" This is also a nice way to let volunteers know you understand what they are giving up to work for you and that you appreciate it. I also include in my pep talks or training how difficult the odds are of winning the campaign and how important it is that we, not the opposition, win. This brings out the best in your workers.

Scheduling the Volunteers

More than anywhere else in the campaign, I try to accommodate volunteers' schedules for canvassing. Generally I set up four time slots for people on a given weekend. However, if none of those works for individuals, I send them out whenever they can go. Nine times out of ten there will be someone else who can or has to go at that time, so I can provide a partner. If I can't get a partner for the individual, I usually go along myself. I do this because it's safer and a great stress re-

Activity: Canvassing (City & Date)				
NAME	PHONE #	CB?	9:30 AM–12:00	2:30–5:00 PM

FIGURE 7.4   Example of a 5 by 8 Inch Canvassing Activity Card

ducer. It is also good for the candidate or campaign manager to canvass. In this way he or she becomes more empathic to the efforts of the canvassers, gets a better understanding of the voters, and demonstrates his or her willingness to work as hard as the volunteers. Volunteers love to canvass with the candidate or campaign manager.

Do special things for your canvassers. If someone says she does not like to do hills or that she wants to do her neighborhood, let her know that a packet will be set aside for her and then make sure to follow through. This further eliminates potential no-shows.

A big part of a good canvassing effort is placing the right volunteer in the right precinct. For example, if you have an area with a senior population, place your oldest canvassers in that area. If you have canvassers whose dress is odd or in some way inappropriate, put them in a more progressive area or have them work lawn signs. Peers should canvass peers. Remember that when that canvasser knocks at the door, he or she represents the campaign. I generally let people know before they canvass that they must present themselves well to the public and look nice.

Sometimes you will have volunteers in areas of swing voters, and many times these swing voters are overwhelmingly registered with one party over another. (Swing voters are people who do not always vote party lines but rather tend to vote issues.) I try to place a can-

"You can't hold a man down without staying down with him."
—Booker T. Washington

vasser who is in that party in that area. For example, if I am working for a Democrat and need to canvass a neighborhood that is predominantly Republican, I get my Republican volunteers together and have them canvass the neighborhood. That way when someone answers the door and says they vote party line, the canvasser can say: "I know, I'm a Republican and I usually do too, but this election I'm working for a Democrat because . . ."

"There are very few people who don't become more interesting when they stop talking."
—Mary Lowry

Bad Weather

There are bound to be days scheduled for canvassing when the weather turns out to be bad. When I am working on a campaign, I pray for a drizzle and I tell my canvassers to pray for rain and dress accordingly. Why? Because when it rains more people are home and your campaign gets bonus points for getting out in bad weather. People open the door and feel sorry for you and admire your dedication. I have also noticed that volunteers don't mind canvassing in bad weather. Think about it: If it is a sunny, glorious spring or fall day, wouldn't you rather be out doing something other than canvassing? If the weather is lousy, canvassing is a good thing to do with your time.

Although volunteer recruitment has already been covered in depth, one very effective technique I have found for getting more people to canvass is to ask every person who has agreed to canvass to bring a friend. This makes it more fun for that individual, increases your volunteer numbers, and helps to reduce possible no-shows. Because canvassing is conducted in pairs, it is an ideal activity for friends or couples. It is also safer in twos.

Often canvassers will ask if they can bring their children to help. Depending on the age of the kids this is fine. I started canvassing for my mother when I was in middle school. I believe in children having a hand in an election so they can celebrate the win with their parents. I especially like kids to canvass when I'm working for a library or school funding measure. After all, they have a stake in the outcome, and it doesn't hurt for the voters to have the stakeholder at their door.

Remember, put no campaign literature in or on mailboxes and also be sure your campaign material does not become litter. When residents are not home, instruct volunteers to wedge it into doorjambs, screen doors, and trim boards so that it cannot escape into the wind.

Because it is much more effective for the candidate to knock on the door, the candidate should also canvass and cover as much ground as possible. Don't, however, overdo it. Pace yourself. Start early enough in the campaign so that you canvass as many homes as possible. The personal touch really works. Candidates often get hung up talking with voters, so be sure to send a partner along to help cover the area.

In Summary

It bears repeating that it is critical to a successful campaign to have a large number of people turn out to volunteer. Canvassers feel good when they are clearly part of a larger effort. They are further reinforced in their commitment to the campaign when they show up and see friends and neighbors there working as well.

1. Carefully select your canvassing volunteers. Use people who are in relatively good shape and individuals who are able to walk for two hours at a time. Save apartments or areas of flat, heavy concentration for individuals who are out of shape.
2. Select the right volunteer for the right precinct. Peers should canvass peers. Have volunteers canvass their own neighborhoods.
3. Accommodate the schedule of the canvassers. If someone cannot make the scheduled time, find a time when he or she can and find that person a partner. This is a great way to finish up partially completed precincts.
4. Use the same 5 by 8 inch cards to sign up volunteers for the canvass that you use for other campaign activities.
5. Call back (CB?) your volunteers to make sure they will still be coming. Remember, do not ask if they still intend to canvass. Instead, remind them to bring something or ask what time you told them to come in case you made a mistake. Reschedule volunteers who forgot about the canvass.
6. Ask volunteers to bring a friend.
7. Have your canvassers read what they will be dropping at homes before they start out. They should be familiar with the material.
8. Set up a role-play door-knocking demonstration as part of the volunteer training before volunteers head out the door.
9. Do not serve coffee or tea to canvassers before they head out, only juice or water. Remind them to use the bathroom before they leave.

> "The reasonable man adapts himself to the world; the unreasonable one persists in trying to adapt the world to himself. Therefore all progress depends on the unreasonable man."
> —George Bernard Shaw

☞ Know the law: Remind your workers of the law: no brochures in or on mailboxes. Remind them also to secure materials left at doorsteps to prevent litter.

Activating the Right Voters

A dramatic example of the effectiveness of combining canvassing and getting out the vote (discussed in Chapter 8) is provided in figure 7.5. Identical ballot measures were placed before Ashland voters in 1993 and then a year later in 1994. Our supporting campaigns were exactly the same with two exceptions: first, in 1993 both high- and low-priority precincts were canvassed, whereas in 1994, only high-priority precincts were covered. Second, only in 1994 did we make a voter ID and GOTV effort. The combination of activating only high-support precincts with a GOTV worked. The same measure that lost in 1993 by 326 votes passed in 1994 by 447 votes.

In figure 7.5, note the decrease of "no" votes in the low-priority precincts between the two elections. Because these precincts were not canvassed in 1994, fewer voters were activated to get out and vote. The increase in the "yes" votes for the low-priority precincts in 1994 over 1993 is a result of the voter ID and GOTV effort.

Because the 1993 election was a "mail-in," it had an overall higher voter turnout than the walk-in 1994 election. Mail-in elections always have a higher voter turnout.

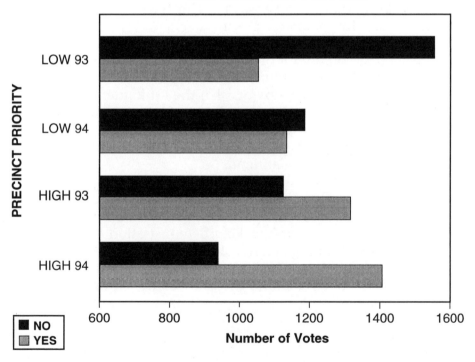

FIGURE 7.5   A Case for Canvassing and GOTV

Getting-Out-the-Vote (GOTV)

While canvassing is about activating people who you *think* will vote for your cause, a GOTV effort is about activating voters who you *know* will vote for your cause. Finding out how they intend to vote is called "voter ID." Getting them out to vote on election day is called "getting-out-the-vote" or "GOTV."

GOTV is also different from canvassing in that you are not just going to specific precincts but rather to specific voters. Obviously this means you need to identify how the person intends to vote. This can be done in one of two ways: by canvassing or phoning.

1. To ID voters while canvassing, you must ask every household you canvass how voters will vote and mark it on walking lists. These lists can be bought from a voter ID service, such as a voter contact service, or from the county elections office.
2. To ID voters by phone, call people in favorable precincts that are inclined to vote for your candidate and simply ask.

Whether you ID a voter by canvass or phone, the campaign must keep track of how each person intends to vote (supportive, somewhat supportive, undecided, somewhat opposed, opposed) and get a current phone number for election night. If your lists come with phone numbers, great. If not, set up a clerical team to fill in the blanks. Don't forget to check the Internet as a possible resource for phone numbers.

> "One thing the world needs is popular government at popular prices."
> —George Barker

A GOTV effort is most effective in elections where there is great voter apathy and an anticipated low voter turnout. Your mission is to increase the voter turnout of *certain* segments of the population only; that is, those voting the way you want them to vote. Getting-out-the-vote means urging these supporters to go to the polls, return their absentee ballots, or vote early in states where that is possible.

The Pleasure of Your Company

If you're involved in an election where a controversial measure is also on the ballot, there may be a high voter turnout that significantly affects the election, irrespective of your campaign's efforts. For example, a few years back I was working for a progressive Democrat who was to be on the ballot along with two ballot measures intended to limit the rights of a targeted minority. Our campaign had a well-organized GOTV effort and had been doing voter ID from September through November. The committee working in opposition to these two ballot measures also had a great GOTV effort, which helped ours even more. We had the state Democratic caucus running tracking polls and we knew we were neck and neck with our opponent and that the two ballot measures were going down state-wide. What we had not anticipated was the precincts of the sinners turning out in huge numbers to vote "yes" on these two ballot measures and, as long as they were there, they voted against our candidate as well. Both ballot measures failed in Ashland, three to one, but our county was only one of two state-wide to endorse this hate legislation.

Unfortunately, we realized too late that we spent far too much time identifying and getting out our vote where the proponents of the two ballot measures had already done it for us. Had we left this task to them, more volunteer time and energy could have been freed up for voter ID and GOTV of our persuadables in marginal precincts. To avoid this error, I now do cooperative GOTV efforts with other campaigns or, at the very least, call and see what other campaigns intend to do for this effort.

It's always a good idea to be aware of other ballot items that may affect your turnout or that of the opposition. If no other campaign is conducting a strong GOTV effort that will help you, do not let anything keep you from running a comprehensive GOTV effort for your campaign. There is nothing as important to winning a close election as a good GOTV.

Identifying Your Voters: Voter ID

Before you can get-out-the-vote, you need to identify voters who will be supporting your candidate or measure. One way to get the information you need is to get printed voter walking lists from a voter contact service firm. In my state we have a firm that can put together just about any combination you could think of. To find one in your state, try contacting elected officials, campaign firms, or call 800 information for voter contact services. *Note:* If you are working on a local election where no similar election was held at a statewide level, you must first conduct a precinct analysis. You then tell the voter contact service which precincts you want walking lists for.

Explain to the voter contact service that you want to use these lists to identify voters for a GOTV effort. The service will list potential supporters based on past precinct voting trends and list them according to precinct by street address and in numerical order. The voters on each street will be listed on a separate page. Across the top of the page will read: "supporting," "leaning support," "undecided," "leaning no support," and "not supporting" (or a number rating system correlated with these categories). Next to each registered voter's name will be a number from one to five that corresponds to the categories from "supporting" to "not supporting."

As indicated before, you may also get walking lists of identified priority precincts from the county. If you do this, you must do the precinct analysis first (see Chapter 6) and tell the county which precincts you want. Once you have the walking lists, you are ready to do your voter ID.

Canvassing for Voter ID

If you intend to do voter ID while canvassing, you need to reorganize the contact service's walking lists to coincide with your canvassing maps. Your canvassers must have the contact list that goes with the canvassing area they are assigned to. This is a lot more work than you might imagine. *Do not let just anyone help you with this task* or you'll spend days undoing and redoing. Once you match a walking list to a canvassing map, place the list *inside* the canvassing envelope.

If you are canvassing for a GOTV effort, you will need twice the number of canvassers normally required *or more*. At the door, each of your canvassers must ascertain whether the house will be in favor, opposed, undecided, or leaning in some way. If voters are leaning support or undecided, your campaign should be ready to follow up with literature or a phone call to bring them into your camp. If no one is home, you must have clean-up teams going out to re-knock or do the voter ID at phone banks to determine how people intend to vote.

> "There is no knowledge that is not power."
> —Ralph Waldo Emerson

The idea here is to identify individual voters that you are sure will vote for your cause if they vote. You use the results of your voter ID to compile lists of those who will vote for you, your candidate, or your cause. List your "yes" voters according to city and precinct. You must include a phone number. Remember, if some of these names come without phone numbers, set up a clerical team to look them up before election day.

If this sounds like a lot of work, it is. If you intend to do a GOTV effort, you will need someone to watch over it specifically and carefully. And everyone who has volunteered at some time during the campaign must work on election night. Actually, getting volunteers to work election night is not difficult. People who work on a campaign often have excess energy on campaign night and love to be part of the final big push. Coordinating all the people for a GOTV by canvassing is a job and a half, so be prepared.

Although it puts a heavy burden on the phone bank team, I tend to prefer voter ID by phone for a number of reasons:

1. Some areas have only 40 percent of the households with anyone at home during the canvass. That means that the remaining homes have to be called or re-canvassed anyway.
2. It is generally easier to get phone volunteers than canvass volunteers, and canvassing for voter ID uses large numbers of volunteers.
3. I believe people will tend to be more honest on the phone. It is hard for individuals to tell candidates or volunteers face-to-face that they will be supporting the opposition, especially if volunteers made all that effort to come to the person's doorstep.
4. Voter ID by canvass will sometimes get individuals that are not supporting to vote.

Voter ID by Phone

Conducting voter ID by phone works anywhere. Your goal should be to target between 10 and 15 percent of the total number of votes you need to win. If you live in a small area and are working in a non-partisan race, you may try to contact as many as 70 percent of the registered voters. As the area and voting population increase, your voter ID efforts must also expand. Always start with the precincts that will give you the most return for the effort.

From a voter ID service or from the county (much cheaper), get a list of registered voters by precinct in alphabetical order. The best use of time is to call only high- and medium-support precincts. To identify your supporters, you need to set up phone banks and systematically call every registered voter in the designated area. Again, county lists often do not have all of the phone numbers, so you may need to set up clerical sessions to look up phone numbers before your phone banks begin. Phone banking to identify supporters, if you can do it, goes much quicker than canvassing.

In your first round of phone calls your campaign has a couple of choices: blind calls or persuasion calls. In a blind call the volunteer asks questions regarding the candidates or issues but does not reveal for whom he or she is calling. In a persuasion call the phone caller immediately lets the voter know which organization is behind the calling effort. I happen to prefer the persuasion call over a blind call because it saves time by eliminating one step. If you start with blind calls and the voter is undecided or has a question about one of the candidates, your volunteer cannot field the question or attempt to persuade. Your campaign must be ready to follow up that call to try to persuade the voter and later with direct mail or brochure.

If the first call is a persuasion call and your volunteer finds an undecided voter, he or she can immediately provide reasons for that voter to move to your candidate or cause. The caller may also offer to send information to move the voter from undecided to supportive. A campaign can also use an endorsement group to pull along voters with a persuasion call. For example, your targeted precinct is one where parents have been very active in a neighborhood school or have voted heavily for school projects. By having teachers call, you can ask your callers to identify themselves as just that, teachers calling on your behalf. Or if your targeted precinct has been very supportive of environmental issues, you might have members of the Audubon Society call on behalf of the campaign. Or you can use people from within a particular precinct to call their neighbors: "Hello, is this George? Hi, I'm Shirley Smith. I live just down the street from you . . . " Indirect supporters can be very persuasive.

Last-Minute Efforts to Persuade Voters

The weekend before the election I always drop a persuasion piece to my high-priority and swing precincts. If I am working on a candidate campaign this piece may outline the differences between the two candidates, the voting record of my opposition, and so forth. If I'm working on an issue-based campaign the flyer may include who supports the effort and why as well as who opposes it and why, or it could highlight the benefits of the ballot issue. If I'm working on a write-in campaign the drop might be the actual mechanics of the vote: what to press and where and what to write. Whatever you do, keep it short and to the point. People are inundated by this time and have a very limited attention span.

> "To do great and important tasks, two things are necessary: a plan and not quite enough time."
> — Anonymous

If you do not have the money to send something by mail, hit the streets with your volunteers. Single-sheet flyers are cheap and people need to be nudged so they remember that the election is just days away. If you have limited money for a direct mail piece, send a post-card. For direct mail, ask the county clerk to download the registered voters for the desired party affiliation (Republican, Democrat, Independent, or other) minus the absentee voters in the precincts you want. Take that disk to a mail house and have them pull duplicate names to a single address. That way each address gets just one piece of mail. This saves money for the campaign and clutter for the voter.

On election day an estimated 5 percent of the voters go to the polls still undecided. Some of these voters will undervote your race (vote for candidates and issues they're decided upon but skip yours) and some will decide in the voting booth. For these voters, there are a few things your campaign volunteers can do to pull them over at the last minute:

1. Move existing lawn signs from one location to another the night before election day. People get used to seeing a lawn sign for the month before the election and if a new one goes up in a neighborhood, or, better yet, ten new ones, that will get noticed.
2. Hand paint specialty signs for a specific neighborhood and place them the day before the election. "Elect Mayor Daniels for a central bike path." "For more parks, elect Daniels." The message should be personalized for that neighborhood. This looks like the upwelling of new support. (I have used the reverse side of old lawn sign stock for this.)
3. Start calling your identified supporters a couple of days before the election to remind them to vote, underscoring how close the election will be and how their vote could make a difference in the outcome. Then ask them to call five friends.

Avoid Untargeted Activities

I have never worked for a candidate who has not wanted to stand at the entrance of the county fair, or set up a table on the plaza in the heart of our community, or hand out flyers at the co-op, or walk the boulevard with sandwich boards on election morning. This kind of untargeted activity can really work against your GOTV effort by reminding those to vote who you would prefer stay home. Getting-out-the-vote is about getting *your* voters to the polls, not all voters.

On the other hand, I have worked on campaigns where certain neighborhoods, areas, and even entire cities within a district support one candidate over another by huge numbers. If your objective is to increase voter turnout in just these areas, waving signs on street corners or in front of malls works very well. People love to acknowledge this kind of hard work with a vote.

However, there are far better ways to use a candidate than doing high-profile, low-return activities. I like to keep the candidate busy and out of my hair on election eve and day. It's a great time to have him or her be on the phone for GOTV or canvassing a high-priority precinct. It is also an excellent time for the candidate to call and thank supporters and volunteers for their time and money.

Once you have identified your supporters, there are two ways to find out if they have voted. One is poll watching and the other, much simpler method, is phoning.

Poll Watching

Poll watching represents the last chance to get your supporters to the polls. Chances are you've worked hard to get to a win and, without a doubt, poll watching can mean getting the critical votes you need to push your effort over the top. People have great intentions of voting but somehow things just come up; they get busy or will simply forget to vote unless they are reminded. I have not missed a vote since I registered at age eighteen, but there were a couple of elections that I nearly forgot. Even recently I have sometimes postponed voting and then on my way to an evening city council meeting remembered I hadn't voted. It happens.

Poll watching is a labor-intensive campaign activity that can make all the difference. It's also something that needs plenty of preparation. Forms must be filled out and returned to an election officer at the county to get permission for poll watchers to do their job. It is not an activity that can be put together at the last minute, so prepare ahead of time. Find someone who will oversee this activity and support that person with your volunteer base. Each poll watcher will need lists of people who have been identified as supporters, listed alphabetically and by precinct. Ideally this list would also include all members of the party with which your candidate is affiliated and supporters highlighted within that list. However, if all you can get together is a list of identified supporters, don't worry.

Be sure to provide each poll watcher with more than one list so that when volunteers come to retrieve the list to start calling no-shows, time isn't wasted transferring names. Also be sure that the poll watcher has a clipboard and a couple of good writing utensils. I prefer pencils with good erasers.

> "I wanted to look nice if we won, and if we lost this would be nice to be buried in."
> —Bob Borkowski, assistant coach, on why he showed up for a game in a black, pinstriped suit

Things to Do for a Successful Poll-Watching Effort

1. Check with your county clerk or election official, prior to the election, to determine what is required of your poll watchers. Are there forms that must be filled out and returned? Does the clerk require that training be conducted by his or her staff? What are the requirements for a poll watcher? In my area it is legal for poll watchers to review the poll book as long as they don't interfere with the work of the election board. In other areas they can only listen for names as they are being called out.

2. Place poll watchers in high-priority precincts (where high numbers of your supporters have been identified) and provide them with an alpha-sorted list, clipboard, writing utensils, and a cell phone. It is also a nice touch to send them out with a folding chair or stool.

3. Have teams of poll watchers at the polls noting which of your identified supporters have voted throughout the day. As the name of the voter is called out, the poll watcher will check the list of supporters to see whether that individual is among those who have been positively identified.

4. Relay this information back to phone banks. Approximately two hours before the polls close, call supporters who have not yet voted to urge them to get down to the polls.

5. Tell the phone bank volunteers to impress upon the voters how important it is that they get to the polls, that you predict a *very* close election, and that every vote will count. The supporter who hasn't yet voted must have a sense of urgency to get to the polls and vote.

6. Offer rides to get supporters to and from the polls. If there is a sleeping baby or sick child, a volunteer may offer to come stay in the home while the single parent votes.

With the poll watcher, the phone bank, and the transportation effort, you will have a lot of people involved and you may find that the best hope for pulling it off is to combine efforts with other campaigns. Only a well-organized, well-run campaign can pull off an effective poll watching effort. That is one reason well-organized and well-run campaigns win elections.

Format for Poll-Watching

There are two basic steps in the poll-watching process:

1. Volunteers observe the voters all day (from the time polls open to two hours before they close) in selected precincts to

see who votes. Those who vote are marked off by running a dark line through their phone number and name.

2. Two hours before the polls close, the final poll watcher of the day takes the precinct list to pre-assigned phone banks where callers divide the sheets and call all identified supporters who have not yet voted to urge them to get to the polls before they close.

Note: If your last poll watcher wants to stay at the polls longer, he or she can call in names by cell phone to the phone banks.

Precinct Captains

Each precinct where poll watching is to occur must have a precinct captain responsible for the precinct team. Each captain has four specific duties:

1. Prior to election day, the captain makes sure phone numbers are looked up and written on the precinct lists and your identified voters must be highlighted on the lists as well. It is best to assemble a clerical team for this activity. If the voters' phone numbers cannot be found in the telephone directory, run a line through their names as though they had already voted.

   In this process of writing phone numbers, be sure not to separate the precinct sheets. This task should be completed no later than the Friday before the election.

   Note: If your campaign has not identified supporters prior to election day and the intent of your poll watching is to call all registered voters in your highest priority precincts, then be sure to cross out people you know have left the area or voted absentee.

2. The captain is responsible for recruiting four poll watchers and one standby. These five people need to be certified, trained, and supervised. Poll watchers should meet with the their team captain the weekend prior to the election. Signed certificates for each poll watcher should be provided to the precinct captains at that time. Your county clerk or county election office will supply you with all the information and forms you may need.

   > "The important thing in life is not the triumph but the struggle."
   > —Pierre de Coubertin

3. The captain is responsible for setting up the phone bank for his or her precinct and recruiting the phone volunteers to work for the last two hours before the polls close. The last days of the campaign are the most demanding. It is impor-

tant that poll watching operate independently of the campaign manager, candidate, and campaign team. However, the precinct captains should look to the campaign structure for volunteer names to call and possible locations to secure.

4. The captain must be present at his or her precinct when it opens and supervise the precinct off and on during the day to make certain that all goes smoothly. Two hours before the polls close, the captain must be present at the phone bank to make certain that the doors are open and that the telephone volunteers use the recommended format in their calls. The recommended format for these calls is presented in figure 8.1; the general protocol for phone banks is covered in Chapter 3.

Poll Watcher Responsibilities

1. Arrive a few minutes early at the polling place.
2. Give your signed certificate to the election judge, who is a member of the polling board.
3. Do not engage in conversation with the election board. You, of course, may answer questions, but do not discuss other topics with the board.
4. Listen for the names of voters as they arrive and state them to the board. Cross the names out on your list as the people are voting.
5. Two hours before polls close, the fourth poll watcher should take the precinct list to the designated phone bank.

In close elections, the poll watchers and phone banks that follow will often supply the margin of votes needed to be victorious on election day. However, because of the amount of organization and labor-intensive demands of this activity, few campaigns conduct poll watching anymore. *If at all possible, do it. Voter ID, poll watching, and GOTV absolutely make the difference between winning and losing in a close race.*

Regulation of Persons at the Polls

☞ Know the law: In all aspects of a campaign, it is important to know the law; in poll watching it is imperative. The polling place has special regulations that cover everything from how close individuals may stand to the polls if they are not voting and not a certified poll watcher to what may be discussed by those present. The campaign manager should contact the county clerk prior to the poll watching activity and get the regulatory information to the precinct captains in written form.

ELECTION DAY PHONE SCRIPT

Hello, this is _____ .

I am a volunteer worker for *(name of the campaign)*.

I am calling to remind you that the polls will remain open until 8 P.M. and also to encourage you to vote. This will be a very close election and we really need your support for *(name of person or ballot measure)* to win.

Your polling place is located at _____ .

Will you need transportation to the polls?

> ## If transportation is needed, they can call the following numbers:
>
> _____
>
> _____
>
> _____
>
> _____

FIGURE 8.1 Election Day Phone Script

Authorized poll watchers are allowed in the polling place and must sign a specific section of the front cover of the poll book. Only as many poll watchers are allowed as will *not* interfere with the work of the election board.

Poll watchers must have written authorization from one of the following:

1. For the purpose of challenging electors at the polling place, either from the county clerk or a political party;
2. For the purpose of observing the receiving and counting of votes, from a candidate.

Poll watchers *may*:

- Take notes
- Have access to poll books, so long as it does not interfere with the work of the board

> "The only thing that hasn't changed is our ability to think differently."
> —Albert Einstein

- Challenge persons offering to vote at the poll
- Challenge entries in poll book
- Wear campaign buttons

"Democracy is a contact sport."
—Ray McNally of McNally Temple Associates Inc., in Sacramento, California

Poll watchers *may not:*

- Campaign in any way
- Circulate any cards, handbills, questionnaires, or petitions
- Fail to follow the instructions of the election board
- Take poll books off tables

All members of an election board should familiarize themselves with specific election law violations.

Phoning

If you do not have enough people to watch the polling places all day, don't worry. I recently worked on a campaign where we came up with an approach that was nearly as effective and won handily because of the GOTV effort. For this process you will need a good precinct analysis. Remember, your precinct analysis will tell you where your support is. It will show you where people have voted for causes similar to yours in the past. Your precinct analysis will also tell you where people live who will *never* vote for your cause or candidate. If it is clear that a precinct has traditionally voted against campaigns such as the one you are working on, don't canvass it, don't call them, don't activate them. Forget them for the GOTV effort. Instead, look for precincts that have been split: those that have narrowly supported or narrowly defeated past campaigns similar to yours. These are the precincts you should call and voter ID. Then on election day call only the *identified "yes"* voters.

As for those remaining precincts that have overwhelmingly supported past campaigns similar to the one you are now promoting, it is not so necessary to voter ID them. You know they will tend to vote your way.

On election day, while your volunteers are going down the list of supporters in the marginal precincts calling the *identified "yes"* votes, they can call *all* of the voters in the high-priority precincts. Should your campaign have time before election day, you may want to ID the voters in the high-priority precincts as well, but this is not as important. Look at the phone calling on the day of the election as your one last canvass in a high-priority precinct. Call everyone. If your precinct analysis is accurate, you will turn out strong support that might have stayed home otherwise. *Remember, you are not changing minds, just the turnout.* Minds are generally made up.

One important caveat: *Don't duplicate calling lists.* Each phone banker or phone station needs a separate calling list. When the caller reaches someone who has already voted, he or she needs to cross off the name so the person is not called again. For those who have not voted, it is up to you to decide whether you want to call them again. If the election is close, you may want to urge them one more time to get down to the polls. However, in general, more than one call is an annoyance and counterproductive.

In Summary

1. Identify who your supporters are, by either canvassing or phoning.
2. Persuade undecided voters with direct mail and follow-up phone calls.
3. Drop literature or send a direct mail piece to the high-priority and swing precincts the weekend before the election.
4. Call your identified supporters two to three nights before the election to remind them to vote.
5. Turn your support out on election day by:

   A. poll watching to see who has voted and who has not among your identified support;
   B. placing new signs, moving signs, and using people with placards;
   C. calling those who have not voted by two hours before the polls close.

The Absentee Ballot and Early Vote

Voting absentee used to be a service to the voter who was temporarily out of the area or unable to get to the polls. However, at least on the West Coast, it has now become the vote of convenience. As ballots become longer and more complex, the busy and conscientious voter is choosing to vote absentee. In a recent California election it took my parents more than an hour to vote their twelve-card ballot. And they *knew* how they intended to vote on each of the issues. Is it any wonder they would choose to do it at home?

With long, complicated ballots, you run the risk of voter fatigue. Voter fatigue occurs when voters actually lose interest in voting as they spend more and more time getting to the end of their ballot. Because many states set up ballots with the local elections at the end, this is something for your campaign to keep in mind. If your measure is the last item voters will hit on a ballot, encouraging vot-

> "If the only tool you have is a hammer, you tend to see every problem as a nail."
> —Abraham Maslow

FIGURE 8.2   Newspaper Headlines Concerning Absentee Ballots

ers to register and vote absentee at home may help minimize the
undervote for those items at the end of a long ballot.

The absentee ballot has traditionally been a more conservative
vote, in part due to the age of the absentee voter. Moreover, with
the Republican party and Republican candidates putting more resources and energy toward registering voters absentee, it has become even more conservative. In my area, an absentee count has often turned losing candidates into winners and often will reverse a
winning funding measure.

There are a number of reasons it is to your advantage to register as
many of your supporters as possible to vote absentee or early:

1. Often campaigns don't heat up and get nasty until the final
   three weeks. As voters are becoming more and more disillu-
   sioned with negative campaigning, their response is to stay
   home on election night. If a candidate or party has a huge
   percentage of the turnout locked in before things get nasty,
   they're at a decided advantage.
2. If you know who will vote absentee or by early vote, then
   your campaign can concentrate on these voters prior to election day, closer to when they actually will vote.
3. Nasty weather can affect voter turnout on election day.

In the 1998 mid-term November election nearly half of the registered Oregon voters requested absentee ballots. Of those who requested absentee ballots, 74 percent returned them. Of those not requesting absentee ballots, only 41 percent turned out to vote. The

absentee ballot represented over 58 percent of the total voter turnout. And that was unusually low for us.

Although Oregon voters approved permanent vote-by-mail in the November 1998 election, prior to that time they could register as a permanent absentee without re-registering to do so at each election. These lists were available from the county clerk for a small charge and about 40 percent of the names also had phone numbers listed.

This means that with a little effort any campaign can access a large group of likely voters, ID whom they intend to support in the election, send persuasion mail to the undecideds, and make sure those supporting your efforts return their ballots by election day.

In many states the option to register absentee is open to anyone for the asking up to the day before the election. Those who request absentee ballots within the three weeks prior to an election are the most likely to actually vote. Your county election offices are often able to provide updated lists of those requesting absentee ballots as the election draws near. When someone makes the request, that voter should be contacted by the campaign.

Most states that have absentee voting require that voters make that request prior to each election except, as is the case in California, if a voter has a permanent disability. Then voters can register to vote absentee always, unless they miss an election, in which case they have to start again. Some states require a reason for the absentee ballot.

Some states have early vote. With early vote, the registered voter may go to a designated polling place between certain hours and vote just as though it were election day. Depending on the state, this can take place anywhere from four to forty days before an election. As with absentee voting, early vote gives a campaign an opportunity to lock in votes prior to the election. It does, however, require that a campaign peak twice: once for the early vote or absentees and once for election day. Direct mail, advertising, canvassing, and everything else must be done earlier for these voters.

> "Vote early and vote often."
> —Al Capone

Voters love the convenience of absentee and early vote and those who use them tend to be some of the most likely of the likely voters. In Texas, early vote represented 40 percent of the voter turnout in some districts in 1996.

If your state or county has early vote or absentee voting:

1. Check past elections to determine the number who requested or took advantage of this option (and, for absentee, look at the percentage of those returning their ballot who requested to vote absentee).
2. Determine the percentage that these voters constituted for the overall voter turnout.

3. Find out whether a list of those requesting absentee ballots is available to your campaign through the county clerk or election office.
4. Determine whether you may acquire periodically updated lists of those who actually vote absentee or early as the election draws near. (That way you will not be continually contacting those who have already returned their ballots.)
5. Set up a clerical team to look up the phone numbers of the voters if the list of absentee voters does not include them.
6. Hound your supporters to vote early if you are in a state that offers early vote.

Absentee ballots present some unique challenges to the grassroots campaign. There is an inexpensive way to deal with absentee ballots if lists are not available from the county election officials.

Assign the task of finding out about the absentee ballot to a team. One person must be willing to go the county clerk's office and find out who has requested absentee ballots on a daily basis. This person keeps a running list. This should be done on a regular basis because voters requesting the absentee ballot will often fill it out and return it the same day they receive it. Once you know who the people are making the request, you must try to persuade them to vote for your candidate or cause. Forget the precinct analysis for the absentee voter. You are no longer hoping these people will *not* be voting. You know for a fact most *will*. As I said before, these are among the most likely voters. To persuade these voters you have a number of choices:

1. Use direct mail to persuade.
2. Send volunteers or the candidate to their homes to canvass the voters.
3. Have the candidate, a friend, or a prominent citizen call the voters.
4. Send a personalized letter from the candidate or from a well-known, respected local leader of the same party affiliation as the voter.
5. Use some combination of all these techniques.

Mail-in Elections

While this section is tailored for Oregon and Washington, states that currently conduct mail-in elections, many of the activities can also be used to increase the voter turnout for absentee ballots.

Vote-by-mail is a no-brainer. It increases voter turnout, reduces the cost of running elections for the taxpayer, and makes life easier for those of us running for office or helping others run. It makes it easier to secure funding for schools, parks, libraries, and needed improvements for government buildings. For state and local government to provide the option of both absentee and poll voting with tax dollars is a costly luxury we should relinquish everywhere.

In mail-in elections, the county mails all ballots to the homes of registered voters within a specific voting district. To give voters ample time to review the ballot items, ballots are mailed about three weeks prior to the due date when they must be at the county clerk's office for tabulation. The cost savings to county and state governments is about 50 percent, with the added bonus of increasing voter turnout anywhere from 10 percent to 30 percent. Higher turnout and huge savings to the taxpayer are pretty strong endorsements.

For the purposes of your campaign team, the difference between a mail-in election and poll voting lies primarily in timing. In a normal election most of your canvassing occurs and nearly all of your ads appear in the three weeks prior to the election. With a mail-in election, more than 50 percent of all the voters who return their ballots will do so in the first week after receiving the ballots. That means if you wait to do your canvass and to place your really great ads in the final three weeks, you will be doing so after the election is essentially over.

Depending on when you can place lawn signs, you might even choose to eliminate them from your campaign plan. After all, if you are restricted to placing signs thirty days before an election and voters return their mailed ballots in the first week after receiving them, is it worth the money and effort? Many believe that the impact of lawn signs comes in the first week and that lawn signs will still probably do the job they are intended to do. However, this point should be discussed by your campaign committee.

In general, if you are involved in a mail-in election, your campaign must peak the day the ballots are mailed, not the day they are due back. Your canvassing must be completed the day the ballots are mailed, and your ads must start at least a week before the ballots leave the county clerk and peak during that first week that they are received by the voter. Even though many voters will return their ballots immediately, your campaign or cause should continue to have a presence in the media until the day the ballots are due. You must be prepared to spend more money on ads to span the three weeks between when ballots are mailed and when ballots are due.

> "Trust in Allah, but tie your camel."
> —Arab proverb

GOTV and Voter ID

After the ballots are mailed, your campaign's primary focus must turn to the get-out-the-vote effort. A GOTV effort for a mail-in election is remarkably easy and painless. It is also the best thing about mail-in elections. With a mail-in you do not need to voter ID by either canvassing or phone banks as described earlier in this chapter. The voter ID and GOTV take place in the same call, as described below.

Many counties keep track of who returns the ballots as they are received, and for a nominal charge they will print a list of those who have voted *(activity list)* or those who haven't voted *(inactivity list)*. To do a GOTV, you want to know who has *not* voted in that first week or so. Some counties do not have the capability of separating the active and inactive lists. If this is the case, consider setting up a clerical team to prepare lists for your GOTV effort.

When vote-by-mail was first introduced in Oregon, over 60 percent of all the voters who intended to vote did so within the first week. These percentages have now leveled off to 40–50 percent the first week, followed by 10–20 percent in the second week, and 40 percent in the final week. If you are involved in a vote-by-mail campaign, call your county clerk to determine the habits of your constituency in previous elections. You need to know the percentage of people who return ballots in the first week. Then plug this number into the formula outlined below.

Predicting Turnout

Usually counties will run a couple of days behind, so about ten days after the ballots are mailed, call up and ask for the number of ballots already returned. The number they give you will be anywhere from 50 to 80 percent of the total turnout for the election. Call your county clerk for voter tendencies in your area. With this information you can figure out what the actual turnout will eventually be.

In past elections, I have used this information to help me calculate how many more ballots I need to win. Let's say you're working on a school election that in the past lost by a 45–55 percent margin. First you must figure what the turnout will be. You do this based on the percentage of the total turnout that is usually received the first week, and with simple math you can calculate how many people will ultimately vote. Multiply that number by 55 percent and subtract the result from the total voter turnout. The difference is what you predict you will lose by, and it also gives you the number of ballots that *must* come in during your GOTV effort to pull off a win.

Calculating the Predicted Turnout

Let's say you live in a city with 6,000 registered voters where 60 percent of those who will return their ballots do so in the first week. Ten days after the ballots are mailed, you call and find that 2,400 voters have returned their ballots.

We know that 2,400 = 60 percent of the total number of ballots that will eventually come in.

Set up the following equation: 60/100 times X = 2,400. (We put 60 over 100 because it is 60 percent.) Now we have to isolate the "X"; multiply both sides by 100 and then divide both sides by 60. X (total number of votes) = 4,000 ballots that will eventually come in, or a 66 percent voter turnout.

In the past, school elections for money have failed in your city by 55 percent, so multiply 55 percent by 4,000, which equals 2,200. This represents the number who will be voting against the school tax measure if you do nothing. Subtract 2,200 from 4,000, which equals 1,800. This is the number who will be voting for your school measure. Subtracting 1,800 from 2,200, you can see that if you do nothing you will lose the election by 400 votes. That means you need to increase the voter turnout of your supporters by 400 plus 1 to win.

After making this calculation for your situation, do the following two weeks before the ballots are mailed:

1. Order a list of registered voters in your high-priority/swing precincts (you determined these when you did your precinct analysis) from the county.
2. Have a clerical team look up phone numbers. (Don't forget to check the Internet for local phone directories.)
3. Find phone bank locations and set up phone banks to begin calling the voters in your favorable precincts to ID them for support for your ballot measure or candidate.
4. Spend time persuading undecided voters to support you.
5. Follow up with all undecided voters via direct mail or phone calls from friends, colleagues, co-workers, the candidate, or prominent citizens. Keep on the undecided voters until you know where they stand.
6. Call people who should be supportive of your candidate or cause in lower priority precincts based on party affiliation, age, income, and education, only if the odds are really against you and you cannot get the number of votes you need to win from the high-priority precincts. Be sure to keep track of whether the responses are "yes," "no," or "maybe."
7. Follow up "maybes" in the lower priority precincts and leave the "nos" alone.

Once the Ballots Are Mailed

1. Order the inactivity list (alphabetically by precinct) from the county clerk about seven to eleven days after the ballots are mailed.

"The people who win elections are those with the guts to keep on running when nobody else gives them a prayer."
—Christopher Matthews, *San Francisco Examiner*

If your county does not separate those who have voted from those who have not, line up a clerical team to highlight which ones have not yet voted.

2. Set up another clerical team and have them look for anyone who has said they will be supporting your candidate or cause and has not yet returned a ballot. This is also a good time to transfer the looked-up phone numbers from the first list you were calling.
3. Set up phone banks and call all your identified supporters to get in their ballots.

Don't Quit Now

Five to seven days before the ballots are due, order another inactivity list. Have all volunteers go over copies of the list to identify and call any friends they find. The hope is that if friends call friends, they can move them to get their ballots in or influence the votes of the still undecided. In one campaign when we did this, I called a friend to get her ballot in and found out that she was a "no" vote. While I could not convince her to vote "yes," I did convince her to not return her ballot.

Last-ditch Effort

As each day progresses toward the campaign, more and more people will have returned their ballots, making late campaign activities less effective. But even if you have done nothing in the way of voter ID or calling up to this point, there is still hope.

On the Friday preceding election day, you will need to get one last inactivity list. Again, request that names be organized alphabetically and according to precinct. That weekend, two to three days before the election, when it's too late to return a ballot through the mail, set up your phone banks. Your job is to call *everyone* on that list. Start with high-priority precincts where you will be most successful and then work your way through the rest as votes are needed. (Remember, you're doing this *only* if your campaign has not had the time or people to voter ID prior to this point. If your campaign has identified voters, follow the steps I listed above but avoid the non-supporting group.)

Your objective is to conduct voter ID and GOTV in the same phone call, so when you contact someone, you must first determine if he or she is supportive. If so, ask if a volunteer may come pick up the ballot.

If the voter called is not supporting, get off the phone. Don't worry about activating "no" votes. The chances of a non-supporting person who hasn't already mailed in the ballot driving to the library or county offices is minuscule. Collect ballots all weekend, and on Monday or Tuesday morning have campaign workers deliver all the ballots to the county. Your final push is on election eve and election night.

For those called who say they are supporting your cause, but for whatever reason failed to get their ballot in, offer to pick up the ballot. In this case, ask the voter to tape the ballot to the screen door or shove it in the jamb, so a volunteer can quickly pick it up without knocking. It's my experience as I do more and more write-in elections that most people don't want you to pick up their ballot. I used to think that it was because people didn't really trust the volunteers, but now I believe differently. I think that for many people it is embarrassing to admit that they still have not voted, and it makes matters worse that you're going to drive to their homes to pick up the ballot. Close to three-quarters of the people we call that are supportive and still have their ballots volunteer to drive them immediately to a drop-off box. Because I am generally anxious I push the voter a little bit and say, "Hey, we have someone driving right by your house to get another ballot; let us save you the trip." If the voter says, "No, I'll do it," I let it go.

For the final two nights, Monday until 9:00 P.M. and Tuesday until one hour before the polls close, I have phone banks going full tilt. I also line up runners for these nights. (More are needed for Tuesday than Monday night.) Runners are people whose sole job is to go out and pick up ballots as phone banks turn them up. It's best to use two runners per car so the driver doesn't have to park. While the driver slows down, the passenger hops out and pulls the ballot off the screen door or from the doorjamb and takes off. For runners to be efficient, I generally have the city divided into four quadrants. As soon as a phone volunteer has a ballot to pick up, I put the address and name on a card or piece of paper and route it. I continue to do this until a driver returns and I have enough ballots to pick up in a certain area.

On election night, depending on how many ballots need to be picked up, all my callers may become runners. When the phones shut down, everyone goes out to pick up the last of the ballots.

In May 1997 we had a vote-by-mail bond measure to cover the city's portion of the damages from our New Year's Day flood. It was the second election in which I had worked under the double majority limitations imposed on the state in the November 1996 election. (Under the state's double majority, for any money measure to pass you must have 50 percent of the registered voters turn out and win 50 percent plus one of those voting.) We had been on the phone for four nights straight, starting with the high-priority precincts and

> "Spend the time to make the foundation right or you will pay in time and money all the way to the roof."
> —Tony Nunes, builder

working our way down the list. Because we needed 50 percent turnout, none of us cared if the voter was for or against the bond measure by then and my callers wanted to press on past 7:00 P.M. All the runners were out getting ballots to drop off at the public library.

> "Out of the strain of the Doing, Into the peace of the Done."
> —Julia Louise Woodruff

Finally, at 7:30, with hundreds of calls under our belts for the night, we shut down the phone banks and each picked up a handful of addresses so we could go retrieve ballots and get them to the library by 8:00. Now our library, like most old Carnegies, is situated on a temple-like hill with a horrible ingress and egress, no on-street parking, and a small lot with only eleven spaces. Although many of the people we called said they would drive their ballots in that night, it was still a push to get the ones who could not. As I pulled up to the library, cars were lined up around the block with voters wanting to drop off their ballots. Eventually, people just left their cars and walked in their ballots. Because we were all on the same mission and because Ashland is so small and everyone knows everyone, it turned into a kind of social gathering.

By the time I worked my way into the library, the ballot box provided by the county clerk was jammed full and the ballots spilled over onto the counter. In a close mail-in election, those last-minute votes will win you the campaign. We won.

9

Direct Mail

In this chapter
Ethnic and Gender Gaps
Direct Mail to Persuade Voters
Direct Mail to Hit Your Opponent
Direct Mail on a Budget
Mail Preparation

Whereas canvassing is about activating voters who are inclined to vote for your candidate according to the past voting patterns of their neighborhood, direct mail is about activating voters around a specific issue that transcends voting tendencies. As discussed in the chapter on brochures, the first thing you do with your campaign committee is to develop a theme and message for the campaign. Remember, to develop a theme, you look for external forces outside of the campaign. Find indicators to predict where your community is going or wants to go, as well as the opportunities and constraints. You also look for fears, concerns, worries, hopes, and dreams of your constituency. Your message is how you communicate this theme to the voter in a concise sentence or two. Through the process of identifying why and who will vote for your cause, you identify groups with which your candidate or campaign will develop a relationship. This process and the message are developed early to activate special interest support that can lead to endorsements, money, and, yes, votes.

Direct mail can cultivate a relationship between your campaign and the voters based on issues. These issues should resonate with your base vote *and* the swing vote. The purpose is to lock in your base vote and move swing voters your way, regardless of party affiliation or prior voting tendencies.

For example, you are working for a pro-choice Republican running against an anti-choice Democrat. You have a list of pro-choice voters who tend to vote party. Your job is to point out to swing voters that their Democrat is anti-choice. You're banking on their ide-

> "Public officials are not a group apart. They inevitably reflect the moral tone of the society in which they live."
> —John F. Kennedy

als influencing their vote. Believe me, it works. The strategy you use here is the same as you use in an issue-based campaign. With these voters you stay on this message.

"The world is moving so fast these days that the man who says it can't be done is generally interrupted by someone doing it."
—Elbert Hubbard

This method works because you are offering the voters simple, additional information to help them decide about an issue or candidate. You're providing a shortcut for the voter needing to make a decision. Direct mail is a way to get a specialized message to individual voters regardless of where they live or how their precincts tend to vote. You can run your entire campaign on direct mail; all it takes is money. However, in a grassroots campaign where resources are limited and jurisdictions somewhat smaller, direct mail can best be used to augment the more comprehensive, less-expensive campaign.

Direct mail is more than a letter or brochure stuffed into an envelope. It is the most selective of all media forms and, because of its selectivity, there are distinct advantages to using direct mail rather than TV, newspapers, or radio. Using direct mail, a campaign can align an exact issue with an exact voter in a specific house. To do this effectively requires research on the part of the campaign, as you must know your opponent's stands on specific issues and you also must know the issues that will swing a particular voter. Ideally you will find areas that matter to the voter in which your candidate and the opponent differ dramatically from one another. These are called "ticket splitters." A ticket splitter is an issue that is so important to the voter that it, and it *alone,* will determine how that person's vote is cast. In general, ticket splitters are emotional issues and do not track party lines.

It is important to remember that your direct mail is only as effective as the list to which it is mailed.

A number of issues tend to influence voters to break from party lines:

Military issues: For example, you are running against an incumbent who was one of two "no" votes in the state senate on a bill designed to protect job security of National Guard volunteers after a military rotation. This is information that veterans should have.

Libraries: Your opponent voted to close the public library during tight budget years while voting to increase his salary. Friends of the Library, district schoolteachers, volunteers associated with the libraries, and faculty and students at a local college should know this.

Woman's right to choose: Your school board opponent voted against sexuality education in the high school curriculum, and teen pregnancy increased dramatically. Supporters of NARAL, Women's Political Caucus, American Association of

University Women, Planned Parenthood, and the Presbyterian and Unitarian churches should know this.

Environmental issues: Again, environmentalists and anti-environmentalists do not track party lines. Positions about issues in this area should be delivered to a specific voting constituency.

Other ticket splitters:
- Air quality
- Traffic (congestion, bikes, pedestrian walkways, mass transit)
- Airports, especially general aviation
- Seniors
- School funding, teacher salaries, school infrastructure
- Unions
- Children's athletic and extracurricular programs
- Small businesses
- Land use, development, and parks
- Taxes
- Historic preservation

Ethnic and Gender Gaps

The gender and ethnic gaps play their biggest role in direct mail. Throughout the Dole/Clinton presidential campaign, the women's vote was a hot issue. What Newt Gingrich laid out, Bob Dole wore around his neck. In 1996, women across America, irrespective of income or education, had an underlying concern about their personal economics. Men tend to worry about problems when they actually happen, but women think more about "what ifs." Bob Dole's attacks on welfare moms played well to angry white men but made women anxious. Many women, working full time, raising kids, sometimes without a father, worried that they were just one paycheck away from being a welfare mom, almost irrespective of their financial security.

When Dole went after Medicare and seemed uninterested in shoring up Social Security, many women worried that they were the ones who would eventually be responsible for taking care of aging parents, and this political posturing became a source of economic anxiety for women. When the California GOP went after affirmative action, women became uneasy. Women interpreted these types of issues in many ways and worried how this direction would affect them personally. No matter what Dole said to win the women's vote, it backfired. Perhaps because of his age, generation, or reference point, he simply did not speak to women's fears, frustrations, and anxieties. Clinton, on the other hand, with his father dying before his birth and having been raised by his mother and an alco-

> "Once the game is over, the king and the pawn go back into the same box."
> —Italian saying

Dole Trying To Close Gender Gap
He tells women he's the one to trust

Most female voters do not endorse the social Darwinism espoused by the Republican far right.

Fewer in Number, Elders Flex More Voting Muscle

FIGURE 9.1   Newspaper Headlines Concerning Voter Groups

holic stepfather, didn't even have to think about it. He just got it. As more and more women, including pro-life Republicans, moved away from Dole, the GOP must have been very disoriented.

Similarly, when the California GOP took a hard line against affirmative action and immigrants, the very people under attack registered and then voted against Republican candidates in droves. To make matters worse, their turnout doubled and their percentage of the total turnout increased. In Florida and Texas, where the GOP had been wooing Hispanics, blacks and immigrants, their efforts were rewarded in 1998 with votes. Statistics and issues such as these are weak spots that can be capitalized upon in direct mail.

It is always helpful to look at trends to see if they are one-year glitches or becoming more pronounced, thus providing your campaign with a road map. For example, following California's proposition 187 in 1994, which cut off a variety of state services to illegal immigrants, Latinos began registering and voting in greater numbers. According to Paul Maslin, a Democratic pollster, in the 1980s Latinos made up 7 percent of the California electorate and voted three to two for a Democratic ticket. That amounted to two points in the polls for the Democrats. In 1998 Latinos made up between 14 and 15 percent of the electorate and voted four to one for the Democrats. That adds up to nearly a nine-point lift (E. J. Dionne, Jr., Washington Post Writers Group, *San Francisco Chronicle*, May 2, 1998).

Direct Mail to Persuade Voters

It is important to know what is going on within voting groups to help shape your direct mail so you may either highlight or distance your campaign from the problem. Remember, direct mail has about a three-second life. You must first get the receiver to open it, and then there must be something there to grab the person's attention:

1. Use direct mail to persuade swing voters. Do not waste campaign resources by sending direct mail to the saints or sinners. However, do not completely ignore your base support.
2. Send a persuasion piece to anyone targeted as undecided in your voter ID phone banks and canvassing effort.
3. Use direct mail to reinforce your message, campaign theme, and other media packages.
4. Use direct mail to reinforce news events.
5. Be smart and creative about direct mail. For example, you're trying to pass a library levy, have the campaign generate letters for teachers to sign and send them to the parents of their students.
6. Use direct mail to build a relationship with the campaign, the community, and an issue.

Direct mail is a sophisticated medium and should be treated as such. In 1996, I received a direct mail hit piece from Gordon Smith, a Republican running for the Senate, that was directed at his opponent, Democrat Ron Widen. Apparently, in an interview with a Portland newspaper, Ron Widen did not know the cost of a loaf of bread, a gallon of gas, or Oregon's unemployment rate, among other things. Personally, I didn't know these things either and cared less that Widen didn't know. However, there were some who thought he should. The direct mail piece I received from Smith

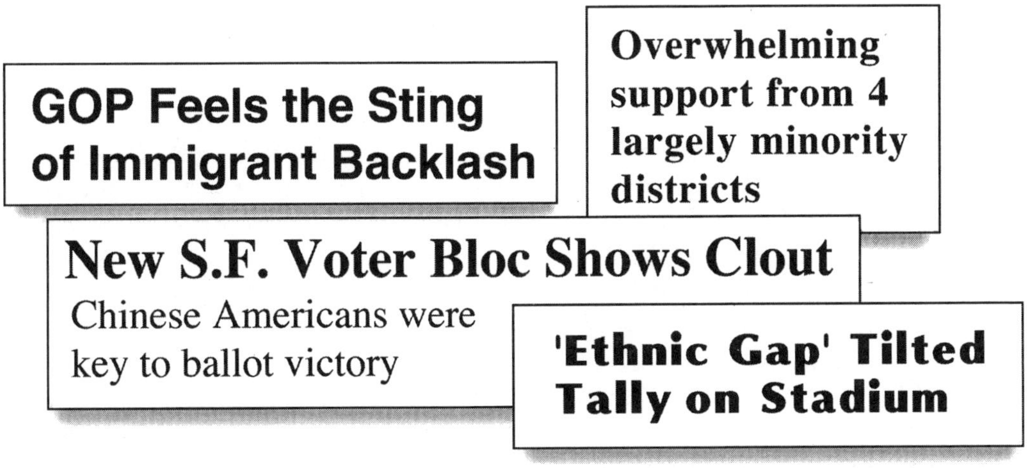

GOP Feels the Sting of Immigrant Backlash

Overwhelming support from 4 largely minority districts

New S.F. Voter Bloc Shows Clout
Chinese Americans were key to ballot victory

'Ethnic Gap' Tilted Tally on Stadium

FIGURE 9.2   More Headlines Concerning Voter Groups

painted Widen as an out-of-touch Washington politician and combined his inability to answer these questions with related votes in the House and general trends in Washington. It was a good direct mail hit piece.

The next day I got another direct mail piece from Smith. I am not registered Republican and I could remember receiving only one Republican direct mail piece in the past. My precinct, even the city, may come out high as swing voters, but the majority here vote Democrat and "yes" on progressive issues. The front of the second Smith piece had a picture of him walking through a grassland with someone else, maybe his brother, maybe a farmer. Smith was not wearing a ball cap but his walking companion was; both had on jeans and jackets: Smith's was open, his partner's zipped up with "Smith" and a star over the breast. Both men were looking down at where they were walking and the picture was slightly out of focus. On the bottom it said: "One U.S. Senate candidate shares the values of rural Oregon." Great cover.

Inside the brochure were four pictures. The first was of Smith's family and their horse and a caption reading: "A Senator who's one of us." The second was a panoramic view with the caption: "Defending our property rights." The third was of some farmers with the caption: "A Senator who shares our values." The last was a picture of Smith with his son and their bird dog. Both Smith and his son held a gun. The caption on the final picture read: "Standing up for Oregonians."

The back of this direct mail piece had a picture and a quotation from the executive director of the Oregon Farm Bureau and a list of groups endorsing Smith. It was a very effective piece, obviously sent only to rural Oregon. But as I looked through this piece, with the exception of the family group, all I saw were guys doing guy things.

The next day I got another piece from Smith. This one was printed on the same stock as the other two, glossy 11 by 17 inch paper, but whereas the others were folded in half and opened right to left, this was a tri-fold opening bottom to top. The outside was solid blue with white lettering that read: "Have you heard what women say about Gordon Smith?"

Inside were pictures and quotes from four women: the president of Crime Victims United in Portland, a mother of two from Salem, a teacher from Silverton (a very nice small rural town), and a small business owner from an affluent city outside of Portland. Each had appropriate quotations for her special interests: crime, families, education, and a balanced budget. Three out of four described how Smith was not like other Republicans regarding their particular issues. This was a killer piece.

Through direct mail, Gordon Smith took his campaign to a home of a single mother in the rural part of the state, hit his opponent, and established himself as part of my geographic world and then my personal world.

Following are some tips to make your direct mail more effective:

1. Have no paragraphs with more than six sentences, no sentences with more than twenty words, and keep as many words as possible to two syllables.

2. Keep text brief and on point. Cover no more than three issues in each piece.

3. Personalize wherever possible on letters: the salutation and signature, a handwritten or typed P.S., and especially a hand-addressed envelope (use a clerical team). Use a stamp, even if you're sending by bulk mail. Remember to include a remittance envelope. If possible avoid business envelopes and use something along the lines of a 5 by 7 inch so it looks like an invitation rather than junk mail.

4. Make sure the piece looks crisp. The direct mail reflects on the candidate's taste and organization. If the piece looks shoddy, it tells prospective voters that the candidate thinks they aren't worth anything better.

5. Get a professional to organize "a look" and allow enough money for high-quality production. Consider direct mail that doesn't go in an envelope.

6. Plan the release of your direct mail. Make it coincide with a relevant news item or legislative action that will reinforce your campaign message. For example, you are running against an anti-choice state representative. A vote comes before the legislative assembly on parental notification for minors prior to having an abortion, and you know your opponent will vote "yes." Have a hit piece ready for your pro-choice voters with this information and more.

7. Decide in advance what your direct mail will say, how it will look, to whom it will be sent, and when it will be sent.

8. Use color; it lends credibility. However, avoid colors that clash with each other.

9. Use only professional photographs.

10. Have someone not involved with the campaign glance at a mock-up of every piece. If that person does not get your salient points or message within two seconds, go back to the drawing board. Your pictures should say what your text does.

11. Do not needlessly clutter a piece. Use graphics that enhance rather than detract from your message. Avoid the use of too many fonts and use none smaller than 12 point.

> "Words that come from the heart enter the heart."
> —Old saying

Direct Mail to Hit Your Opponent

I do not consider pointing out how my opponent has voted as negative campaigning. While I try to avoid it in debates and ads, in the privacy of the voter's home I will point out the past voting record of my opponent or how the opposition has lied in campaign materials.

To hit your opponent or the opposition effectively with direct mail, you must do your homework. Know from where the money for the opposing campaign is coming. Know past voting records, if it is a candidate, and, as with issues, follow the money and follow the endorsements. Look at the principles on which the opposition is basing its campaign; that is, their campaign message. If their voting record directly opposes their message, it speaks to integrity. Campaign themes, such as voting records, are fair game. For example, if the brochure for the opposition has pictures of children and speaks of strong school support, yet the voting record of the candidate shows no school support, point that out clearly and often.

When at all possible, hit your opposition in a clever way or with humor. One of the best direct mail opponent hits I have seen using humor came out of New Jersey. New Jersey has unbelievably high auto insurance premiums. An assemblywoman ran for her first election campaign on a platform of going after auto insurance rates. However, once elected, the only legislation she introduced was for pet insurance. In the next election, her opponent used direct mail to deliver a full glossy close-up of a trimmed and fluffed poodle, wearing diamond-shaped sunglasses and a bow in its hair, sitting behind the steering wheel of a very nice red convertible. The caption below the dog read, "She promised to fix our insurance problem. . . ." On the inside of the brochure was a close-up of just the dog looking straight at the camera with text that said, "Unfortunately [name] is fixing the wrong one." The picture was surrounded by text elaborating on this woman's voting record and ineffectiveness in office.

Another clever ad had a cutout of the busts of James Madison, George Washington, and Thomas Jefferson on card stock. Directly below their busts were their signatures and below those a single question: "Who wrote the Declaration of Independence?" When you flip it over the back says, "[Name of candidate] doesn't care if our kids never know." The brochure goes on to explain that this candidate voted against a measure brought to the state legislature by parents making the Declaration of Independence, the Constitution, and the *Federalist Papers* required reading in schools.

A voting record is not only a verifiable fact, but a fact that goes to the very essence of why we have elections. In a county-wide campaign, I usually have one volunteer researching voting records. This can bring interesting information together for the campaign to use in direct mail or debates.

Direct mail is different from targeting neighborhoods for canvassing in precinct analysis but similar in that you are directing your pitch for voter *interest* areas rather than simple voting proclivity patterns. Also keep in mind that, by using direct mail, you can address subjects that, if put in the paper, might activate a lot of nasty letters-to-the-editor. Well-targeted direct mail reaches potential friends of the campaign and lets them know where you (or your opponent) stand and where to send money. Used properly, direct mail is very effective.

I usually mail or walk a persuasion piece to voters the weekend before the election. During my last run for mayor, I did this as I had in previous elections and for other candidates and issues. Each point I listed about my opponent had been said during one of the five debates we had or was part of the public record and his voting history. However, I made a fundamental mistake. I did not reference any of these items. When the piece came out, voters felt it was unfair to bring these things up at the last minute when they did not appear to have come up during the campaign. At that point it was useless for me to explain when and where they were said. I could have avoided this problem by putting dates and events next to each item. Always reference your comparison pieces.

Direct Mail on a Budget

Most campaigns are, of course, short on money. If that is true in your case, consider combining direct mail with canvassing. I recently worked on a campaign where we walked direct mail stuffed in the brochures to neighborhoods. In this particular campaign, we were trying to fund an open space/parks program. Each neighborhood of the city was slated for a park in the plan. We drafted a specialized campaign piece pointing out what kind of park each specific neighborhood would get. We then asked four to six supporters from that neighborhood to sign their names under the piece, and volunteers walked it into the appropriate neighborhood as part of our canvassing effort. In this way the campaign piece became both a personal letter and an endorsement. We also had neighbors canvassing neighbors. The technique was extremely effective and was certainly a contributing factor in our city's becoming the first in Oregon to pass a food and beverage sales tax. The open space program won state recognition in the "Cities Awards for Excellence" Program.

Walking direct mail becomes more difficult (if not dangerous) when you are dealing with hot-button issues such as choice or land use. This is where your precinct analysis will help. In most small

"The first and greatest commandment is, Don't let them scare you." — Elmer Davis towns and counties, specific issues will be important in certain neighborhoods. If you can connect the issues with the neighborhoods, walking direct mail can be very effective and far cheaper than mailing it or printing up three or four different campaign brochures.

Walking direct mail to the door is also a good way to time your mailing. In one campaign I worked on, we walked a hit direct mail piece three days before the open space election. In the piece we pointed out nothing more than who was financing the other side. It worked for two reasons. First, it obviously showed that our side was rich with volunteers and not money, as close to 100 people walked the streets for that canvass. And second, because of the timing, the opposition did not have time to respond before election day.

To save money you might also consider sending a postcard. Be aware, however, that oversized postcards cost just as much to mail as a letter. On the other hand, one sheet of card stock can make four postcards, saving your campaign money in paper stock and printing. Figure 9.3 is an example of a direct mail postcard for a write-in candidate.

As the campaign progresses and your issue or candidate looks like a winner, more money will come in to support your efforts. Chances are that even though you may have only budgeted for one or two direct mail pieces initially, there may be additional opportunities before election day.

Mail Preparation

Using volunteers to prepare your direct mail is a great way to save money. Once you have decided what you are going to do and the direct mail piece has been written, printed, and is back at your home in boxes, you need to perform the following tasks:

1. Organize a clerical work team to assemble your direct mail. If there is a letter or brochure, that needs to be stuffed into an envelope along with other enclosures. Using a clerical team is a great way to get this done. If you are mailing out a simple information piece, you can cut costs and work by printing your message on one side of a single sheet of paper. Have your clerical team come in and fold the piece in half, stamp it, address it, and, if needed, place a return address on it. You do not need to staple. Using a bright color here can increase the likelihood that someone will look at it. Keep the message simple. You may also choose to do mass invitations to a fund-raiser on card stock using half sheets of 8 1/2 by 11 inch paper and send them as oversized postcards. However, if it is a nice fund-raiser, you may well want the invitation to

> "Americans will put up with anything provided it doesn't block traffic."
> —Dan Rather

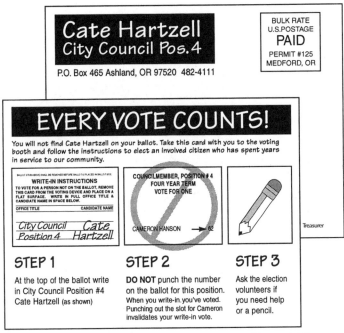

FIGURE 9.3   Example of Postcard for Direct Mail/GOTV Effort

be in an envelope that looks classier. Whatever the task for your clerical work team, have it all lined up and ready to go.

2. Address the stuffed or folded (if it is a single page with no envelope) mailing. Hand addressing and stick-on stamps really increase the number of people who will open the item and look inside. However, if you are mailing to specific precincts, you may prefer to hire a voter contact service to print labels.

3. Keep addressed pieces separate according to zip codes. Once things are bundled according to zip codes, take the bundles to the post office and ask for directions on how many they want in each bundle, which post office stickers go on which, and what forms to fill out. If lingering at the post office is a hassle, bundle all mail with the same five-digit zip code in groups of ten or more per pack with rubber bands. Packs should be no greater than two inches thick. The rubber bands go horizontally and vertically. Bundle groups of less than ten with the same zip code with other envelopes matching the first three zip code digits. For example: *97520, 97523, 97540, 97501* go together. You must know the count of your entire mailing. Make sure that each component of the mailing is exactly the same. For example, I once did a mailing with a number 6 remittance envelope stuffed inside. However, I ran out of the number 6 envelopes and stuffed a

> "The only thing that saves us from the bureaucracy is its inefficiency."
> —Eugene McCarthy

slightly larger one I had in stock. You can't do this. Each component of each piece must weigh the same.

4. Take your bundles to the post office to fill out the paperwork and place appropriate post office stickers on the front of each bundle. The post office will provide stickers and forms.

5. Hire out direct mail rather than using volunteers, if you can afford it. Take your camera ready art and your mailing list printed in a specific format for labels (call ahead to get the specifics) to a mailing house, and they will take care of everything else, including getting it to the post office.

6. Be aware that some colors of ink will not work for post office scanners. Check these things out ahead of time.

7. Mail one piece to your home so you know if and when it will arrive at your targeted areas.

Often near the end of a campaign, when the committee suddenly decides to create and send another direct mail piece, the grassroots campaign does not have the ability to pull together the people to get the piece out on time. This is a great time to consider a mailing house. A mailing house only needs the camera ready artwork and a list, on paper or disk, of who will be getting the mail. Again, if you're activating your base and the swing voters to vote, go to the county and ask for the full registration list, on paper or disk, for the targeted precincts you want to send the mail to.

The mailing house can then download the parties you want onto their label machine and eliminate duplicates going to the same home. Be aware, however, that mail houses are often flooded by last minute requests from political candidates.

10
Media

The media have a way of legitimizing your cause or your candidate. People are always saying, "It must be true; I read it in the paper" or "They wouldn't print it if it wasn't true." Don't waste the legitimizing effect of the media. Promote yourself and your ideas in a believable way rather than tearing down your opponent, and you'll get the most from your media budget.

Your campaign theme and message must be at the center of your media efforts. Although there will be times when you must answer attacks, do so immediately and then get back on your message as quickly as possible. Use each question to bring the topic around to your message. As I indicated before, once you lay out your campaign, assess your strengths and weaknesses, and establish your message, the media will be your best avenue for bringing this message to the voters. If you take too long in establishing who you are, the opposition will define you first, and the rest of the campaign will be spent digging your way out of a hole.

While I dislike negative campaigning, it is inherent in the process. After all, you are running because you embrace values different from your opponent's. If you are working for or against a measure, there is a reason, and as you define that reason, you not only define who you are but who your opposition is. The inverse is true also. If your opponent is telling the voters what he or she represents

> "The charm of politics is that dull as it may be in action, it is endlessly fascinating as a re-hash."
> —Eugene McCarthy

"Did you ever get to wondering if taxation without representation might have been cheaper?" —Robert Orben

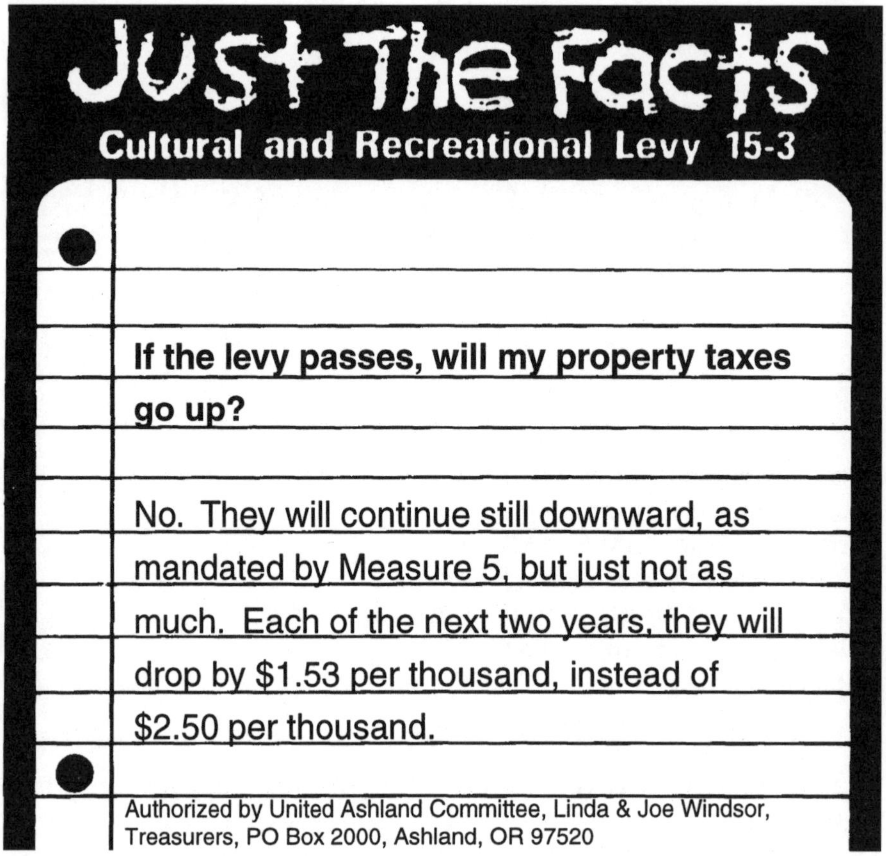
Just The Facts
Cultural and Recreational Levy 15-3
If the levy passes, will my property taxes go up?
No. They will continue still downward, as mandated by Measure 5, but just not as much. Each of the next two years, they will drop by $1.53 per thousand, instead of $2.50 per thousand.
Authorized by United Ashland Committee, Linda & Joe Windsor, Treasurers, PO Box 2000, Ashland, OR 97520

FIGURE 10.1 Example of Information Ad

as opposed to you, your opponent is defining you or your campaign. If nothing comes from your side, that definition gains credibility.

Establish your campaign theme early and stick to it. Raise your money early and schedule your media buys early.

In this chapter I have included examples of ads. In general, I use three ad formats when I am working on a campaign: emotional ads, information ads, and endorsement ads. Figure 10.1 is an example of an information ad. Sometimes I mix together the style of my ads, for example, an endorsement ad with pictures that elicit an emotion. Ad styles can be combined; they are not mutually exclusive. Within the context of television and radio there are also three types of ads: establishing, comparison, and response/-attack.

Timing Your Ads

Once your candidate or measure appears in a campaign ad in the paper or on TV or radio, the ads must continue to appear. It will hurt your campaign more than you realize to run some early ads, then take a break before running more ads. Your first ads will make the biggest impression. Choose them carefully. If you start and then stop, it gives the appearance that the campaign is faltering or without funds, that is, support. Voters generally don't want to back a losing team.

Not long ago the Pew Research Center (www.people-press.org) conducted a study that showed that while voters preferred to get their information about a candidate from news reports rather than paid advertising, 63 percent of them were not aware of a candidate until after they saw a paid advertisement.

Once you start a media campaign, work it like the fireworks on the Fourth of July. Start with a little at first, then add more and more, climaxing with the finale just before the election. Your money determines when you can *start* advertising, not when you will end. You always end a day out from the election.

If your campaign war chest is very lean there are two approaches you can take.

1. Schedule your ads so you have some presence throughout the campaign and use additional money to fill in where you are lean as support grows. If you're working on a winning campaign, fund-raising for ads will get easier.
2. Decide when you want to start advertising and schedule buys for a week or two at a time. This can help in a couple of ways. First, it gets your candidate or ballot measure right out there to bring in additional money; second, the opposition may think you are grossly underfunded and, therefore, not a serious threat. If you are not perceived as a threat by the opposition, their campaign may ignore you and spend neither time nor money on negative ads against your campaign. The possible downfall with this approach is that when you are ready to buy space, none is available.

"What we are voting on is far more important than buying cereal. The last thing we should be doing is advertising that dumbs us down."
—Cindy Wilson, freelance public relations and marketing specialist

For newspaper advertising, go to your local paper and talk to the person who sells display ads. For television you will need either to have your production company do the scheduling or, if you're handling that part of the campaign yourself, to go to the ad sales representative and set up a schedule. In either case ask if there is a special rate for political candidates. If you're working on an issue-based campaign, there may not be any break for TV ads, so add at least 20 percent to your TV budget buys.

Because most campaigns run their media with greater frequency as they get closer to the election, media buys become scarce. In TV, as with radio, there are just so many seconds in the hour. Unlike a newspaper that can add more pages, TV and radio have limited amounts of time to sell. Depending on the popularity of the show, the time when you might consider a buy is even more restricted. If you do not secure your media buys early, sometimes as much as weeks out, there won't be any airtime left to buy.

You do not have to deliver finished products the day you buy ad time. All of that production can happen later. But you do have to have the money: You must have cash in hand in August or September if you're going to buy thirty seconds on the evening news for November 1. This is where early endorsements and early money pay off.

> "I do not take a single newspaper, nor read one a month, and I feel myself infinitely the happier for it."
> —Thomas Jefferson

Advertising Formats for Newspapers

All political campaigns have a tendency to look messy. There are literature dropped at the voters' doors, lawn signs all over town, and political ads in the paper. If you can organize your efforts and give a sense of continuity and neatness to your particular campaign, by all means do it. If you have a campaign slogan, put it in all your ads, on your lawn signs, and in the brochures. You should have an easily identifiable logo and put it on everything. I use my lawn sign as my logo and I have a miniature made up for canvassers' buttons and as the trademark on all my media ads.

If I am running ads for a candidate, I like the newspaper ads to look a bit like a newspaper story. I place the candidate's picture as a fairly prominent part of the ad, under which is the logo. I place a headline of my choosing and then have the copy run alongside the picture. Figure 10.2 is an example of this type of ad. Candidate ads should be no more than three paragraphs long, on one subject. Below the copy I place the campaign slogan.

I might have five or six ads of this nature that I rotate in and out with different pictures and text. Generally, I like to run small ads such as two by four column inches, which is two columns wide by four inches long. Not only are small ads cheaper, they tend to be placed on top of other ads, directly under newspaper copy. I have seen local races effectively place ads half this size and do it on each page of the paper. If you have lots of money, you can make the ad any size you want. If properly placed, on the back page or across from the editorial page, for example, large ads can be very effective.

Another effective newspaper ad is an individual testimonial. One campaign I worked on used the same format as outlined previously but used quotations from prominent citizens about the candidate as

CATHY GOLDEN ON INDEPENDENT MANAGEMENT AUDITS

"Ashland city government is long overdue for a management audit by an outside professional firm. It just makes good economic sense.

Management audits consistently pay for themselves in money saved, improved service, and higher staff morale. And they let taxpayers know exactly what they're getting for their money."

Cathy
GOLDEN
FOR MAYOR

Building a Better Community

FIGURE 10.2   Example of Candidate Ad

the text. Don't make the mistake of using a picture of the person who is being quoted. It is important to get the candidate's face in front of the public at every opportunity. I have also pulled great lines from various letters-to-the-editor and used them in a large testimonial ad. There might be ten quotations spread out, as well as a picture of the candidate, logo, and slogan. The result is very effective. Figure 10.3 is an example of an endorsement ad.

In my first run for mayor, I was characterized as a no-growth candidate. My feeling was that growth itself wasn't the problem, but rather the effect it had on our quality of life. Some would say it is too fine a distinction, but I argued that if we did all we could to mitigate the effects of growth, we would probably be okay. One of my small information ads referred to building moratoria as being a result of poor planning for growth. Later, when I was endorsed by the Board of Realtors, I blew up the building moratorium piece and added a footnote headline saying that the realtors had endorsed me.

By coupling the real estate community's endorsement with my advocacy of good planning, I took the bite out of my opponent's no-growth charge and replaced it with a responsible growth idea. If

"Never argue with people who buy ink by the gallon."
—Tommy Lasorda

FIGURE 10.3   Example of Endorsement Ad

I had not been endorsed by the realtors, I would simply have said, no surprise there.

If you are placing a ballot or revenue measure before the voters, it is generally best to go for emotion in your ads. You can and should run some information ads, but a better response can often be had with a picture and very little copy. For example, for our open space plan we ran ads that juxtaposed pictures of open fields filled with grazing sheep with a more current photo showing the same fields filled with wall-to-wall housing. The caption asked the voter to leave some of the community untouched. Similarly, we ran other ads comparing pictures of forested hillsides before and after development. When running a campaign for a school issue (tax base, school board, and so forth) we show lots of pictures. Pictures personalize what people are voting on. Use professional photography in all ads.

I worked on a campaign where we hoped voters would pick up after-school functions to offset a state-wide property tax measure that was undermining school funding. Because of the wording of our city charter, the city could pick up only programs that would enhance the recreational and cultural aspects of our city and the vicinity. Getting voters to spend additional money for extracurricular activities can be tricky. Many of the activities did not exist when the older half of the voting population was in school. At least 15 percent of the voters were two generations beyond having children in the schools. We needed to convey the importance of extracurricular activities as a critical part of helping our students. To do this we had one ad that juxtaposed two transcripts of the same student. One had nothing but an excellent GPA; the other had the same GPA plus a list of all her ancillary activities showing involvement and leadership. The caption read: "Which student would you rather hire?" We ran another ad that was identical but said, "Which student is more likely to get into a great college?" Without using a lot of words we were able to get to the heart of the challenges facing our students today.

Ashland is a town of 18,000 residents; however, each year, because of the Oregon Shakespeare Festival, over 150,000 people visit throughout the theater season. A few years back we put together a prepared food and beverage tax to fund future park land acquisition and fix our ailing wastewater treatment plant. The opponents to the tax first argued that this was a tax on tourists and later that it was a tax on locals. They were correct; the tax did reach both locals and tourists, as it should, because these services were used by both. To make this point dramatically, we ran an ad with a picture of the city's central plaza on the Fourth of July when more than 30,000 people drop into the city for the day. The ad captured the idea that 150,000 visitors each year use our parks, have their bedding laundered, and flush toilets. Through this ad we stayed on our message of parks and wastewater treatment plant updates while redirecting the opposition's energy back on them. This tax measure passed. It was immediately referred back to the voters and passed again. Emotional ads can be very effective. Figures 10.4 and 10.5 are examples of emotional ads.

> "All reformers, however strict their social conscience, live in houses just as big as they can pay for."
> —Logan Pearsall Smith

Endorsements and Endorsement Ads

Endorsements from support groups, editorial boards, and business and community leaders can mean both money and votes for your effort. As you get endorsements, incorporate them into your brochure, newspaper ads, direct mail, TV, and radio. Craft them into press releases and send them to the local papers and news rooms.

TIME IS RUNNING OUT!

OR

YOU DECIDE

The revenues generated by Measure 15-1 will help preserve the land that gives Ashland its unique character.

Paid for & authorized by the *Good for Ashland!* Committee, Hal Cloer, Treasurer, PO Box 0, Ashland. OR

IT'S GOOD FOR ASHLAND! VOTE YES ON 15-1

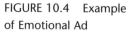

FIGURE 10.4   Example of Emotional Ad

150,000 VISITORS TO ASHLAND A YEAR:

- **FLUSH TOILETS**

- **TAKE SHOWERS**

- **HAVE THEIR SHEETS AND TOWELS LAUNDERED**

This creates considerable sewage flow.

Visitors should share in the sewage solution.

The revenues from Measure 15-1 will come from a good blend of locals AND visitors.

Paid for and authorized by the Good For Ashland! Committee, Hal Cloer, Treasurer, PO Box 0, Ashland, OR.

Photo by Christopher Briscoe

IT'S GOOD FOR ASHLAND! VOTE YES ON 15-1

FIGURE 10.5   Another Example of Emotional Ad

In the media, endorsement ads are examples of the best kind of testimonial ads, and they can take many forms. You can list the hundreds of people who support you, hopefully showing a broad cross-section of your community. You can also pull quotations and names from letters-to-the-editor, as indicated earlier, or have a page of logos from businesses that endorse you under a caption. Figure 10.6 is an example of an endorsement ad.

Campaigns routinely postpone putting together an endorsement ad with hundreds of names until the last minute. Regardless of whether you intend to run one, you should prepare from the beginning as though you will. You can save hours of last-minute phoning if, right from the start, you ask everyone you talk to whether you can use their names in a newspaper endorsement ad. This will not only make producing an endorsement ad much easier, but it tells you whether the person you are contacting is in fact a supporter and how public the person wants to go with his or her support. Some believe that endorsement ads are ineffective. But when you hear that your opponent is doing one, suddenly everything gets dropped while your volunteers start calling lists of people who might sign on for a counter ad. This gives your volunteers the impression that the campaign is very disorganized. It also takes time away from canvassing, phone banking, fund-raising, and maintaining lawn signs at the end of the campaign when volunteers are stretched to the limit. The last hours of a campaign are precious, so don't needlessly burden yourself with these ads. Take care of this business as you go.

In one campaign on which I worked, the candidate said that he didn't want to do an endorsement ad. Accordingly, we never collected names for such an ad. Then at the end of the campaign, his opponent came out with one of the best endorsement ads I have ever seen. The ad had a few great pictures of the opponent doing something wonderful—with babies and dogs, a few very tasteful lines about America that even had me with a lump in my throat—and then one full page of names. A full newspaper page of names. Even if we had started calling then and there and did nothing else until the election, we couldn't have made the 500 calls that it would have required to run a similar ad. The ad went unanswered.

When doing an endorsement ad, keep a separate list of names in a computer or create a field for the endorsement ad sort. This is a time when access to a computer really helps. Being able to sort the endorsement list alphabetically helps you find duplicate names. However, when it comes time to run the endorsement ad—and hopefully you will have hundreds of names—do not put the names in alphabetical order. Random listing of names gets people to read through more of them looking for friends and family, and random order allows you to put your big names in prominent locations, es-

> "It's the responsibility of the media to look at the president with a microscope, but they go too far when they use a proctoscope."
> —Richard M. Nixon

"Poor ads disengage consumers from the category. They make you feel like the category is not worth entering. Consumers ask, 'Is that all the category of government is?'"
—Joel Drucker, Oakland, California, marketing and communications consultant

OPINION
Mail Tribune

Editorial Board

Gregory H. Taylor, Publisher
Wm. H. Manny, Editorial Editor

Robert Hunter, Editor
John N. Reid, Executive Editor

Editorials
Golden for mayor
Why mess with success?

The case being made against Ashland Mayor Cathy Golden comes down, really, to the fact that she's too successful: too successful at putting her stamp on the city, at getting the council and the bureaucracy to follow her lead, at getting her way.

Oh, to have such shortcomings!

Critics say that Golden can be brusque or imperious. But when public hearings drone on, a mayor must keep people on point. Some view that as being rude or insensitive; but others see it as insisting on respect for all who wish to speak, for those who must debate and vote after all the talking ends.

The mayoral role DeBoer envisions for himself is as a "facilitator," a neutral referee. That's not what this unique, dynamic city needs.

Golden, who has served eight years, is an activist with much to be proud of. If she's ruffled some feathers, she's also helped use the food-and-beverage tax to finance needed parks and sewage-treatment, and got voters to support a city levy to support Ashland schools. She addressed aggressive, harassing panhandlers.

To succeed like that, it takes someone willing to tell people what they don't want to hear. That's a quality all too rare in political life.

Ashland succeeds in part because it has a council and mayor who know where they want to go. You can't argue with success.

Authorized by The Committee to Re-Elect Mayor Golden, Hal Cloer, Treasurer, 1036 Prospect, Ashland

FIGURE 10.6   Example of Endorsement Ad (made more striking by adding shading and placing at angle in box)

pecially at the tops of columns. If you know you are going to do an endorsement ad and you are not using a computer, periodically give the typesetter a list of the names. In the final days of a campaign, when it is likely everyone is going to your typesetter asking for things to be done yesterday, showing up with 450 names on every scrap of paper imaginable makes for the most interesting conversations. Prevent this by planning ahead. Figure 10.7 is an example of an endorsement ad using hundreds of names.

In one campaign, we ran the endorsement ad on shocking 4 by 8 inch yellow paper as a door hanger. At the top front was the candidate logo with a "Join us in voting for [candidate]." It was followed by hundreds of names. We did an early Saturday canvass, hanging them on all doors in the city.

As I mentioned above, the prepared food and beverage tax was referred immediately back to voters after it passed. To say that the first campaign was divisive and emotional would be a gross understatement. As the mayor, I asked that the council place the measure on the ballot, which it did narrowly, and I also ran the campaign to get it passed. Needless to say I was closely associated with this tax. Restaurant owners were so angry about this tax that they began placing postcards in every restaurant in town, one side asking the patron to tell me what they thought of the tax and the other side with my name and address at city hall. I'm sure the idea was for the restaurants' patrons to tell me how disgusted they were with the tax. But many of the tourists who visited these restaurants came from out of state where restaurant taxes were commonplace, and many Ashland residents and even those visiting from other parts of Oregon didn't seem to care. So many of these postcards came to my office with glowing remarks about Ashland and how happy they were to be contributing in some small way to the beauty of our community.

Finally, when the opponents gathered signatures to refer the matter back to the voters, I took a few of the postcards I had received and printed them verbatim in an endorsement ad to keep the food and beverage tax (see figure 10.8).

Letters-to-the-Editor and Free Media

If you don't have the funds for a sustained paid advertising campaign, start by encouraging letters-to-the-editor. Letters-to-the-editor can carry a campaign until paid advertising can begin. Depending on your area, using the letters-to-the-editor section of the local paper can be a very effective media tool. Such letters show that a voter cares enough about a candidate or ballot measure to take the time to write a letter, put it in an envelope, put a stamp on it, and get it to a paper. Letters-to-the-editor can be the most effective endorsement ads going.

"Diplomacy is the art of saying 'Nice doggie' until you can find a rock."
—Will Rogers

FIGURE 10.7   Example of Endorsement Ad Using Hundreds of Names

We *LIKE* the Meals Tax

We've been coming to Ashland since 1970. OSF is the impetus, but we've come to love the charm of your city/area. We make three trips a year into your economy. Since the ambience of the area attracts us, we don't object to contributing to ambience things like park areas, and mundane things like sewers. We're not paying the total cost with our 5% meal tax, just a contribution (maybe $25 a year). It's a small price to pay for the joy we get in return. How would the critics finance these things? And if you don't have them, folks like us wouldn't come. Don't be foolish, there's no free lunch – and we had a picnic in the park last night. 5% was only $1.50.

– R.S.
Eugene, OR

I applaud the wisdom of your voters in implementing this tax. I hope it continues.

– B.C.
Edmonds, WA

As frequent summer vacation visitors to Ashland, my wife and I are pleased to make a small contribution to the well being of your beautiful city through the tax. We feel it to be a good idea, not unreasonable.

– J.R.M.
Portland, OR

Paying 5% on our meals is a small price to pay to help keep Ashland the lovely city it is.

– T.W. **Talent, OR**

As a frequent visitor to Ashland, I welcome the opportunity to help pay for parks, open space and water treatment. The 5% tax seems appropriate to me.

– K.R.D. **Corvallis, OR**

I think you would be CRAZY NOT to collect this tax. These services benefit tourists, like us, therefore we should pay for them. This tax should focus more on visitors who put demands on your open space and utilities. Restaurant oriented taxation does that.

– J.H.J.
Winters, CA

I think the restaurants are foolish to oppose this tax. I support it and think we should have one in Eugene.

– G.S.
Eugene, OR

Good for you! Deal with your real problems ... I'm glad to chip in my share.

– M.P.
San Luis Obispo, CA

Although I work at a local coffee shop and am surrounded by opposition to the meals tax, I still support it. Please stick with your aims and goals no matter what pressure the restaurant owners put on you 'Good Job!'.

– **Ashland, OR**

We have been annual visitors to Ashland for the past 16 years, and we do not feel burdened to support this sales tax for Ashland's parks and sewers (both of which we USE).

– R.K.
Los Altos, CA

Save our funding for park acquisition

VOTE NO ON 15-1 and YES ON 15-2

Paid & authorized by the Good for Ashland Committee, Jean Crawford, Treasurer

FIGURE 10.8 Example of Endorsement Ad Using Testimonials. Take power directed at your campaign from the opposition and send it right back.

Vote for Daniels

Ellie Daniels would be an excellent school board member. Elle has devoted her life to education as a volunteer in the classroom.

We need people in decision making positions who know first-hand what is going on with our children. Elle Daniels has my vote.

C. Golden,
Ashland, OR

FIGURE 10.9   Example of Letter-to-the-Editor

If you are going to use letters-to-the-editor in your campaign effectively, you should have someone overseeing that activity. The person in charge needs to call people who have promised to write letters and make sure they get them in. The coordinator should also be prepared to write several different sample letters to give people guidance and help move them along.

It is important to get letters in early. Early letters get read. Later in the campaign season, readers become numb and rarely read the last-minute opinions of their neighbors. Keep the letters short. A good rule is one to two paragraphs on one subject. People do not read long letters in the paper. What you really want are a lot of short letters that will get you more boldfaced titles that people will notice at a glance. Also, short letters are often printed more quickly, and because short letters are great space fillers, they are sometimes printed after the paper has said, "No more letters." Figure 10.9 is an example of a letter-to-the-editor.

Be sure to have your supporters send copies of letters to all of the local papers. You never know who reads what.

Many papers will not print letters received a certain number of days prior to the election. Get this information. Almost everyone likes to procrastinate, and you and your coordinator need to make sure the deadline is met. If you're depending on letters for media advertising, being too late could be fatal to your cause. Keep in mind that, because many papers must first verify authenticity of mailed letters by phone prior to printing, hand carrying the letter means that it gets printed sooner. Letters that are typed, e-mailed, and faxed also get printed faster.

Other Free Media Coverage

Most newspapers have a public interest section that lists who is speaking when and where. Look for this section. Find out how often it runs and when the deadlines are. If your candidate is talking or one of your committee members is giving a presentation on your ballot measure, be sure it gets in the community activity section of the paper. Figure 10.10 is an example of an announcement in the community section of the paper.

I once saw a notice in a community activity section that a particular candidate would be canvassing that week in a neighboring town. It really got my attention. At first I thought how odd, surely no one cares when or where this person will be canvassing. But to the average person, it appears that the candidate is stomping the beat, making herself available to the regular folks, even if that candidate never makes it to the reader's front door.

Getting on the Front Page and Creating Media Events

A few of the "absolutes" are discussed here, but an excellent book covering every aspect of creating a media event is *Making the News* by Jason Salzman (Westview Press, 1998).

When you announce that you will be seeking office, it is important to call all of the press. To get the print, radio, and television media there, you will have to schedule the announcement for the convenience of the media, not for your or your supporters' convenience.

▨▨▨ **COMMUNITY** ▨▨▨

Dogs need vaccines and licenses

The Jackson County Animal Care and Control Center reminds the public of its on-going license checking program. All dogs over six mouths of age are required to have rabies vaccination and a dog license. Citations will be issued for violators.

In responding to the public's request, the center will being informing the public of the areas that will receive concentrated checking in the near future. The White City area will be the next on the list.

However, people are reminded that officers work all areas of the county. License checking may be done in any area at any time.

The goal of the license checking program is to achieve voluntary compliance, so people are urged to be sure their dogs are vaccinated and licensed.

House candidate to speak

Bev Clarno, Republican candidate for House District 55 will be the featured speaker **Wednesday** at the luncheon meeting of Jackson County Republican Women at J.J. North's in Medford. The luncheon will begin at 11:30 a.m., reservations are requied. For more information call 000-0000.

County fair entry books available

The Exhibitors Entry Book for the Jackson County Fair, July 19-24 and the Harvest Fair and Wine Fest, October 8-9, is now available from local Grange Co-Ops, the Jackson County Library and at the Fair office at the fairgrounds. Anyone interested in entering the fair competitions, both 4-H and Future Farmers of America (FFA), or Open Class must obtain an entry book.

Oregon poet will read in Ashland

Oregon poet and artist Sandy Diamond will be reading from her new book, "Miss Coffin and Mrs. Blood; Poems of Art and Madness," at Bloomsbury Books 7:30 p.m. on Monday.

▨▨▨ **CORRECTIONS** ▨▨▨

Christensen runs for city recorder

Barbara Christensen has obtained a petition to run for city recorder in November. Her name was misspelled in Thursday's paper, due to a reporter's error.

FIGURE 10.10   Example of Announcement in Community Section in Local Paper. On this day two candidates got some free ink.

Call the local papers to find out their deadlines. Ask what would be the most convenient time for a reporter and photographer to attend your announcement. If you know some of the media cannot attend, have printed news releases faxed or delivered to those who will miss the announcement.

As a general rule, if one form of media has to miss an announcement, I would rather it were the print media. Keep in mind that television news crews like to attend these things no earlier than late morning because they all work at night. Getting your face in front of the camera is important. If you can do that, you can cover the print media with a prepared speech and a studio photo. If your an-

"Politics is short, very focused. To compete with all the commercial advertising you have to punch through."
—Former Lt. Gov. Leo McCarthy

nouncement is too late for the newspapers to be there, be sure to get them the information they need before they hit deadline. You want your announcement covered everywhere on the same day.

To find a good date and time to announce a candidacy or to kick off a ballot measure campaign, you have to know what else is going on when you plan to announce. You don't want to announce on major holidays because people don't watch the news or read the papers as much on those days. For the same reason, you don't want to announce on a three-day weekend. If it is a nonpartisan race with only a general election, I like to announce in June so that I can participate in our Fourth of July parade. The objective is to do whatever you can to get your name out in an inexpensive and effective way.

Recently a candidate announced his intention to seek a state legislative office. He said that if people wanted him to, he would run, but that he needed a groundswell of support. So this guy wants us to beg him to run and support his campaign. People work for a candidate exactly as hard as a candidate works for himself or herself. No one is going to beg. The media barely covered his announcement, figuring he really wasn't serious yet. Bad start.

Press Conferences

If there is an opportunity to call a press conference, do it. When I was working on our food and beverage tax campaign, the opposition called a press conference to announce a funding scheme for open space that would make our tax unnecessary. They gathered together a broad range of local interests to support their scheme. To counter, we called a press conference as well.

We also had a broad range of local interests represented at our press conference. We took advantage of the occasion to point out why the funding proposed by the opposition would fall short of the community's needs. We also went one step further and used the press conference as an opportunity to promote our campaign. Not only were we able to undo any damage the opposition's proposal might have caused, but we used the opportunity to advance our own campaign goals. We kept our campaign message out front. Politics is motion: take energy that is coming at you and redirect it at your opposition.

Regular Campaign Events

In general, I do not invite the media to coffees, fund-raisers, or other special events. Not only am I worried that the event may be poorly attended and the coverage will work against us, but I have also noticed that people want this time with the candidate. If the media are there, there is a sense that everything is staged and those in attendance are merely props. Do not, however, hesitate to include the media if a big name politician is willing to endorse you or your measure. I once worked for a candidate who chose to turn down the governor's endorsement and visit because he felt that the governor was not all that popular, especially in our district. That was a mistake. A big political figure can get you the only page of the paper that is not for sale—the front page—not to mention all of the leads on the evening news.

Challenging the Opposition

There are a number of other tricks you can use to get on the front page of the papers. Challenging your opponent to a series of debates is a time-honored way to get local front-page coverage. Another way to capture media interest is to announce that you are challenging your opponent to campaign on a limited budget. If you issue the challenge, you have to come up with the amount, so set it where you can live with it but doubt that your opponent can.

If you're an incumbent, this technique can really work to your advantage. In small city elections, incumbents are better known and don't need to spend as much as outsiders to get their names out. Because the public thinks incumbents are compromised, this has the appearance of making them look more pure.

However, let me caution you here. If you propose a spending limit and your opponent is unwilling to go along with it, you have a problem. You do not want to hobble your campaign by having to live under a certain amount of money when no one else is. If your opponent is unwilling to rise to the challenge, be prepared to drop the idea. Campaigns involve a huge amount of time and energy expended by many people. The idea is to run and get elected, not to run and then if you lose, run again.

Press Events

Whenever possible create press events. This is where your research can really pay off. Use what the opposition is claiming and then look for inconsistencies in past actions, voting records, and money trails. Dribble this information to the press so that it comes out in increments. Look for where your opposition is getting money and support, and if this is inconsistent with their message, get this information to the press. Look for the opposition to hook and then hammer them. For example, you are running against an incumbent who claims to be a clean air advocate. You point out that his voting record is inconsistent with that claim, knowing full well that there were other favorable clean air votes that he will pull out to make you look silly. That is okay; the hook has been taken. If he doesn't

> "If Hitler invaded Hell, I think I would find a good word to say about the Devil in the House of Commons."
> —Winston Churchill (In response to criticism for siding with Stalin during WWII)

respond, your accusation stands, but if he does, you have a hammer. In this case you hook him with the clean air vote and then hammer him with a history of contributions from polluting companies and other non–air quality votes of his that would indicate he is bought and sold by these companies. This is where your homework pays off. Make sure the opposition campaign is honest and true to its voting record and message.

If you find ten inconsistencies with the opposing campaign, use them for ten press releases or press conferences, not one press conference with a list of ten. Use supporters to point out your strengths as well as the problems with the opposing candidate or measure. For example, the Board of Realtors endorses you, an anti-growth candidate. Call a press conference for this announcement and ask the realtors for help with a reason. In their endorsement they should include not only why they endorse you but also why they are *not* endorsing your opposition. Negative campaigning from a third party is best because it doesn't come from your campaign.

Take advantage of events that are already happening, like the Fourth of July parade. Show up for events that are likely to get media coverage and let the press know that you will be there; for example, if a special speaker is scheduled to talk at a regular meeting of the AARP. When considering these events, look to your persuadable vote and not your base. Sending a candidate to events that reinforce his or her stand on a particular issue or to an event that is largely supported by the candidate's base takes precious time from the candidate and can be unnecessarily wearing.

It is also important to look at the downside of attending an event. In other words, who will be influenced to vote for the candidate because of his or her participation and at what cost. One great example of this occurred in 1994 when George W. Bush was running for governor of Texas. He decided to attend the opening day of dove-hunting season to show he was one of the boys and supportive of liberal gun policy. Of course the press was invited by Bush's team. When Bush finally did pull down a bird, however, it was not a dove but rather a bird under protection. This did not play well and he was fined on top of it. One would have to question if this was an appropriate outing for this candidate, even if everything went right. Was this a group of persuadable voters or part of his base? And at what cost did he participate?

In Summary

1. Create news through research, package it in discrete pieces, and get it to the press.
2. Appear at events.

3. Challenge your opponent to debates or to keep within campaign spending limits.
4. Use ammunition coming at you and redirect it at the opposition in press releases and press conferences.
5. If you're an incumbent, create events by attending others' events.
6. Create a media event when you announce your candidacy or campaign kickoff.
7. Create media events with your campaign activities. For example, let the press know that 100 people canvassed your city in two hours on Saturday.
8. Use endorsements as media events.

Fielding Questions from the Press

If you're calling press conferences or thinking up ways to get on the front page of the papers, you need to consider that the press will ask questions that you may not feel ready to answer. The best advice I can give is, if you're not ready to answer, don't.

Whenever members of the press call me on the phone with a question I have not considered or feel unprepared to answer, I tell them that I am in the middle of something and ask if I can call back. I ask them the latest time I can call them so they don't miss deadline. If it is a complicated issue and they give me a couple of days, I take the time so I can do some research before I call them back. If they say they are on deadline and need it right now, I say I'll call back in five minutes. Even a short amount of time can be enough to get your bearings straight. Call your media advisor, campaign manager, partner, or supporter with specific expertise, and come up with an answer. It is a good idea to write down specific points you want to touch on before you call the reporter back. Make these short and quotable, but deliver them with spontaneity.

One important note: If you ask a reporter to "go off the record," the reporter must agree or else you are not officially off the record. For example, if I am about to share something with a newspaper reporter as a way of giving background and I do not want my name to appear with the information, I will say, "May we go off the record?" I then wait for the reporter to say "yes" or "no." It does not work to say something and then tell the reporter, "and by the way, that was off the record," or "please do not print that." Sometimes after the interview is over reporters will engage a candidate or representative of the ballot issue in small talk. You may be thinking that the interview is over. It's not.

If you're upset about an issue, cool down before you head out to face the press. I cannot stress how important this is. Because tem-

> "If there's more than one person—including yourself—in a room, consider anything said to be on the record and a probable headline in the morning paper."
> —John F. Kennedy

pers flair when you're in the midst of a political campaign, think how what you say or do will read the next day in the paper and choose your words carefully. I hear people say that the papers took their comments out of context or distorted what they said. I have rarely found that to be the case. More often, I have *wished* I had been misquoted.

Media Tips

1. As the candidate, you want to project the image of a credible community leader. You must remember that reporters do many interviews and miss very little. What kind of clues are you giving to the reporter that speak louder than your words? Avoid nervous behavior. Don't click your pen repeatedly, jingle change in your pocket, or twist your hair. Avoid verbal ticks, like "um," "if you will," "you know," and "to be honest." A friend of mine refers to people "toeing the ground." It's exactly what it sounds like: The speaker looks down and moves his foot, marking a half moon with his toe. This is a signal of his insecurity. When people cross their feet while standing, this also signals insecurity. Stand with your feet no farther apart than shoulder width. Arms crossed? Hands on your hips? Nope. Stand with arms straight down. Speak in a clear, firm voice and look directly at the reporter.

2. Be sure you know your subject well. Practice with family or campaign supporters. Discuss talking points around the campaign table and repeat these to yourself until they come out in short, concise sound bites. Reporters do much better if you're to the point and they don't have to do a lot of work to figure out what you're saying.

3. Although you may have the reporter in front of you at that moment, your voters will be reading what you say a few hours later. Think about your audience and talk to your base and swing voters.

4. Try to keep a positive spin on everything. Reporters like to print controversy, but if that will hurt my cause, I do not go there. Remember you do not have to answer the question being asked. You just have to sound like you're answering it.

5. Don't answer a question that hasn't been asked unless that is your intention. Candidates, especially those new to the arena, tend to talk on and on. They often will hear one question when another is asked or want to offer up more information than is necessary. Shorter is better, always. Keep on your message and do not let a reporter pull you off.

6. As I said above, if members of the press call unexpectedly, ask what they are calling about, ask when they hit deadline, and then tell them you're in the middle of something and will call them right back. Take a moment to think about what you will say, call someone for help, jot down some notes, then return the call.
7. In general, return all calls promptly.
8. Avoid going "off the record."
9. Never speak when angry. Calm down, then do the interview.
10. Select where the interview takes place. Think about the backdrop and if it can further your message through a visual effect.

Radio and Television

To be successful as a candidate or in passing a ballot issue, it is important to have a mix of media. When you first sit down to assess your preliminary budget, research the cost of radio and television and consider what they can do for your campaign. Generally speaking, anyone running for a city council seat or even mayor in a small town within a large county might be well advised to discard radio and television and focus on the other media mixes listed above. However, if you're a candidate running for a county-wide seat, state senate, state representative, or mayor of the county's largest city, you should consider television and radio. If volunteers and money are at a premium, give up something like lawn signs, which at best serve only two functions: name recognition and showing community support. Given the cost and time demands of a good lawn sign campaign, television and radio may be a better use of resources.

Television has a huge reach, especially in rural areas with limited cable penetration and only a few local stations. In my county, for example, we have three local stations. Although anyone living within a city has the option to hook into cable, only about 60 percent do. Some of the residents in the unincorporated areas where cable is not available have satellite dishes, but they are the exception and not the rule. Regardless of whether a home has cable or dish, the primary access to local events is through the local stations.

Television can legitimize a candidate or campaign issue more quickly and effectively than any other medium. However, television is not for everyone. Raising enough money to have an effective ad campaign, whether you're urban or rural, can be difficult. And while you may have friends who are professional photographers volunteering their time and energy for your brochure, a sister doing the graphics for lawn signs and newspaper ads, and hundreds of volunteers going door to door, television is not something you can leave to just anybody. Every step, from the storyboard and script to

> "The suspense is terrible. I hope it will last."
> —Oscar Wilde

production, editing, and the time it airs, costs money. Lots of money.

The huge advantage of TV, and to a certain extent radio, is that the market has been thoroughly researched. Local stations know what gender watches what show at what time on what day. They even know how many times a viewer will see the ad given the number of gross rating points (GRPs) you buy. If you have done all your voter targeting and know exactly what message you want to get to what age group and income, the most predictable means of communicating is television.

We have two newspapers in Ashland (other than give-away tabloids). One is based in the county seat and one right here in Ashland. Each paper claims circulation to about half of Ashland's population. However, many households subscribe to both and others subscribe to neither. There may be days when I am unable to read the paper altogether just as there are some days when I do not watch TV or listen to radio. When I do read the paper I see the ads just as I do when I watch TV. However, with TV, I notice ads more.

According to a 1995 Bruskin/Goldring Research (New York) study on "Media Comparisons," the average adult watches 3.6 hours of television each day and listens to 2 hours of radio but spends less than 30 minutes with newspapers. As a nation we have become professional television viewers, knowing what we like and why we like it. Especially when it comes to ads, everyone's a critic.

Given my age, gender, and education, media experts are able to predict which shows I'm likely to watch. So if your targeting turns up my demographics as a likely support, your television ad rep will tell you where to place your ads and how many times they will need to air for me to see them. For example, a purchase of 600 GRPs, a typical buy for political campaigns in October, translates to 89.6 percent of the people watching TV seeing the ad 6.7 times, according to David Townsend, who heads Townsend, Raimundo, Besler & Usher, a political consulting and public affairs firm in Sacramento, California.

A purchase of 1,000 GRPs the week before an election for a hotly contested seat means that 94 percent of the people watching will see the spot about 11 times. Now, if you're running a campaign in Nebraska, a relatively inexpensive television market, you will pay about $110 per GRP in a state-wide race. That translates into $110,000 for the final week of the campaign. If you live in California, however, the same 1,000 GRPs will cost you $1.6 million. Compare either of those to a local campaign where viewing is restricted to a few stations. For example, in southern Oregon and other comparable small communities across the nation, 1,000 GRPs will cost around $32,000. Take into consideration that 1,000 GRPs in a small

> "Television allows you to be entertained in your home by people you wouldn't have in your home."
> —David Frost

market would be overkill and a fraction of that buy may be all you need to achieve a presence and establish credibility.

In any TV market, as gross rating points increase so does the number of times a viewer might see the ad. Obviously, the larger the GRPs, the greater the number of people reached and the greater the frequency with which they are reached. For example, according to the Television Bureau of Advertising, Inc., "A total of 100 GRPs in one week, placed in all time periods, can reach 56.7% of all people or homes an average of 1.8 times. Raise the figures to 200 GRPs and reach can go to 73.5% for an average frequency of 2.7 times" *(How TV Works Can Help You Win—A Very Basic Primer for Political Advertisers,* TvB, 1985).

While I would not begin to try to lay out a television or radio campaign for you here, following are some important points to keep in mind:

1. This kind of advertising requires a great deal of money if you are to do it effectively. Be prepared. Do not start until you have enough money to see your ads through to election day.
2. As I said before, *buy early.* There is just so much airtime for sale, and other campaigns will compete with you for that time. If you wait to get your airtime until just before the election, there will be none to buy.
3. Treat TV and radio like canvassing. Do not run ads on programs watched by people who will be voting for you anyway. Similarly, do not advertise on programs where you will activate "no" votes for your cause. Ask to see some of the demographics on those who watch particular programs. Radio and TV stations know exactly who listens and watches what and when. Don't spend money preaching to the choir. Concentrate your efforts on the souls that can be saved, not on the saints and certainly not on the sinners.
4. Use radio. Radio is inexpensive to produce and a great buy. It is perhaps the biggest bang for the buck.
5. Radio and TV are very different art forms. Do not have the same people who do your TV spots do your radio ads.
6. In my area political ads may not be placed just before, during, or after the news. There is also a preferred rate for candidates that is not available to issue-based campaigns or political action committees. If you're running an issue-based campaign, add about 20 percent to the cost of the GRPs.
7. Consider doing ten-second TV spots. These are relatively inexpensive to produce and air. Also, because of their length, they get better placement when air time is at a premium.

"Political ads are giving Americans a choice between bad and awful, distorting and undermining debate, increasing campaign costs and driving voters from the polls."
—Curtis Gans, Committee for the Study of the American Electorate

Rules and Regulations

The following are general rules and regulations as they apply to political advertising. However, be sure to get media packets from your local stations and familiarize yourself with individual station requirements.

1. You must be a qualified candidate for public office or an authorized campaign organization to promote a candidacy. Political action committees and non-candidate (issue) campaigns do not fall under the political advertising guidelines.
2. Reasonable access for political "use" will be provided to all legally qualified federal candidates during the forty-five-day period before a primary or primary run-off election and the sixty-day period before a general or special election.
3. While candidates may request specific programming, the station reserves the right to make reasonable good-faith judgments about the amount of time and program availability to provide to particular candidates.
4. All ads must comply with the visual sponsorship identification requirements of the Communications Act. In other words, they must all have a disclaimer. The disclaimer (PAID FOR BY) must last at least four seconds and be at least 4 percent of screen height. Who or what follows the disclaimer depends on who paid for the ad and whether the candidate authorized it or not.
5. Any spot for a political candidate, or on behalf of an announced candidate, must include video and/or audio use of the candidate's image or voice.

Fat-Free TV

There are a number of ways to stretch your campaign dollars should you decide to do television advertising.

Know Who You Are and Know Your Opponent. It's important to do as much front-end work as possible. Research the candidate. Anyone creating your ads should know both the strengths and weaknesses of your candidate. While the strengths may be accentuated in ads that establish a candidate, there should also be clear ideas, established at the beginning, of where a candidate may be vulnerable. Once your candidate has been attacked, the media consultants may have to respond with a finished product to the television stations within hours. By knowing your candidate's weaknesses, you begin the groundwork for response ads before attack ads come out. If they never materialize, all the better.

To get to know the candidate better, the media team should sit down with the candidate, spend time with the candidate, and observe him or her on the stump. The candidate should also provide a packet that includes background, newspaper articles, current family photos, some childhood photos (especially ones that help underscore an image you want portrayed), career history, and a list of names and phone numbers of close family and friends that the media consultant can contact.

Your campaign should also research the strengths and weaknesses of the opponent. Even if you do not intend to run negative ads, by researching the opposition's fatal flaws you can juxtapose your candidate's strengths with your opponent's weaknesses and never mention them. They become implied. "Jane Doe will not miss important votes" *implies* that her opponent did. However, more than looking into the opponent's record, the media team should take some time to watch him or her in action. They should go to a campaign event, a debate, or a speech, and then craft a commercial or two *for* the opponent. This exercise helps to provide some perspective.

Streamline Production.　Many don't worry about multiple takes or mistakes out in the field because most can be fixed in production. However, minimizing the amount of time the editors spend on your ads saves money.

1. As a candidate, if you're delivering a speaking part, know your part. Be fully prepared. Never, never use a TelePrompTer. People can tell. It makes the candidate seem insincere and contrived. And the message is: "Without a text, I can't be trusted."
2. Bring a change of clothes, especially if you're establishing events that are quite different and supposedly took place over a period of time. For example, a shot at a daycare center, one at a business, and another with seniors will all look fabricated if you have on the same thing for each shot.

Recently I saw an ad for a woman running for congress in Washington State. The ad began with her talking to the camera while walking through a hilly outdoor area in a skirt and pink silk blouse with white pearls. It was bizarre. My first thought was: She was out for the day to make ads and this is what she wore. Sure enough, in nearly every subsequent shot, she had the same pink silk blouse and white pearls. How much trouble can it be to bring a change of clothes? Especially if you are going from woods to senate chamber, why not dress appropriately?

> "Man is the only animal that laughs and has a state legislature."
> —Samuel Butler

3. If the ad involves testimonials, impress upon those in-volved that they need to know what they will say and then deliver the lines accurately.

4. Find locations that convey message and image. Think about these ahead of time and share your thoughts with the media specialists.

5. Consider using photos with a voice-over. Still photographs of the candidate as a child, at work, as a parent, as a spouse, fly fishing, and so on can be a very effective way to evoke a feeling of intimacy and establish a candidate. (Figure 10.11 is an example of such an ad.) Don't forget to add newspaper stories as a method to increase credibility of accomplishments.

6. Get enough baseline footage so more ads can be cut without sending the crew out again. Figures 10.12 and 10.13 use footage from other ads.

7. Try using just music and no voice-over. Because TV is so noisy, if a thirty-second ad appears with only music, everyone looks. Figure 10.14 is an example of this type of ad.

8. Consider using stock photos and film clips. For a relatively small cost your campaign can purchase stock images to convey a message or create an emotion. Rather than send a professional photographer to an old growth forest or a wastewater treatment plant that uses wetlands for polishing, why not purchase this footage? Images of the great halls of government, people shaking hands, crowds, a child with the American flag, piles of money, orchestras, you name it, are already available and professionally done. The Image Bank (www.theimagebank.com) is one source but there are others.

9. Send a professional photographer to early campaign events. Use these images for ads.

10. Make ten-second ads from thirty-second ads.

> "Endeavor to speak truth in every instance; to give nobody expectations that are not likely to be answered, but aim at sincerity in every word and action—the most amiable excellence in a rational being."
> —Benjamin Franklin

Buy Smart.   There are a few ways to reach your targeted audience and hit that critical mass if dollars are short. Because television costs are based on the size of the audience, the bigger the audience, the higher the cost. However, purchasing less expensive time periods, when the audience is smaller, may allow your campaign to actually air your advertisements more frequently for less money.

If you know you will be advertising on television but really don't have the funds to keep a critical mass presence for more than a week, buy your TV time starting with election eve and work your way back. As money becomes available you can add commercials to

ANNOUNCER: "Carol Moseley Braun was born and grew up on Chicago's south side. Her mother worked in a hospital and her father was in law enforcement. Carol was an honor student in high school and worked her way through college.

"Winning a scholarship to the University of Chicago Law School, she becomes a prosecutor in the US Attorney's Office. She received the US Attorney General's Special Achievement Award. Carol marries, has a son and is elected to the Illinois House.

"As a legislator she earns a reputation as a tireless worker for improving education and bringing property tax relief to Illinois homeowners. Braun makes history by being the first woman elected Cook County Recorder of Deeds. She changes the agency and is recognized as a national leader.

"Now Carol Moseley Braun is running for the U.S. Senate. After her stunning victory in March she has traveled Illinois campaigning for jobs, education, health care, protecting the environment, and a woman's right to choose.

"Carol Mosely Braun for the U.S. Senate. For working and middle class families for a change."

This one-minute spot used only stills and voice over with no video. Credibility is increased through the use of archived newspaper reports. Carol Moseley Braun (Illinois Democrat) became the first African-American woman to be elected to the United States Senate following this successful 1992 election.

FIGURE 10.11   Example of an Establishing Ad That "Tells a Candidate's Story"

Peter Navarro doesn't understand San Diego. He favors allowing city employees to strike. He proposed increasing fees on new houses by 1000% and the city's economic development agency said his plan would have doubled unemployment.

Now he's taken contributions from the pornography industry and only returned the money after he got caught. No wonder major law enforcement agencies and the ten past chairmen of the Chamber of Commerce endorsed Susan Golding for mayor.

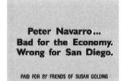

Susan Golding (Republican) vs. Peter Navarro (Democrat) San Diego, CA Mayoral race, 1992.

Peter Navarro, bad for the economy, wrong for San Diego.

FIGURE 10.12   Example of "Attack" Ad and Use of Images from Other Ads to Save Production Costs

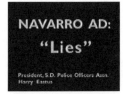

ANNOUNCER: "San Diegoans are outraged at Peter Navarro's commercial attacking Susan Golding on her exhusband. One paper called it, 'the dirtiest commercial of the campaign'. The chairman of the Chamber of Commerce called it, 'a sleazy smear' and the president of the police officer's association called it 'lies.'

"Voters deserve better No wonder every major newspaper has endorsed Susan Golding. The LA Times said, 'Golding has vision and energy.'

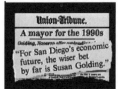

Susan Golding (Republican) vs. Peter Navarro (Democrat) San Diego, CA Mayoral race, 1992.

"The San Diego Union Tribune said, 'for San Diego's economic future the wiser bet by far is Susan Golding for mayor.' "

FIGURE 10.13   Example of "Response to Attack" Ad Using Images from Other Ads to Save Money

This ad used no voice over; only music (The Barber of Seville). 1987 Denver, CO mayoral race between Fredrico Pena and Don Bain.

FIGURE 10.14   Example of Humor Used in Negative Spot with No Voice-over, Only Music

more and more days out from the election; however, by purchasing the time closest to the election first, you don't run the risk of that very coveted time being unavailable later. Smaller-rated avails (availabilities) are usually the last to go, so there may even be some opportunity for in-fill close to election day, but don't count on anything. Buy early.

As I said before, you can buy ten-second (dime) spots. Dimes get a candidate's name and a quick message before the voters. One approach that can work well is to cut three or four thirty-second spots that air with frequency in less expensive time slots starting a few weeks out from the election. As the election week approaches move your dimes into time slots with higher and bigger reach. The ten-second spot tends to reinforce the thirty because people are already familiar with the look and message.

I once worked for a candidate who had a background in television production. He knew quite a few people in the business and headed up the media team. He also produced some of the best local ads I have seen in this area. However, one night I was home watching David Letterman and one of my candidate's ads came on. When I asked him why he had an ad in this time slot and this show, the candidate said that he watched David Letterman, as did *a lot* of his friends. Folks, the object of this exercise isn't to have friends at work

> "The difference between genius and stupidity is that genius has its limits."
> —Albert Einstein

say: "Hey, I saw your ad last night." The object is to influence targeted voters. If you have to woo your base, you're going to lose anyway. Make the assumption that they will vote for you and spend your money on media to influence the all-important swing voters.

Be Creative, Organized, and Focused

> "Victory goes to the player who makes the next-to-last mistake."
> —Savielly Grigorievitch Tartakower

1. Make your script tight and punch through. Line up your arguments from strongest to weakest. Do not compensate for a long script and bad editing by talking faster. Remember the adage: "I would have written you a shorter letter if I had the time." Take the time. This is a little like backpacking. Lay out everything you're going to take and then reduce it by half. Then half that amount.

2. Use language that reflects that of your voters. Don't talk over people's heads. Talk about issues the way real people would talk about those same issues.

3. Show clear comparisons between the candidates.

4. Be both specific and realistic about promises and programs you want to bring to the voters once elected. Be sure your goals are achievable. Making unrealistic claims or promises insults people's intelligence.

5. Take the stealth approach. Lead the opposition to believe that you're struggling for media buys. Lock in some great spots and then back-fill with smaller rated avails later in the campaign.

6. Consider talking head endorsements as a way to show support and credibility. Using prominent, respected community leaders can be an effective tool to establish credibility for an outsider. Using on-the-street people can show that an incumbent is still connected to everyday people.

7. Use black and white. What color does for direct mail, black and white does for TV. It's an effective tool to get noticed and create mood, intimacy, and a sense of history for the candidate.

8. Use humor. Do this especially if you're on the attack. In 1987 Don Bain mounted an unsuccessful campaign against Mayor Federico Peña of Denver. The ad started out with white lettering scrolling onto the screen reading: "Mayor Peña spends a quarter of a million dollars on a squad of personal bodyguards to protect him from crime." As this message scrolled the first notes of the *Barber of Seville* played. The next frame had "The mayor goes shopping." And the music picked up. In each activity the mayor was surrounded by bodyguards moving in time with the music. No words were spoken in

ANNOUNCER: "My job was to find Dee Huddleston and get him back to work. Huddleston was missing big votes on social security, the budget, defense; even agriculture.

"Huddleston was skipping votes but making an extra $50,000 giving speeches. I just missed him. (Sir...)when Dee skipped votes for his $1,000 Los Angeles speech. (Let's go boys, we got him now .)

"I was close at Dee's $2,000 speech in Puerto Rico. (Have you seen Dee Huddleston? Thank you very much, come on boys.) I can't find Dee. Maybe we ought to let him make speeches and switch to Mitch for senator. (Dog barking)"

Kentucky Republican Mitch McConnell (Republican) vs. Dee Huddleston (Democrat) for United States Senate 1984.

FIGURE 10.15   Another Example of Humor Used in Negative Spot

the ad; there was just music. And of course the implication was that if Mayor Peña spent as much money and energy on doing something about crime he might not need to spend so much on personal bodyguards. (See figure 10.14.) Another humorous ad, one that is quite well known in the industry, was for a 1984 U.S. Senate race in Kentucky. In the ad, the challenger Mitch McConnell, Republican, went after incumbent Dee Huddleston, who missed a number of key votes while giving speeches in exotic places for honoraria. In the ad, McConnell attempted to track Dee down with four bloodhounds, searching his office, the beaches, and hotels. "Switch to Mitch" McConnell won. (See figure 10.15.)

"Only those who will risk going too far can possibly find out how far one can go."
—T. S. Eliot

9. Again, use still photography and create motion by zooming and panning. By mixing childhood photos with more current images you can establish a candidate and tell a story

about that person in a controlled, evocative way (see figure 10.11).

10. As I outlined in "Streamlining Production," use no talking, only music as a tool to get people's attention (see figure 10.14).

11. Use professional equipment, good camera operators, proper lighting, and thoughtful settings. You're spending a lot of money and time, so don't cut these corners.

12. Make video look like film. Many in the industry prefer to use film because it creates a more reflective feel. Few campaigns, especially local, can afford this. However, if you start with video or film, then do all your editing on video going back to film, you can save quite a bit of money. The final product is film but the process to get there is video.

13. Use motion. When a candidate speaks directly to the camera, have him or her moving forward, either to a set camera or a camera that moves with the speaker. This implies the candidate is someone who is going places, moving forward.

Bumper Stickers and Buttons

Bumper stickers are an inexpensive way to familiarize the community with your name or ballot measure. Although bumper stickers are predominantly used in large city, county, state, or federal races, they can also be quite effective in the small election simply because they continue to be a novelty in that context.

This is one time I would move away from my strong recommendation of placing your campaign logo on all your materials. Ideally you want your candidate or measure before the voters, nothing more. Bumper stickers are small and hard to read, so clarity is what is important. In one campaign we placed the logo along with the name. Even though the logo was printed in a modified fashion, it was still difficult to read.

An added bonus is that bumper stickers are occasionally left on cars if a candidate wins, giving the community the impression that the individual is well liked in office. People who like to display bumper stickers are often willing to kick in a dollar or two to buy them.

Three words of caution. First, should you decide to print bumper stickers, be sure to print them on removable stock. If people know they will easily come off after the election, they are more inclined to place one. Second, urge people to drive courteously while displaying your name on their cars. If they are rude on the road, the only thing the other driver will remember is your name. Finally, using bumper stickers, like lawn signs, is an untargeted campaign activity.

Buttons are walking testimonials or endorsements. If supporters actually wear them, it further serves the goal of getting your name in front of the voting public. My experience is that very few people put them on each day, and they tend to be added clutter and expense. However, because all canvassers should have some sort of official identification with the campaign, I recommend the following.

At a stationery store, purchase a box of the type of plastic name holders used at conventions or meetings. Ask the graphic design artist who put together the lawn sign logo to make a miniature version of it for the plastic badges. Also ask the designer to lay out enough of these to fill a sheet of paper. Reproduce on card stock as many as you think you will need. Keep the original to make more throughout the campaign. Cut out your miniature lawn sign logos and slide them into the plastic holders. Print these on brightly colored paper. After the campaign you can reuse the plastic name badges.

> "The significant problems we have cannot be solved at the same level of thinking with which we created them."
> —Albert Einstein

11
The Candidate

In this chapter

Once you declare your intention to run for office, you become part of the public domain. You are fair game for just about any criticism people might feel inclined to level at you. Should someone write a letter with an outright lie in it, you essentially have little recourse. You can defend, but you cannot sue. Some political analysts think candidates should ignore attacks and lies. However, far more think that unanswered allegations imply truth. Either way such attacks are a problem. You can defend yourself, but when you decide to run, you give up your right to whine. It is great preparation for office.

This chapter is about projecting a positive image before the voters and thereby minimizing the potential nit-picking that the public might do. You will also find suggestions on how to redirect negative questions at your opponent, turning the ammunition back on that person. As a candidate, this is not a time to be defensive. Take criticism as a gift and an opportunity.

Prior to declaring my intention to run for mayor, I was at a picnic with my family in a nearby city. The Historic Society was sponsoring the event on a glorious summer evening on the lawn in front of a 100-year-old museum. The speaker was the secretary of state, who

> "Any good politician knows what's good for the community is good for him or her."
> —Rick Shaw

within a few years would be our first woman governor. I remember being impressed by her speech and filled with pride at the prospect of joining ranks in the elected arena with women of her capability.

As I was eating, a friend shared a comment she had just heard about me. A woman attending the picnic had said, "How can Cathy ever hope to run a city if she can't leave her children at home?" I was stunned, enraged, offended, and more. But once I calmed down, I thought about her criticism. If she felt this way at an *outdoor picnic,* imagine the criticism at a more formal event. Rather than react in a defensive way, I realized that my actions were more potent than my words. If I were elected, I could lead by example and thereby serve as a role model for young women in the community. However, if I moved off my campaign message to beat up potential voters on the double standards that exist in society, I might never hold a position of leadership, serve as a role model, and accomplish the goals that prompted me to run in the first place. I did not let the criticism distract me. I also choose to not drag my children through the political process with me. I would add that children need a family life of their own and are better off not serving as political props.

> "A mayor does not create a new vision of a city from the inner workings of his own mind. Rather, he collects it from scattered hopes and buried dreams of people he has listened to in the course of his own political journey."
> —Former mayor of Boston Ray Flynn in his 1984 inaugural speech

The Lay of the Land

Each elective office has specific powers and duties associated with it. For example, as mayor of the city of Ashland, the city charter says I am the chief executive of the municipal corporation and shall closely oversee the workings of city government. Laced throughout the document are other stipulated duties associated with the office such as appointment of department heads and my duties in relation to the city council. It is a charter that sets up a strong-mayor form of government.

Before I ran for mayor I spent a great deal of time familiarizing myself with council business and city documents, but I never actually read the powers of the office of mayor. Then, within my first six months in office, the city council set about stripping the powers of my office. Their intention was to do it through a simple resolution, which unlike an ordinance does not need a public hearing. As they put it, they didn't want to "take" the powers, they merely wanted to "share" them with me and to "help" me do a better job. I was young, just thirty-five, and felt both attacked and betrayed. No help came from the city administrator, who wanted the department head appointment power to fall under his jurisdiction, and none came from fellow councilors, who wanted input on department heads' appointments and city boards and commissions.

Many department heads, who technically worked for the mayor, aligned themselves with the administrator. Many did not want to work for a woman, especially one as young and inexperienced as I. Behind my back I was called names—my favorite was the "meddling housewife"—and was often spoken to in a patronizing and placating manner. I represented an upset and a change of the status quo, a move from a good old boys' system. The city council, in concert with the administrator and the city attorney, were in effect changing a strong-mayor form of government as outlined in the charter to a weak-mayor form of government, all without going to the people for a vote.

Things heated up quickly. I did not want to go down in history as the mayor who lost the powers of the office. I floundered in meetings as I tried to find my footing. I simply could not figure out how to stop the train. Then another southern Oregon mayor told me he thought his city's charter was modeled after Ashland's, and if they were the same, what the city council was doing was illegal. He said, "Read your charter." Simple, obvious, good advice. I did just that.

At the next meeting, armed with information, I held my ground, recited the powers of my office verbatim, and threatened to take the council's actions to a vote, through the initiative process, if they persisted. They backed off. Four tumultuous years followed, during which time three department heads and the city attorney left.

Before you run for office, know the powers that the office holds as well as the duties. As the mayor, I serve on the budget committee, handle land use appeals, and have the power to appoint and dismiss department heads and the city attorney and appoint members of boards and commissions. I give the yearly state-of-the-city address and the patriotic speech on the Fourth of July, prepare the annual evaluation of the city administrator and attorney, levy taxes, and perform a great deal of constituent work. City council members are the policy board, yet they also serve as the appeals body for land use matters, must approve the department heads I appoint or dismiss, are members of the budget committee, are appointed as liaisons to city boards and commissions, and also levy taxes.

Not only must you know the jobs and responsibilities of your office, you must also attend meetings and familiarize yourself with the lay of the land. Wouldn't you prefer to know before you run for office whether you're suited for the kind of work that goes with that office? You should also know something about the system: how land use laws work, who gets what part of the property tax, the revenue stream, the expenditure stream, and which follows which.

> "If you get to be a really big headliner, you have to be prepared for people throwing bottles at you in the night."
> —Mick Jagger

In the 1998 California primary, gubernatorial candidate Al Checchi gave a speech to the Democratic Leadership Council followed by questions and answers. During this time he alleged that the state collected all property taxes. Knowing this to be false, reporters followed up, asking Checchi to explain. Again he said the state claims all real estate taxes. He was asked twice again and still did not change his answer. He did not know something as basic as how property taxes were distributed and yet he wanted to be governor. Details such as this are not missed by the press or the voters.

It is also important to know the lay of the land of your community. Recently, an Ashland candidate appeared in a debate at the Rotary Club. Prior to making a point he asked if there were any business people in the room. He was not joking.

So what do you do if you make a mistake? I believe in owning up to it. A while ago, the Southern Pacific Railroad divested some very important real estate in the heart of our city. We had hoped to obtain a portion of it to create a pocket park; however, the option to buy was quickly secured by a developer and there was a small waiting list in case he backed out. The neighborhood was upset. After many calls from the city trying to cut in line without success, I gave up. I explained to the neighbors that it was hopeless and we needed to look elsewhere for a park. However, they would not give up and finally, somehow, got the parcel for the park. Sometime later at a council meeting, I was chastised by this group for giving up and calling the situation hopeless. I smiled and said: "Best crow I ever ate."

More recently, Mayor Brown of San Francisco attacked a *San Francisco Chronicle* reporter for exaggerating a problem regarding homeless vandalism and drug abuse. When later reports corroborated the reporter's allegations, the mayor apologized and indicated that he wished he could retract his words.

Many people are propelled forward into the public arena as a spokesperson for an issue that somehow poked the electorate. Often, in the heat of the fight, these individuals decide to take on public office to further champion their cause. Just a word of caution. Single-issue candidates generally make bad elected officials. Government has become a complex business that needs all elected officials engaged in the many facets of the public corporation. Too often, single-issue candidates have trouble with the wide array of duties of a given office and, once elected, sit on dial tone until the governing body hits a topic that connects their main switchboard with thinking. Such a situation can be unsatisfying and frustrating for the office holder, fellow office holders, and the community.

As a candidate you should never work on other campaigns, either issue- or candidate-based. Voters are suspicious of candidates who seem to have an agenda, and you will end up losing them all.

Packaging the Candidate

A political candidate is selling a lot more than political views. People are looking for an individual who will represent their community, city, school, or county in a professional manner. Elected officials fulfill the role of custodians of the public trust. If the community believes in the candidate, they will believe that their money is in good hands. To meet voter expectations, the candidate must always look the part.

If the candidate's clothes have a spot on them, no matter how small, he or she should change clothes. A candidate should not have any holes in his or her clothes; shoes should be polished; clothes buttoned; and the buttons should not be pulling or strained from a poor fit.

Because people associate weight loss with happiness and success, an overweight candidate may choose to diet and lose weight during the campaign. Canvassing can really help in this area. Whatever improvements can be made in a candidate's appearance and dress, make them. Attention to appearance will project a positive image, and the candidate will look and feel the part. The candidate and the campaign cannot afford to cut corners on personal appearance and dress. A crumpled look may be endearing at home but not on someone running for public office. Inattention to personal appearance translates into inattention to detail and thus incompetence.

Dress in a consistent style. This gives the community the impression that you are stable and know who you are. Do not do things out of character. We all remember the picture of Michael Dukakis in the military tank. A cowboy hat and boots worked for Ronald Reagan but not for Bill Clinton. In an effort to appeal to younger voters, Bob Dole began dressing in khakis and running shoes in his 1996 bid for president. Bill Clinton, who began his first term in office jogging in shorts and a tee shirt that hung below the bottom of the shorts, had moved to the golf course, a more presidential activity, by his second run. Off the course, Clinton was rarely seen in anything other than a black suit. He was "The President" and looked the part of a president. One candidate in eastern Oregon wore Pendleton shirts and midway in the election changed to three-piece suits because his numbers were sagging at the polls. Following his makeover they went down further. Behave and dress in a way that is consistent with who you are.

Recently a candidate for a mayor's race in a large metropolitan city countered accusations that he was "uptight" by jumping into the shower with a couple of radio disc jockeys. Voters want stability in office and run from those who act out of character or in an unpredictable manner. If someone accuses you of being uptight, say that's right, that's the kind of person who can do what this city (county, state) needs. Then move back to your message with specific examples of what the city needs and how you will meet the challenge.

"The Constitution gives every American the inalienable right to make a damn fool of himself." —John Ciardi

Image over Ideology

The uninterested, undecided, and persuadable voters will decide on a candidate based on who they think the candidate is (image) over what the candidate says (ideology). Again, the 1984 polls indicated that more Americans embraced the ideology of Walter Mondale than that of Ronald Reagan, yet they voted for Reagan in overwhelming numbers. People in this important and elusive group are making their decisions based on who they *think* the two candidates are.

Ideology comes into play with your base support. While a candidate may craft theme and message to get at the persuadable voter who does not care about ideology, he or she must not forget the base. A candidate must know what issues are important to the base. If there is any hesitancy on the part of the base to support the candidate, it must be addressed quickly and within the parameters of the theme and message. Although crafted to sway the persuadable voter, the theme and message must allow for the possibility of reconnecting to the base support if it wanes. For example, in the 1996 presidential race, California's environmentalists were upset with Clinton's policies regarding issues they cared about most, so much so that many were threatening a move toward Green Party candidate Ralph Nader. To lock them in Clinton set aside for future generations 1.7 million acres of southern Utah, the Grand Staircase-Escalante National Monument, an action that did not require congressional approval. For Clinton, Utah was a lock for the GOP. There was nothing he was going to do or say that would move that voter base to him, so the giveaway cost him nothing there. However, his action locked in his critically important environmental base in California and produced campaign workers.

I Yam What I Yam

People running for office often are embarrassed about their resumes and anxious to beef them up in an effort to present the image of a more credible-looking community leader. Given the right context during the course of any campaign, a weakness can be projected into a positive characteristic. What may feel like a painful biographical note to the candidate can actually be an asset. For example, if a candidate is embarrassed because he dropped out of high school, he is overlooking the possibility that his GED followed by working his way through college carries more weight because of his early struggles.

Candidates and campaigns who are tempted to embellish a candidate's history should think long and hard before doing so. It is a crime to place any false statement into the voters' pamphlet and it only takes an accusation by the opposition to activate an investigation.

FIGURE 11.1   Headlines Can Sway Votes

In 1994 Wes Cooley was elected to the second congressional district of Oregon. During the campaign he had claimed in the voters' pamphlet that he was a member of Kappa Delta Phi. When that was found to be false, the Secretary of State gave Cooley the benefit of the doubt and let it go. However, in his re-election bid two years later, Cooley made more claims. He listed "Army Special Forces, Korea," among his qualifications, although he never was in Korea. He claimed during the investigation that it was a top secret mission and all very hush-hush. But the pressure didn't let up. Because of his constant denials, the press took on the investigation and in so doing turned up far more than the Korea fabrication (see figure 11.2). Cooley had failed to get building permits for home improvements, the contractor had not been paid, and he and his wife were secretive about their marriage date so she could continue to collect benefits as a Marine's widow. Cooley backed out of the race and later was indicted.

What is instructive about this story is that more ex-GI voters could probably relate more to someone who was drafted and never went anywhere than to someone who claimed to be part of a secret, special mission. More people do average things than the opposite. More have attended state-owned universities than private colleges, graduated without honors than with them, and never made the football team. Don't miss an opportunity to build relationships with the average citizen by trying to make yourself *look* more qualified.

> "Voters want fraud they can believe in."
> —Will Durst

Manners Matter

As important as they are, there is more to looking the part of a serious public servant than dress and appearance. The candidate must adopt the kind of manners a mother would be proud of. Do not chew food with your mouth open or chew gum. Cover your mouth when you yawn. Recently, a U.S. representative, running for the U.S. Senate, called and asked to meet with me to "touch base." Dur-

Cooley's problems multiply

Army records disprove Korean combat claim   **Cooley says 1993 was wedding date**

Reports say Cooley ran over the rules

Cooley, wife entangled in

Media Closes in on Cooley Wedding D... ...ry

Cooley quits

FIGURE 11.2   Lying Can Lead to Negative Press Coverage

ing our forty-five-minute meeting he must have yawned five times, and not once did he cover his mouth. I cannot remember what we talked about, but I remember his uvula.

If appearing as a dinner speaker, the candidate should eat at home prior to the event or eat very moderately at the event. The candidate cannot afford to have a stomach upset from nervous energy and certainly can't afford to burp through the speech. One candidate I worked for would eat a full meal at the head table before rising to give his speech. During the speech he would need to burp but for some reason he always turned his head sideways to do it. I watched as he did this a couple of times and noticed the audience turning their heads with the candidate's. The bright side is that at least we knew he had their attention.

In general, eating and meeting voters don't mix well. I'm going to state the obvious here: Avoid drinking alcohol in public. People have tons of issues about alcohol and it's not worth the grief or uncertainty of how your drinking, even as little as one glass of wine, will play. One uncomfortable incident occurred during my first run for mayor. In the downtown area a new micro-brewery had just opened up and they really wanted me to pour the first glass. This would be a great photo opportunity. However, as an outsider and young mother of two, I was worried that if the local paper had a front page picture of me swilling down a beer, I could have a problem. The newspaper photographer hovered by the bar where I poured the first glass and the owners were urging me to try the beer. I told them that I was allergic to alcohol and handed the glass to my husband, who took the drink instead of me.

When appearing in public, bring along a sweater or light jacket to cover up nervous perspiration if need be. Wear deodorant and clean shirts. Previously worn clothes can carry body odor that might be activated with nervous perspiration. Go light on perfume and after-shave. Bring breath mints, but don't be a candidate that pulls out the little bottle of breath freshener and squirts it mid-sentence. In fact, avoid all public grooming: hair combing, putting on lipstick, and the like. Avoid problems by thinking ahead. For example, when I get nervous my mouth gets dry, so I always go to the podium with a glass of water.

As I said before, a woman candidate should leave her children at home. Besides allowing her to be more focused, this lets voters see her in a professional role. It is difficult for many people to accept a woman as a leader if their only image is one of children clinging to her. This is absolutely *not* true for men. In fact, men are given bonus points for being seen with their children (see figure 11.3). Society assumes that men are professional, and seeing a man with his children gives the voters the idea that they are getting a glimpse into his private life. He seems warmer.

Groomers

Given the importance of image, it may be a good idea to get a "groomer" for the campaign. I generally have a friend whose only campaign job is to let me know how I look and to make suggestions about what I should wear and how to better project my image. In all three of my campaigns for mayor, I had a groomer who proved to be invaluable. In my second run, when I was to be on public access television in a debate with my two male opponents, my groomer advised me to dress conservatively. Both of my opponents showed up dressed very casually and looked less than professional to the television audience.

The next debate of the campaign was covered by the media, but not broadcast live. My groomer predicted that my principal opponent, having looked casual for the public access television debate, would dress conservatively for this one. He advised me to wear my hair differently and wear a boldly colored dress I had rarely been seen in. The idea was that I should stand out to the live audience.

I selected a red dress from the dark depths of my closet. My opponent, as predicted, wore a three-piece black suit and appeared quite intense, severe, even funereal. Because the debate was before a live audience, I took time prior to the debate to say hello, chat with

> "You'd be sur-prised how much it costs to look this cheap."
> —Dolly Parton

Photo courtesy of SOHS

While Jeff Golden chats with supporters, daughter Sarah Beth gets an eyeful of photographer.

Golden celebrates wir

New commisioner's daughter accompanies him

Candidates each bring their own style and special approach to politics, sometimes they carry a lot of political baggage.

But only Jeff Golden carries a baby on his back.

For much of Tuesday evening – ev live TV interview – the Ashland D wore a baby backpack that held hi daughter, Sarah Beth, born a year giving.

FIGURE 11.3   Example of Winning Male Candidate Photographed with Child

members of the crowd, and enjoy myself. My appearance was friendly, and I was clearly having a good time. My opponent did not smile and seemed out of place, strapped in his television armor. The difference between us was dramatic, and the debate proved to be a turning point in the campaign.

When I work for other candidates I usually assign a groomer as well. I look for a man or woman with an eye for fashion and detail.

If my candidate needs a haircut, I try to get him or her the best hair stylist our area provides. Have the campaign pick up the cost of the hair cut and a studio photo shoot. The groomer and I will often discuss the kind of look we want out of the shoot and share those ideas with the candidate. For example, if I have a candidate who smiles very little and is somewhat hesitant, I look for a photo where he or she leans into the lens. Whatever may be a weakness of your candidate in personality or appearance, your photo shoot is an opportunity to make it look otherwise. Many believe that a photo starting low, looking up at the candidate, projects power, and one from above angled down, the opposite. Personally I think nostril shots are unflattering and don't do those. I like the photographer to work with the camera coming straight on.

A groomer must be committed to attending debates and observing the candidate's behavior. I usually like to talk with the groomer following an event to see how delivery can be improved upon. I then talk to the candidate and discuss adjustments. All such suggestions, however, should be cushioned with lots of praise. Candidates' egos can be fragile and you don't want them to be self-conscious at the next event.

Pick and choose your events carefully. Do not say yes to every coffee or speaking engagement offer that may come your way. Think ahead about where you intend to spend time and energy and go where the votes are. Take into consideration the personality of your candidate. For example, minimize the amount of time in public for the candidate who is awkward in a crowd.

Stay on Your Message

Don't let your opponent pull you off message. Ever.

The candidate and team must know who will support the candidate and why. The reason that people vote a specific way will become the basis for your campaign message. Develop that message to build relationships between you and the voters. A poll can be extremely helpful in shaping the message.

List all the positives of your candidate and why the team feels voters will support this individual. That list might include programs the candidate has been involved in, stands on controversial issues, prior votes (if a previous office holder), vision, character, and experience. It might be nothing more than a clear list of issues and beliefs that the candidate embraces.

You must also develop a list of issues and concerns that might hurt the candidate's support. (There should be a fair amount of overlap from the positives list to the negatives list.) It is this list that you will use to prepare the candidate for negative questions and for-

"Enlightenment will be extinguished ... unless applied ... to the machinery of political and legislative action."
—Margaret Sanger

mulate strategies to defuse negative perceptions. For example, if the candidate has an image of being slick, the team sends him to neighborhood meetings where he can be seen as one of the crowd. This requires a candidate open to observation and criticism and a close-knit campaign team to develop the campaign message. You also need people willing to do research about your opponent.

"No man ever listened himself out of a job."
—Calvin Coolidge

Once you have developed your campaign message and strategy, stick to it. When hit by your opponent, respond and move the discussion right back to your message. When appropriate, go after your opponent's campaign inconsistencies and weaknesses.

The campaign team will work only as hard as a candidate or campaign leader. So work hard. The public, besides looking for a community representative and leader, is observing everything during the campaign: your stand on issues, your presence and composure, your appearance, your ability to answer their questions. In particular the public is looking for how well you react under pressure and how hard you work to get into office. That will tell them something about whether they can expect you to keep your head and work hard once you are in office.

Staying on message can be particularly difficult for candidates under attack. It is important to respond to attacks, but how you do so determines whether you're on your campaign theme and message or have moved over to that of your opponent. In one recent local campaign, the incumbent was being attacked for running an inefficient office. As the district attorney, the incumbent had an increasing caseload with a stagnant tax base. The challenger had left the DA's office a few years before, gone into private practice, and now wanted back in as boss.

The incumbent, being the first to speak at the debate, stood and said: "I would take issue with anyone who says I'm not running my office efficiently." Boom, he's on his opponent's message. The following day the debate was covered with the headline: "DA denies allegations of mismanagement."

How could this have been handled differently? First, the DA could have laid out to the audience the dramatic increase in caseload, decrease in staff, and marginalized tax base that, with inflation, translated to fewer, not more, real dollars. He could have suggested that his opponent left his job at the DA's office because of a workload that pales in comparison to the current one. He could have demonstrated the number of tax dollars expended today per case versus years gone by. He could have talked about the complexity of crimes being committed that require additional court time or legal process. In short, he could have promoted his achievements and defended his office without actually sounding defensive. His defense would be framed under the umbrella of disclosure.

Avoid Telling Lies

While looking professional, minding your manners, working hard, and being on message, you must find some way to minimize stress. One way is to listen to your campaign team. Another is to do nothing that could result in your telling a lie.

One of the most dramatic examples of a lie gone bad occurred a few years back when a county commissioner was undergoing a recall in another part of the state. The recall looked dead, even though the proponents were able to garner the signatures and actually get it to a vote. It was a vote-by-mail election, and as is often the case in vote-by-mail the computer spit out a few ballots where signatures did not quite line up. One of these was the wife of the county commissioner targeted in the recall. The local election office, in conjunction with the Secretary of State's office, asked the county commissioner if the ballot had in fact been signed by his wife or someone else. The commissioner said his wife did indeed sign it. They ran it through the computers again; it came out as a no match. They asked the commissioner and his wife again; both said she signed it. The Secretary of State's office continued to press. Finally the commissioner confessed to filling out his wife's ballot and signing it because she was in the hospital and authorized him to do so. While the commissioner had easily beaten the recall, he now had to resign, was charged with a forgery felony, and ended up doing time. Obviously he shouldn't have signed the ballot to begin with; however, had he said from the get-go, "My wife asked me to take care of it for her while she was in the hospital. Isn't that OK?" the Secretary of State would have said, "No, don't do it again" and dropped the matter.

Outsider's Campaign Versus Incumbent's Campaign

If you are in government already, you are an insider; if not, you're an outsider. Insiders and outsiders typically run very different campaigns because the voters expect the insider to defend what government is doing and the outsider to challenge it with a fresh outlook. In reality, however, when the need arises, skillful politicians who have been in office for years have waged outsider campaigns against first-time candidates. Insider/outsider is as much a state of mind as a fact. Whatever the actual status of the candidate, insider and outsider campaigns require distinctly different campaign strategies. Whether you are the incumbent or the challenger, your objective is to contrast your strengths with your opponent's weaknesses.

> "The question, 'who ought to be boss?' is like asking 'who ought to be the tenor in the quartet?' Obviously, the man who can sing tenor."
> —Henry Ford

Outsiders

To run an outsider's campaign, you must first legitimize yourself through establishment endorsement (no matter how tangential the endorsement might be). If you're running against an incumbent, the public record he or she has amassed while in office actually defines that person. However, it only defines the incumbent in terms of image, not specifics. If you're an outsider, it's important for your team to define the test the voters will apply when comparing you to the incumbent. Obviously you want to stay away from experience because an incumbent would easily pass that test. Your best hope is to make the test, as applied by the voters, that of change: "Time for a Change," "Let's Rotate the Crops," "The Change Will Do Us Good" are all common slogans of challengers going after incumbents. Ultimately you as an outsider have to present sound reasons why an incumbent should be cast out of office, not why you should be elected.

Attacks on the system are effective if they plant seeds of doubt about how things are being done or where attention and public money are being focused. You cannot just throw complaints against a wall to see what sticks. Instead, know what you're talking about. Find out how things have worked or not worked and explain them to the voters. Remember, you must sound like a potential office holder rather than a malcontent. That requires solutions, not just complaints. This is where your homework really pays off.

Prior to my first run for mayor I went to the local college and checked out ten years' worth of city council minutes and read them all. I also checked out every current report on every system where the city had a consultant study. I read the city's comprehensive plan and the downtown plan. This information gathering put me at a decided advantage. Simply because it was all so fresh in my mind, I could recall the information more quickly. Incumbents who live through the reports while in office will find it difficult to recall the details. I know that I would have trouble remembering specifics of reports that have come out since I took office.

Incumbents

If you are an incumbent, you must show that the average citizen still supports you and how, working cooperatively with other elected officials, you have made the system better. In other words, your campaign makes the test applied by the voters one of experience. This is a strong theme when the economy is booming and when voters have a grasp of the complexities of government. Again, your public record defines who you are. But avoid looking at each vote individually. Although you should not actually use the word, stick close to a theme of "proven" leadership. Make your record the focal point of the campaign.

Your Opponent

You may breathe a sigh of relief when you discover that you are unopposed in your election or groan when you find that at the last minute someone has filed to run against you. However, an opponent in any campaign is a blessing. Without an opponent, your race will be ignored by the press, and the programs and issues you want to get before the voters will be that much more difficult and expensive to get there. If you are involved in a hotly contested race, the press will more likely provide front page coverage, which greatly reduces the amount of advertising you will have to buy.

If you are unopposed in a primary race, you may never build the momentum and party support that are necessary to win the general election. Do not lament if someone declares against you. Thank your lucky stars and organize a great campaign. Bring forward programs you want to begin or to maintain and use the election as a mandate to muscle these into place. Use the election as a reminder of who you are and what you stand for and as a rallying point to get people behind your efforts.

While working on ballot measures, I discovered that some voters need something to vote *for* while others need something to vote *against*. Average voters watch the debate unfold in the paper and on the news. They listen to see who makes sense and who doesn't. Some are outraged by inane arguments from the opposition and decide to vote for your cause although they normally would not, given their voting proclivities. Without the mis-steps and mis-statements of your opposition, you might never get the necessary votes to push your campaign over the top. However, the drawback of an opponent is that negative campaigning might follow. The next section discusses how to best head off negative campaigning and deal with it firmly.

Debates

> Don't use debates to attack your opponent; rather, tell what you know and would do once elected.

> "What is noble can be said in any language, and what is mean should be said in none."
> —Maimonides

Debates can be turning points for a campaign or not amount to anything. I have seen amazing mistakes made during debates that have had little or no consequence and other minor errors blow up. There are a number of ways you and your campaign team can minimize the risk factor and make a debate work in your favor. Small precautions include familiarizing yourself with the room prior to the event and making sure that some friendly faces are in the audience. However, preparation is your best tool for positioning yourself. If you are well prepared, political debates are surprisingly easy and great fun. As a political candidate, you should welcome the showiness of debates, the pressure, and the opportunity to get your opinions in front of voters. When you have successfully positioned yourself as a candidate, people recognize who you are and what you do. You make sense to them.

The central rule of debating is that the voters should know more after the debate than they did before it. Come armed with lots of information. In my third run for mayor I had the advantage of being well versed in city matters; in addition, even though I was the incumbent, I studied like crazy to prepare for all six of my debates. In the first debate, I was shocked at how uninformed my opponent was about city matters. He had seemingly done little or nothing to prepare himself for the event. I thought, boy, this is going to be easy. But with each debate that followed my opponent took, verbatim, statistics and anecdotal examples that I had used in previous debates and presented them to each new audience as though they were his thoughts, his research. I couldn't believe what was going on. It really threw me. I couldn't say, "Hey, you sound just like me," or "That's exactly what I said last week" without sounding petty, whining, accusatory, or on the attack. Every debate was before a new audience that had never heard either of us, so they assumed he was delivering his spiel, not mine. In hindsight, I should have had a campaign supporter at each event and had that person call my opponent on it each time.

To get ready for a political debate, choose eight to ten subjects that are of interest to you and/or the community. You should include issues that are part of your campaign platform. For each of the subjects you have chosen, list the information and points that you feel are relevant on one side of a 5 by 8 inch index card. Use only one card per subject and only one side of the card.

For example, development in the forest interface is of great concern in my community. As an incumbent I would list on the right-hand side of one card all that government (with my help) has done to limit development. On the left-hand side I would list concerns of fire danger and what government, again with my help, needs to do to make the forest safer. If I were running an outsider's campaign, for the same subject I would list all that is being done, how that is not enough, what has gone wrong (being specific), and exactly what I would do to remedy the situation. The information is just listed, not written out. The idea is to be very familiar with the information before the debate and to use the cards to focus on what you want to talk about.

Once you have the subject cards filled out, choose a separate color for each card and make a single stripe along the top in a particular color. For example, your card for budget issues might be red; for forest interface, brown; for park issues, green; for recycling, yellow; for air quality, blue; for transportation, black; and so forth. Once color coded, the appropriate card can be skimmed at a glance and be discreetly in front of you without letting people know that not all your information comes right off the top of your head. By color coding in advance, you can avoid disorienting yourself looking through all the cards to find the one you want. Once you have the information card you need for a particular subject on top of the stack, you can glance at it while looking around the audience. You should appear to be collecting your thoughts rather than reading the cards.

Do not kid yourself that you can guess all the subjects or questions that will come up in a debate. You will undoubtedly prepare for areas that never get a question and have nothing for areas that are covered. Even so, with the preparation done ahead of time, you will be much more relaxed and "on" during the debate. Be sure to bring extra blank cards to jot down thoughts during the debate. This will help you remember on rebuttal what you want to say.

Familiarize yourself with any ballot measures coming before the voters or any initiative petitions being circulated. Either the press or your opponent may question your position, so have a clear idea of where you stand and why.

The importance of your image and how you present yourself cannot be overstated. Smiling and speaking clearly and slowly enough so those in the audience can hear and understand are very important. A certain amount of tension surrounds a campaign in general and a debate in particular and people will notice how you relieve that tension. Being able to relieve this tension with humor is a gift. Be aware that your image is projected in a hundred ways.

Following are some of the more famous examples of debate situations in which a candidate appeared to greater advantage than his opponent.

In a 1960 Kennedy-Nixon televised debate, Kennedy's team checked out the studio location for the debate a few days ahead of time and found it set up with a drab, gray background. To contrast with the background, Kennedy was told to wear a dark blue suit and spend some time under a sun lamp. The hope was that he would project an image of youth and vigor. Kennedy was also told to look directly at Nixon when Nixon spoke and to look directly at the cameras (his audience) when he spoke. This would show that Kennedy had respect for what people had to say, even his opponent, and that he could communicate with the nation. Further, Kennedy's advisors found out that Nixon had hurt his leg while campaigning, so they

"There was a gap between what went on in his mind and what came out of his mouth."
—James M. Cain

requested that the two candidates stand. During the debates, Nixon looked tired and poorly made-up and he was ill. Because of his leg he shifted about and perspired under the hot lights of the studio.

In the second debate between Ford and Carter, Ford was asked about the Soviet sphere of influence in Eastern Europe. He responded that there was no Soviet domination in Eastern Europe.

In a Reagan-Carter debate in 1980, the president said he asked Amy, his daughter, what she thought was the most pressing issue and her response was nuclear weapons. The opposition assumed correctly that Americans would be uncomfortable with Amy Carter as a presidential political advisor and made it a campaign issue. In the same debate, Reagan scored big points by crossing the stage to shake hands with the president.

In a Reagan-Mondale debate, President Reagan said, "The nation's poverty rate has begun to decline, but it is still going up." Comments like this brought the factor of his age to the race, but only briefly.

And, finally, in a 1988 Bush-Dukakis debate, Dukakis was asked if he would change his mind about capital punishment if someone raped and killed his wife, Kitty. Dukakis's response lacked passion and emotion. Some said he framed his answer no differently than if he were asked if he preferred a dill pickle or relish.

> "I will never apologize for the United States of America—I don't care what the facts are."
> —George Bush

Fielding Negative Questions

Think of everything as a gift or opportunity.

You will very likely face nasty questions and innuendoes during a debate. Look at such questions as your opportunity to show how well you respond under fire. People know that being subjected to negativity is part of serving in public office, and they will want to see how you handle it. Never be defensive. If possible, be humble and somewhat self-effacing. If you can come up with a joke that turns the attack to your advantage, so much the better. Find anything that uses the ammunition of the opposition and redirects it at them. If you redirect attacks, it is important to do so with class, without sounding defensive, and with poise. This is your opportunity to sound smart. Being quick on your feet is not a function of intelligence but rather of preparedness, confidence, and poise.

Grace Under Pressure

Your campaign committee should help you list everything that is a weakness: every vote, every mis-statement, every missed meeting, all of it. They should also list everything on which your candidate may appear vulnerable: past voting records, who is paying for the campaign, special interest support, inconsistencies in what he or she has said and done. Once this level of homework is done, you will be much more comfortable.

In general there are four options for responding to an attack:

1. I did not do it.
2. I did it, *but* it's not like you think.
3. I did it, I'm sorry, I won't do it again.
4. Attack the source.

If you are attacked and do not respond, you are assumed guilty. When you do respond, you should do so on the same level as the attack. For example, if you were attacked in a letter-to-the-editor, respond in a letter-to-the-editor.

Fatal Flaws

One way to prepare yourself for attacks is to sit with your campaign team and brainstorm on every possible negative question that might come your way. Practice responding to questions about your weaknesses. This is especially important if you are working on a ballot measure. Listing the "fatal flaws" of your candidate or measure allows discussion within your support group, where the team can determine the best possible responses. These responses may be placed according to topic on your 5 by 8 inch cards for handy reference during the debate. Even if the attack is not *exactly* what your team predicted, this level of preparation lends comfort and organization to the candidate. The result will be better responses in high-pressure situations.

Following are some examples of how to capitalize on negative questions. The last time I ran for mayor, I met criticism of city budget increases by explaining that I was the only member of the budget committee who voted "no" on the last budget. Later in the campaign, my opponent pointed out (during a debate) that when this same budget came before the city council for final approval, the council vote was split. He went on to point out that I failed to cast the tie-breaking "no" vote and instead voted "yes." Why, he asked, if I was so opposed to the budget during the budget process, was I unwilling to vote "no" at the council level?

You can imagine my surprise. Until that moment, I had forgotten that, when the budget came before the council, two members were away and two for odd reasons voted "no." That left only two voting "yes." As mayor, I had to cast the deciding vote. As I went to the podium to respond, I pulled out my color-coded budget card.

> "I really didn't say everything I said."
> —Yogi Berra

From the card, I was able to outline the exact issues about which I had concern as a budget committee member. After relating those concerns to the audience, I explained that I lost my appeal to the budget committee to delve into the issues further and explained that the budget was ultimately adopted by the committee. Having been outvoted at the committee level, I suggested to the audience that it would not be right to, in effect, veto the budget as the mayor. Therefore, I voted to put in place the will of the majority of the committee and council, even if I personally disagreed with some provisions of the budget.

Because I was prepared, my opponent had given me what I could not get on my own: the opportunity to show that I had good reasons to vote against the budget during the budget process and that I was willing to set aside my differences with the budget process after losing the vote. As an incumbent I was able to demonstrate that I was still willing to challenge the process and yet be a team player.

At another debate one opponent brought up a program that I had initiated to clear fuel (dead and dying brush) from the forest interface using volunteers. He cited how the program had been a miserable failure, placing the city at great risk of potential litigation due to possible worker injury. I picked up my forest card and took the microphone. I said that while the outcome of the program had been different from that first envisioned, it had raised community awareness of the need to mitigate fire danger. Moreover, the voters needed to make a decision for the future. Did they want leadership that never tried anything out of fear of failure or leadership that solved problems creatively at the risk of an occasional partial success?

By using this attack as a gift, I was able to direct attention to the limited success of the program and then shift back to my message, which was strong, creative leadership, leadership willing to take risks.

Another approach to leading or negative questions is the "Yeah, so?" answer. For example, the opposition might say, "Since you became mayor, the city has acquired more and more programs that should be run by the private sector." Your "Yeah, so?" response might be, "I'm sorry. How is this a problem? The proof is in the pudding. We are extraordinarily successful at providing a broad range of outstanding programs while saving the taxpayers money." While you may not use these exact words, this is the tone: "Yeah, so? What's your point?"

Attacks Can Backfire

I think it is somewhat unpredictable to attack your opponent during a debate. Do it carefully; it can backfire. I worked for a candidate whose opponent, an incumbent, was receiving lots of PAC money. My candidate wanted to hit the incumbent for taking special interest money. Because the campaign team had heard rumors that the

> "Earlier today the senator called a spade a spade. He later issued a retraction."
> —Joe Mirachi

incumbent always had an effective counter whenever he was hit on PAC money, the campaign team felt an attack was dangerous.

At the next debate, however, our candidate went after the credibility of the incumbent based on the PAC money coming in. Our candidate implied that the incumbent was bought and paid for because so much of his money came from PACs and so little from citizens. True to the rumors, the opponent stood up and said that when he was first elected, a supporter who had given a large contribution to his campaign visited his office at the capital. According to the story, the contributor was looking for a particular vote on a bill and felt that the size of the campaign contribution warranted this vote. Our opponent went on to say that after hearing the demand, he went to the bank and took out a personal loan to pay back the contributor. He concluded by saying that no one owned his vote.

In about thirty seconds our opponent not only killed the whole PAC money attack, but showed that he was poor like everyone else in the room—he had to take out a personal loan to pay off the contributor—and that he had integrity. In hindsight, this attack would have taken on new meaning if our campaign had been able to point out other campaign contributions and votes that appeared to follow PAC money.

In debates you just never know how your opponent will turn an attack around. So unless I have concrete information, I try not to attack unless it is impromptu or on rebuttal.

In 1996 a Democrat and a Republican were facing off for a U.S. Senate seat. The Democrat had been criticizing the Republican for using federal Superfund money for clean-up of his industrial waste in his family-owned business. During a debate, the Republican, who was worth millions, was challenged by the Democrat to pay back the money to the taxpayers. The Republican then stood and said, "I'll pay it back just as soon as you pay back the honoraria you said you would never take when you ran for Congress." The Democrat, in a very flustered voice, said, "Why, why, you've insulted my integrity."

The Democrat should have seen this coming, and when it did, he should have been ready. If he were, he would have then reached into his pocket, pulled out his checkbook, and said, "Deal. I'll pay back all the money I received for giving speeches. You get out your checkbook and do the same for the federal clean-ups, which amount to $XYZ. And, while you're at it, make it out to the federal deficit, because the only way we're going to get our arms around it is if those that *have* stop taking from those that don't." While the Democrat had received thousands in honoraria, the Republican had received millions.

> "The Republican Party stands for: Anti-bigotry, anti-semitism, anti-racism."
> —George Bush

Developing Your Public Speaking Skills

In my first run for mayor, during my first debate, I was elated, excited about what was ahead of me, charged up, and well armed with information. When it was over, I thought I had done a great job, so when someone from the audience came up to me afterwards and handed me a slip of paper, I was certain it was some sort of commitment to get involved in my campaign. The note said: "You said 'um' forty-eight times during your speech and the question and answer period that followed. Why don't you join us at Toastmasters?"

As you progress in a campaign, you will gradually get better at public speaking. I have been mayor for eleven years now, and I still get butterflies before a speech; I don't care how perfunctory it is or how young the audience. After years of making speeches, there are some techniques and tricks that work for me:

1. Arrive a few minutes early to get a feel of the audience and the room.
2. Sit in the car to go over your speech or talk. You will have neither the time nor the inclination to do it once you are inside.
3. Answer questions directly. I have an unfortunate tendency to drift into a stream-of-consciousness when responding to a question. One thing reminds me of another and another and another. Avoid that.
4. Have fun. Remember you are on stage. This is your moment. Enjoy it. Smile a lot.
5. Lose the verbal tics: "um," "you know," "basically," "if you will," "quite frankly," "to tell you the truth," all can distract from your presentation. Every moment does not have to be filled. Silence can be a time to gather power. Never underestimate its force.
6. Have some notes with you about what you are going to say, even if it is a short speech and one you have given a million times. I remember once I was asked to speak at the outdoor local Shakespearean Theater with a standing room capacity of around 1,000. I had never spoken to such a large group, under lights or on a stage like that. I walked out and could not remember one line of my two-minute, memorized speech. Not one. I stood there for what seemed like an hour waiting for it to come to me. Nothing. Finally, with no hope of it coming back, I looked down at my notes. The first line triggered the speech and out it came. Even if you think you won't need them, bring along some notes.
7. Make your speech fun for others to hear. Include something in it to make them feel proud or appreciated. Throw

in some self-deprecating humor. I once watched a candidate give a speech at a Rotary Club meeting. She got up bemoaning the fact that one more lumber mill had closed. It would have been much more effective had she stood up and said: "In Jackson County, small business is big business." She could have followed that up with examples of business people, most of whom were sitting in the room, who were a testimony to our economic strength. She also could have pointed out that the success of communities like ours is dependent upon the volunteerism and commitment of organizations such as the Rotary Club. Give examples. People hate to hear candidates whine. Avoid it.

One speech I gave as mayor was to the Annual Conference of the Engineers of Oregon. I am the daughter of an engineer, and I'm certain my son has all the makings of one. Back then when I got home from work late at night, my son, six at the time, would call me to his bed. Silly me, I thought it was for a kiss. Instead he would turn on the light and bring out from under his bed the most bizarre contraptions I had ever seen. He would then say, "If I could just have a little piece of electrical tape . . ." I told this story to the Engineers of Oregon with the tone of, "You don't know how your mothers suffered." I then pulled out of a bag three or four examples of my son's handiwork. It was great fun.

8. Add some history to your speeches. Some people know the background of their town, but many don't. Call seniors or local historians for ideas.
9. Focus on friends in the audience. I once gave a speech in the middle of a really horrible campaign for a money measure I was personally proposing. In the audience was one of the opponents, making faces and otherwise distracting me. It had to be the worst speech of my career. Now I look for friendly faces and focus on them.
10. Use quotations, jokes, and anecdotes. Although there are exceptions, I usually do not tell jokes but rather incorporate jokes as funny stories within a speech. This is where self-deprecating humor works. For example, at a speech to the Oregon Nurses Association, I followed two women who were not nurses but rather children of nurses. Although I had not thought of this while I wrote my speech, I said that I too was the daughter of a nurse, an operating room nurse. I told them that OR nurses are the only people I know who wash their hands before *and* after they go to the bathroom.

> "He can compress the most words into the smallest idea of any man I ever met."
> —Abraham Lincoln

Even my mom laughs at this because it's true. Give people something of yourself.

11. Collect quotations and incorporate them wherever possible. There are many books out now that offer up food for thought in quotations. Modify the quotations you choose so that they are your own words or fit the moment.

12. Share your experiences on the campaign trail. "The other day while I was canvassing . . ." can be an effective way to make known that you canvass and care what voters think, plus it provides an opportunity to communicate an important idea that is part of your platform.

13. Save correspondence that is entertaining and incorporate it in your speech. My favorite is a letter from a supporter telling me I need to wear more makeup. I never reveal the author's name in this situation.

14. Target your audience with the campaign message.

15. Give your speech to yourself in the mirror or have a supporter videotape a speech and have the campaign team watch and critique it.

16. Avoid "word stir-fry." That is, avoid confusing people with unprepared, incoherent speeches or answers to questions. It makes those listening think you do not know what you are talking about.

Look for opportunities to speak before groups. You need to get your name and face known to the public if you are a candidate, and you need to get your cause before the public if you are working for a measure. With that said, it is just as important to protect the candidate's time from too many activities with marginal returns. Look for speaking opportunities where the audience should be receptive to your campaign message. Focus on the saveables.

When organizing campaigns for ballot measures, I set up a committee of supporters whose sole job is that of a speakers' bureau. If it is a county-wide proposition or measure, the speakers' bureau might be quite large. In an individual city, this committee may be as small as two people. Regardless of the size, the bureau's job is to seek opportunities to speak and make sure someone is there from the committee to explain the ballot measure and answer questions in a knowledgeable way.

A speakers' bureau is a terrific way of publicly involving big name people who want to be aligned with a campaign yet lack the skills to work as a campaign committee member. It is also good for the ballot measure. Whereas an election with a candidate depends on that candidate and his or her stands to build relationships with the voters, ballot measures often encompass only one idea. With a bal-

> "I would feel that most of the conversations that took place in those areas of the White House that did have the recording system would in almost their entirety be in existence but the special prosecutor, the court, and I think, the American people are sufficiently familiar with the recording system to know where the recording devices existed and to know the situation in terms of the recording process but I feel, although the process has not been undertaken yet in preparation of the material to abide by the court order, really, what the answer to that question is."
> —Ron Ziegler, former White House press secretary answering a reporter's question about the Nixon White House taping system

lot measure, the people who attach their name to it create the relationship. You might have the president of the college, the president of the Rotary Club, the mayor, the leaders of every church, and so forth on your bureau. Each of these people brings a following. Their names have grown to represent something in the community, and it is their reputations that draw the vote.

Write-in and Third Party Candidates

The Write-in Candidate

Following the sudden death of a city councilor just weeks before the general election of 1998, a few of us got together to help a write-in candidate. This turned out to be a great campaign. There were lots of volunteers, plenty of money, great ads, well-placed lawn signs, a solid brochure, and a solid candidate. The write-in candidate was both hard-working and would also do anything we asked, from walking districts to modifying her "look." She had been actively involved in city politics, served on volunteer boards and commissions, was smart and well spoken, and did her homework. She got the endorsements, strong endorsements from both local newspapers. Figure 11.4 shows the brochure we used in this campaign. The opposition really ran no campaign other than two or three ads and about as many lawn signs. We made no mistakes during the campaign and still we lost.

Write-in campaigns, under the best of circumstances, are tough to win. Can it be done? Absolutely. There are examples everywhere of people pulling it off. A couple of years ago a woman was elected to the House of Representatives following a write-in campaign in Washington State. Write-ins are really no more work than a regular election. However, write-ins are a little more complicated.

First Things First.
1. Know what the ballot looks like where you live. Go to the county clerk and get a copy of the ballot.
2. Find out just what is expected of the voter at the ballot box. Does he or she have to put down the full name, the position of the office (for example, County Commissioner #3)? Exactly how must it be written? Does punching the opponent's number on a ballot invalidate the vote?
3. ☞Know the law. Are the laws for financial disclosure the same for you as a write-in as for the individual appearing on the ballot?
4. Know when the absentee ballots are mailed. You must both identify support and turn out your absentees on or before election day. This is crucial for a win.

"Experience is a hard teacher. She gives the test first, the lesson afterwards."
—Anonymous

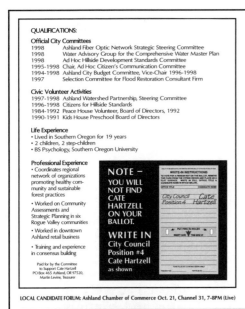

FIGURE 11.4   Example of Brochure for Write-in Candidate. Write-in candidate Cate Hartzell had a difficult challenge to overcome in her attempt to win a seat on the city council: the ballot. Each county has a ballot that is particular to that area. Some lend themselves well to a write-in, some do not. To overcome the challenge in this campaign, a facsimile of the ballot was placed on all campaign materials: the brochure, ads, lawn signs, and direct mail. And yet hundreds of citizens filled their ballots out incorrectly in an attempt to vote for Cate.

5. Know what percentage the absentees are of those who vote: not the registered voters, but those who actually vote. For example, in my county 25 percent of all registered voters request and vote absentee, but on election day they represent 52 percent or more of the voter turnout.
6. Run two campaigns: one for absentees and one for walk-ins.
7. Reinforce in your campaign literature and advertising what the voter will see on the ballot.
8. Get your candidate on the speaking circuit with the opponent(s).
9. Conduct all other business as you would for any other campaign, keeping in mind item number 7 above.

You might think this sounds convoluted, but write-in campaigns are actually more fun than running a regular campaign. Why? Well, no one really expects a write-in to win, so everyone is kind of rooting for you. Also, because they're so rare, the media gives the campaign more attention with feel-good stories *during the news*, especially if the candidate is working his or her tail off in an obviously well-organized effort. This kind of campaign creates a sense of urgency that brings out the best in volunteers, so they really go the extra distance for the campaign.

It is usually difficult to raise money for a candidate who appears to be losing; however, with a write-in, people don't perceive this as the fault of the candidate but rather of circumstances beyond the candidate's control. As a result, if you have a strong write-in candidate, it is surprisingly easy to raise money for him or her.

Finally, because people know the odds are long on a write-in winning, when you lose, your efforts get far more attention than they would in a more traditional race. Depending on the kind of campaign you run, the candidate ends the race with more stature, power, and respect in the community than before the campaign and, ironically, is not portrayed as "the loser."

Problems with Ballots. In our write-in race, we had a very difficult ballot type to work with. On some ballots there is a place to write the name of the candidate right next to the position they are seeking. On our ballot our voters had to write "city council," the position number of the council seat, and the candidate's name, and they had to remember not to punch the corresponding number of the opponent on the ballot itself.

"I have always found paranoia to be a perfectly defensible position."
—Pat Conroy

To visually reinforce all the voter needed to do, we re-created a ballot and then used this as our logo. Our slogan was "Keep the Vision Alive" to remind people that our candidate was only running because a strong environmentalist, with a clear platform, had died.

The message was: "It's about experience and involvement." Who could better hit the ground running as a new city councilor than the write-in candidate, especially given the complicated government of our city?

In fact, although the campaign focused largely on how to fill out the ballot, there were so many mistakes made (failure to put the proper council position or any position on the ballot, failure to stipulate city council, and so forth) that hundreds of votes did not count.

Third Party Candidates

As in all campaign activities, a third party candidate can be a blessing or a curse. If you're a third party candidate you will benefit most by presenting the Republican and the Democrat as one and the same. You and you alone provide an alternative. To win as a third party candidate you must be able to pull from both parties, all age groups, and all income levels.

Third party candidates usually act as spoilers by splitting the vote of one party and thereby increasing the likelihood of a win by the other. Independents can go either way, pulling votes from either the Democrats or the Republicans depending on how they stand on issues. In 1990 a very conservative Independent went on the gubernatorial ticket in Oregon. He ran on an anti-choice, anti-sales-tax, anti-land-use-planning platform and successfully pulled conservative votes from a very popular moderate Republican. This allowed the Democrat to win.

In New Mexico, Republican Bill Redmond won a congressional seat in 1996 in a heavily registered Democratic district by using a third party candidate to pull support from his Democratic opponent. Redmond's win was primarily a result of three strategies: Target the Democrat with negative ads, boost the Green Party candidate to split the Democrat vote, and turn out the Republican base. Redmond's campaign even sent literature to registered Democrats for the Green Party candidate.

If you are involved in a campaign with a third party candidate, think of creative ways this additional candidate can work for your win.

Media and the Candidate

In my ten years as mayor, I have had my ups and downs with the media. Some of those have occurred during elections, some in between. In my first two runs for mayor, I suspected that the local paper was not particularly thrilled about my being where I was. However, in my third run something happened that ended any doubts.

The local paper had been reporting campaign events in what appeared to be a very biased fashion since I declared my candidacy. Small and not so small things were adding up. For example, the paper invited my opponent to do a guest editorial but forgot to ask me. When I asked the editor about it, he lied and said he told my campaign manager. (I didn't have one.) My campaign team was getting more and more indignant, and supporters were writing and calling the paper with direct accusations. Then, while I was delivering an ad to the paper, I overheard a conversation that confirmed all my suspicions. In the doorway of the publisher's office, located adjacent to the drop-off counter at the local paper, stood the editor and publisher in conversation. Because of how they stood they could not see me just three feet away from them.

They were talking about how the campaign was being presented to the community through the paper and laughed about my supporters calling to protest over the biased reporting. The editor said, "I would feel a *little* better if there were complaints coming from both sides, but *that's* not going to happen." The publisher laughed and said, "No, that won't happen." They also mentioned the headlines used to make my opponent's letters-to-the-editor stand out and mine disappear. The conversation lasted only a couple of minutes, but it was quite revealing. When they finished, the editor turned and saw me standing there. I was the mayor. I had been the mayor for eight years, had volunteered thousands of hours to the community; every neighborhood except mine had benefited from my efforts. My face was expressionless as I stared at him. In that moment, as he realized that I had overheard them, his face turned bright red and he turned and quickly retreated to the back of the building.

You and your campaign team may suspect bias on the part of the local media, you may even have those suspicions confirmed as I did, but there is no way to use something like this. A candidate looks weak to the public when he or she complains about the press, not to mention that it is political suicide. The best revenge is to win. Following my win, when the editor called my office and said, "Let's let bygones be bygones," I said, "Fine." I never hold a grudge because there's simply no profit in it.

Although I am amazed when I see candidates, especially presidential candidates, who should know better, go after the media, I can understand why they do. In recent years the media, even local media, have become more vicious and combative. They can be merciless to elected officials who *volunteer* their time to serve the community and then wonder, on the editorial page, why so few enter the fray. I believe that controversy sells papers, and candidates and government are fair game. Although I will respond to anything my

> "You never get ahead of anyone as long as you try to get even with him."
> —Lou Holtz, Arkansas football coach

opponent says about me that is false, I generally ignore any bait that the press floats on the pond.

Candidates are no better. They are vicious with each other and segments of the community, using fear as a political device. Why? Because it works. Candidates say immigrants are responsible for job scarcity, your life is marginalized because of minorities, or corporate executives created the deterioration in your quality of life. Candidates encourage the public to blame their problems on other segments of the population and then fail to see why they are unable to draw communities together, once elected, to solve huge and demanding problems.

There is little interest in personal responsibility anymore. And the role models—candidates, community leaders, and the media—are not doing much better than the public in this regard. Community leaders and the media are missing an opportunity to serve as role models for personal responsibility. However, rarely do these two entities understand how they can move communities, counties, states, and even the nation forward by working together to communicate the hopes and dreams of society through a little civil discourse.

"Whatever else there may be in our nature, responsibility toward truth is one of its attributes."
—Arthur Eddington

Thank-you Notes

There is one overlooked area that goes a long way in a campaign: the thank-you note. I cannot stress how important thank-you notes are. Send them often, and not just in response to monetary donations. I like to have half sheets of a high-quality paper printed with a letterhead and use matching envelopes. If you have the money, let a print shop do the letterhead for you in a different color ink. Blue is very nice on off-white. Jot off a quick thank-you in your own hand to those who put in a little extra effort, who gave you the coffee, who donated items for your special event, who called to turn people out for an event.

12

The Issue-based Campaign

In this chapter
Initiative, Referendum, and Recall
Saving Our Libraries
Building New Schools
Packaging the Issue-based Campaign
Flies in the Ointment: The Double Majority and Super Majority

Initiative, Referendum, and Recall

The initiative and referendum processes arose out of the fundamental controversy about whether government should come directly from the people or through representatives to the various levels of government. Although some direct democracy existed in the early years of U.S. government, the first hundred years were almost solely representative. It wasn't until the late 1800s, when dissatisfaction with government and distrust of the state legislatures became prevalent, that citizens enacted the initiative process. Primarily a Western-state phenomenon, the initiative process began in reaction to laws that benefited a few powerful interests rather than the body electorate. It enlarges the role people have in decision making.

Ironically, today this process has become a tool for special interest groups with agendas relating to natural resources, morality and government, the rights of minorities, and tax limitations. As Oregon's Secretary of State Phil Keisling said, "At key moments in our history, the initiative has held up a mirror to who we are as [a society], reflecting our pettiness as well as grand visions, our mean-spiritedness as well as our generosity, our perils and possibilities as a political community."

The state initiative process enables citizens to bypass the legislature and directly place proposed statutes and constitutional amendments on the ballot by gathering signatures. Each of the twenty-four states with citizens' initiative authority has different criteria to

> "To be successful, grow to the point where one completely forgets himself; that is, to lose himself in a great cause."
> —Booker T. Washington

activate the process. Before you begin an initiative campaign, you should contact your local elections office or Secretary of State.

The state referendum process is different in that it serves as a check on the legislature by forcing an approved law to go to a vote of the people. In this way it allows voters to indicate acceptance or rejection of a statute or constitutional amendment passed by the governing body.

> "I pay my taxes gladly. Taxes are the price of civilization."
> —Oliver Wendell Holmes

Local initiative and referendum are also available in many states, and the requirements and what they may encompass are basically the same as for the state level. Local initiative and referendum both can be very useful tools for school districts, libraries, and municipal and even county government.

In a local initiative, although most of the guidelines are established by state statutes, the percentages of signatures that need to be gathered vary from city to city and county to county. Voters may also refer (through referendum) any legislation passed by the local governing body to the voters. To do this requires a certain percentage of signatures from voters in a specific election (for example, 15 percent of those who voted in the last mayoral election).

Local referendum differs from the initiative process only in the time constraints: Usually something must be referred to the voters a certain number of days after adoption by the governing body, but if you find you hate a law, you can in essence repeal it through the initiative process at any time. Because both the initiative and referendum process revolve around the legislative body there are some inherent problems. If you're not working in conjunction with the local elected officials, be prepared. They have many tricks in their bag.

For example, in the local initiative process, the municipal officer always prepares the ballot title for cities and a county officer does this for the county. Preparing the ballot title provides a possible edge for the governing body. I have seen some titles prepared in such a way that you cannot tell whether a "yes" vote is actually a "yes" or a "no."

Also, in many states you can have only one question or subject placed before the voters in any given initiative. This is more difficult than it sounds. Often citizens throw in a couple of ideas, each of which may strengthen the other and is quite related to the rest. After collecting the signatures or running the winning campaign they find out that the initiative is held to have covered more than one subject when it is appealed by the opposition to a higher court. You shouldn't leave this determination to the local election body. If you intend to do all this work, hire an attorney.

There are many restrictions. For example, in Oregon you can only put legislative, not land use, matters to a vote. Know what your parameters are before spending a lot of time and money.

One additional caution: Those signing the petition must be registered within the jurisdiction of the area that will be affected by the proposed legislation. For example, if your school measure is to be voted on by those within your school district, then only those registered within the school district will qualify as signers on the petition. Similarly, if your proposed legislation affects your city, then only those registered within the city limits would qualify. Be sure to get at least 10 percent more signatures than are required for qualification.

Competing Measures

For local initiatives, the governing body often has the option of placing a competing measure on the ballot but must do so within a specified amount of time.

In a more generic sense, competing measures are two or more ballot items for money that appear on the same ballot. They are usually similar in some way. For example, two county measures may request funding through the property tax, one for juvenile services, the other for adult detention. Counties and cities are often placing competing measures on ballots because there are so many needs that are falling by the wayside. However, this competition increases the likelihood that all will fail; rarely do they all pass. For example, in November 1998 our county placed three bond measures before the voters and all went down. The reason is pretty simple. Among voters there are those that vote "no" on *any* new taxes and those who will vote "yes." Of those "yes" voters, some will vote for more than one money measure and some will choose between the measures. This effectively splits the "yes" vote.

That counties and cities would choose to place two measures on the ballot at the same time indicates some muddled thinking. However, there are situations in which it cannot be helped. For example, your school district is trying to pass a bond measure for a new gym, the city needs money for new fire stations, and the county needs the library system upgraded. Three different governing bodies, all with the right to place items on the ballot, separately create a competing–ballot measure scenario. Ideally they would be talking to one another and spread these items out, but that doesn't always happen.

If citizens have put together an initiative that the governing body doesn't want, a competing measure is a very powerful tool and should be used. For example, a few years back we passed a prepared food and beverage tax to fund the open space acquisition program and state-mandated upgrades on our wastewater treatment plant. It was a divisive campaign driven by local restaurants and the state food and beverage industry on one side and the parks commission,

> "A life spent making mistakes is not only more honorable but more useful than a life spent doing nothing."
> —George Bernard Shaw

environmentalists, and me on the other. No city in Oregon had this tax and the food and beverage industry didn't want it to start here. It was approved by the voters and was immediately referred back to the voters by the losing side through the initiative process.

In the meantime the state legislature decided to place a state-wide sales tax for school funding before the voters. The timing was such that the referral of the F&B tax would happen on the same ballot as the sales tax. I assumed the proponents of the F&B tax repeal would stress that our food and beverage tax would be added on top of a state-wide sales tax, creating a 9 to 10 percent sales tax on prepared food in Ashland.

To head off this predicament, we placed a competing measure on the ballot along with the F&B tax initiative. The competing measure stated that should the state sales tax pass, our F&B tax would be repealed AND if people voted in larger numbers for our competing measure than for the ballot measure repealing the tax, it would override the citizens' initiative. Citizens chose our measure over an outright repeal of the tax. The state-wide sales tax went down and our meals tax remained.

Recall Process

The recall process requires signatures of registered voters equaling a specific percentage of those voting in a specific election. For example, recall for a state office might be 8 percent of those who voted in the last election for governor, whereas a recall of a city official might be 15 percent of those who voted in the last mayoral election. Once a petition is pulled it must be filed within a specified amount of time (depending on the state or local statutes) and a special election must be held within a specific number of days following verification of the signatures. In Oregon the whole process can last no more than 140 days: 90 to gather the signatures, 10 to have them verified, and 40 until the special election. You cannot begin a recall process until someone has been in office for six months after his or her last election. This goes for those who are in their second or third term of office as well.

If you're thinking about recalling an elected official, it is my hope that you will stop and reconsider. Recalls are almost never warranted. I know many who have been subjected to them and they generally take on the atmosphere of a public flogging. It destroys people who serve and it destroys their families. Recalls also scare other qualified, honest, hard-working people, the kind of people we need, from ever wanting to enter public office. If you want to recall someone, get over it. Run a candidate or yourself in the next election.

> "It doesn't make sense to talk about successful corporations in a society whose schools, hospitals, churches, symphonies, or libraries are deteriorating or closing."
> —Clifton C. Garvin, Jr.

Saving Our Libraries

For some reason many voters look at library funding as a frill. Unlike new wastewater treatment plants or dams for more water, both of which can be paid for through revenue bonds, libraries have suffered under taxpayer revolts and ignorance. If your mission is to get money to build a new library or remodel and expand an existing one, there is hope.

Library campaigns must be set up a little differently from other bond measures, in part because it is more difficult to convince people of need. There are basically three steps involved, with a number of choices within each of those steps.

1. Establish a committee to examine needs, opportunities, and direction. Your first step is to get a select group of community members together to usher your project through. Although some may end up working on the campaign, that is not the purpose of this committee. The members' job is to serve as liaisons with the community and the project. Assemble people who represent the many sides of your community and are well respected in their circles. You may select an individual from the immediate neighborhood; a business person; representatives of influential city boards or commissions, such as planning and historic; a builder; a librarian; a member of the Friends of the Library group; or a liaison to the city council. It is also important to have city or county staff there for guidance and administrative support. It does not matter if all the committee members are not 100 percent on board for the project in the beginning; in fact it's actually better if opinions are varied. Don't worry, people will come around or the project won't fly anyway.

2. Select an architectural team once you have the committee in place and are working with the local, hopefully municipal, government. The architectural team should be committed to community process and inclusivity. You want architects interested in what the community wants, not what they think is best for the community. Through community visioning, where citizens are invited to attend a half-day workshop, a clear idea of what people want will emerge. From this the architects can draft architectural renderings and come up with a money figure to place before the voters.

3. Have your governing body place this on the ballot for you. If they don't, use the initiative process described above and consider running for office next time one of them is due to be re-elected. Using the money figure generated by the architectural team and backed by your committee, the council

> "If you're doing what's right, the bullets bounce off."
> —Cathy Shaw

Historic Photograph of Ashland's Carnegie Library (Photo courtesy of Terry Skibby, Ashland Historian)

FIGURE 12.1   Issue-Based Campaigns. In issue-based campaigns use a mix of the old with the new. Civic buildings reflect who we were as well as who we are. As Winston Churchill said: "We shape our buildings, and then our buildings shape us."

or county commission should place the matter before the voters. You now have two months to convince people to support it.

Now you should consider who gets to vote on this issue. In my area, those who live in the unincorporated areas, that is, those outside of the city limits, tend to vote "no" on such things, so I prefer to leave them out of the district and limit the vote to the city. It is also much easier to turn out the vote if the election is just city-wide. Don't forget, those who use the library the most live close to it.

If you think you will have trouble convincing the city council to place the measure on the ballot or you want additional public input and direction, consider having your library friends group print flyers with questionnaires and canvass the city. One part of the flyer can be dedicated to what the community proposed in the visioning process and another part could invite community members to contribute money to the Friends of the Library group. You would be surprised at how much money you can bring in with this small effort. If your Friends group is a 501C(3) organization, this money and effort is restricted in how it may touch your campaign. They must be kept separate and distinct.

If your library project comes in on the high side and sticker shock is a concern, following are some suggestions for getting the price down:

1. Have local donors or organizations financially sponsor different rooms, fixtures, floors, rugs. Determine how much the children's, young adult, or reference section will cost and ask civic groups to fund each room; promise to put their name over the door. Go to likely organizations that might pick up the computer component.
2. Ask either local organizations or the historic society to fund and place all the artwork for the library. Have the walls of your renovated library tell the story of your town through pictures.
3. Determine if there is state-owned furniture that is being warehoused that could be used for the public library.
4. Find out if there are local, state, or federal historic renovation grants available for some portion of the remodel if the library is a historic structure.
5. Consider investing in a great video collection that people can access for free; this helps when your library's funding is dependent upon patronage.

> "This nation cannot afford to maintain its military power and neglect its brainpower."
> —John F. Kennedy

Once you have your library on the ballot at a price you feel people can live with, go through this book and conduct all the steps for winning an issue-based campaign.

Building New Schools

The biggest obstacle that public school districts have in passing operation and maintenance money or construction bonds is that they have evolved beyond the kind of education much of the electorate received. As a result, many voters see computers in the classroom as a luxury, extracurricular activities such as debate and business programs as unnecessary, and connection to the World Wide Web as a frill. I can't tell you how many times I have heard how we need to get back to the basics of reading, writing, and 'rithmetic. The reality our students face has to do with screen-based literacy, collaborative learning, and critical thinking.

To get voters to support the changes needed in our schools, we must educate the populace to understand that our schools are no longer training students for trades and specific jobs. Instead, students are and need to be trained to work with people, be flexible in an ever-changing job market, and think creatively and freely, with access to data. Most of the jobs for today's elementary students do not yet exist.

The bulk of America's schools were built in the early 1950s or earlier and are either falling apart or are woefully inadequate for the electronic demands of the computer age. The task of rebuilding them or constructing new ones, added to all the other costs of public education, is almost overwhelming to the taxpayer, who has become immobilized. But in Ashland we have had great luck and following are some tips to our success. They are basically the same as those discussed above for getting library funding.

1. Set up a committee that represents a good cross-section of the community. The last time we proposed major improvements to our schools, we started out with about forty citizens, all invited, who then worked in focus groups to design a plan and a dollar amount that would work for our community. However you decide to do it, just remember to start broad and continue to widen the involvement all the way to the campaign.

2. Select an architect. Obviously, you can't use a large group to select this individual or team, but this is a really important step and needs the right people. Too often, in an effort to save money and make public buildings salable at an election, we cut corners. We should construct civic buildings with materials that speak of permanence and are compatible with the community and a point of civic pride. It costs no more to build a beautiful building than to build an ugly one. Look closely at what the architect has designed before. Do

the buildings all look the same? Have past contractors had trouble working with the architect? Do a lot of research and homework here, or you'll be sorry.

3. Ask the council to float the issue to city residents if you think you'll have trouble getting it to pass district-wide.

Packaging the Issue-based Campaign

In an issue-based campaign the message is the messenger. You want those in your community who have broad support and leadership standing to usher your project through. I have touched on issue-based campaigns throughout this book but there are many specifics that bear emphasis:

1. Set up a "Committee to Support" of movers and shakers that is separate from your campaign committee, people whose names will appear on ads, in direct mail, and on the brochure.
2. Find the right chair or co-chairs for this committee, people who represent the many sides of your community. This is an opportunity to use an individual who will bring along the saveables, not the saints.
3. Educate the electorate about the changing world. With either schools or libraries you are selling opportunity. You are not asking people to fund needs. The example provided in a previous chapter contrasting two high school transcripts of straight-"A" students reflects an issue that resonates with voters. It asks voters to ensure the success of their children and grandchildren. Who is more likely to get a job or into a good college? There is also an element of self-interest to consider. As an aging society, we must position ourselves to improve the education of those who will take care of us in our old age.
4. Talk about making libraries information hubs once again. The pathways and opportunities libraries can open to a community, young and old, are often overlooked, even by librarians.
5. Be sure to include areas in your library or school design that can be used after hours for community needs. These areas could be computer labs so that the community can learn how to use the Internet and computers or meeting, reading, and study rooms.
6. Conduct a precinct analysis that closely tracks who has voted for similar measures. If you are looking for funding for libraries, examine the last census and determine who has school-aged children, then target those households. Remem-

> "Education makes a people easy to lead, but difficult to drive; easy to govern but impossible to enslave."
> —Baron Henry Peter Brougham

ber, schools are moving more toward training our students to work in groups, and these groups need to gather somewhere to do projects and research. What better place than the public library?

7. Acknowledge the changing face of libraries and schools. For example, because of the Web and CD-ROMs, reference sections are actually getting smaller on the one hand (less need for reference books) and larger on the other hand (computers take up lots of room).

8. Use teachers, Parent-Teacher Organizations, and parents to volunteer for this effort.

9. Pay close attention to the fatal flaws. For example, in a nearby school district a bond measure for schools failed because voters discovered that it included money to pave the parking lot. At no time did the committee tell the voters that state track-out ordinances require paving if remodeling occurs.

10. Have a speakers' bureau that can go before civic groups. This should not be teachers or librarians because they have a vested interest in the bond passing. (Librarians are not, in general, great public speakers.)

11. Create a strong theme and message and stick to them. Remember, a theme is strategic, not tactical. Aim at the souls that can be saved and use the theme as a focus point for your campaign team and "Committee to Support."

Flies in the Ointment:
The Double Majority and Super Majority
The Double Majority

In November 1996 Oregon passed an initiative that included, among other things, a stipulation requiring a 50 percent turnout of the registered voters for money measures to pass. The author of this initiative felt that too many money measures were placed on the ballot during obscure, special elections when officials knew turnout would be low. The only exception to this rule is during even-year general elections, when the double majority does not apply.

The challenge for passing bond measures became one of turning out 50-plus percent of the vote, not just a majority of support. Opponents quickly figured out that if they stayed home their no-show status worked more in their favor than if they actually cast a "no" vote. They would not vote and also urged their friends to stay home so that the tax measure would be defeated before votes were even counted. There was an added bonus: People who had not been

> "We are continually faced with a series of great opportunities brilliantly disguised as insoluble problems."
> —John W. Gardner

purged from the voter rolls after they moved or died suddenly got a de facto vote because they were still part of the registration totals from which the 50 percent must be pulled.

In March 1997 I put together a campaign to raise the necessary local dollars to match FEMA funds for our flood-damaged city. I had never run a campaign under the double majority and set things up as I outlined in GOTV except for one thing: I ran GOTV phone banks for three days instead of five.

Eleven days out from the election, the mail-in ballots showed only a 21 percent return. I was surprised. Ashland had traditionally been a city with good turnout, often in the 60–80 percent range. I ordered the inactivity lists and the next day distributed them to fifty people to look up phone numbers. Three days later the lists came back. Meanwhile only another 4 percent of the votes had come in. Now I panicked. Even if we called on all of the remaining days, we couldn't pull in the votes needed. I set up phone banks for the Wednesday, Thursday, Friday, and Sunday before Tuesday's election. On Wednesday we hit large numbers of college students who had moved, local kids who were away at college, and about ten people who were dead but still on the voter rolls. There was little change in the ballot count on Thursday, but by Friday the return rate had jumped to 35 percent. By Saturday it was 39 percent. I quickly tried to set up phone banks for that night but could not get a location. However, we did call on Sunday, Monday, and Tuesday nights.

The election count showed that 55 percent of those voting supported the flood bonds. However, we lost because turnout was only 49.7 percent. In May we took the same measure back to the voters but never let up on the phones, turned out the required 50 percent and then some, and the measure passed.

Since then I have tracked a number of money elections around the state that have labored under the double majority. What I discovered was that, with almost no exceptions, if 50 percent of the voters turned out, the measure passed. I realized that people who support funding for schools, libraries, civic buildings, and parks love to tell you that they are voting for these things, but when it comes to getting out of their chairs on a cold election night to raise their taxes, inertia sets in. Pro-tax voters are simply less motivated to vote than anti-tax voters.

> "Human history becomes more and more a race between education and catastrophe."
> —H. G. Wells

The double majority has turned out to be a blessing. It creates a sense of urgency on the part of the pro-tax voter as well as the volunteers needed to prod them. I discovered two other things during my research: first, a double majority election works best in cities; and second, because governing bodies are worried about turning out 50 percent of the registered voters, fewer competing ballot measures are offered.

Keep the Vote in the City Limits

In my experience in Oregon, those in the unincorporated areas want little or nothing to do with what government has to offer. They have wells and septic drain fields and often heat exclusively with wood. They want to drive on paved roads, use libraries, and have the sheriff and fire patrol appear promptly, and they want their kids to attend the best schools, but when it comes to tax increases, they're a loud and strong "no" vote. People within city limits, however, tend to want what government provides and are willing to pay as part of a group for these services. Obviously there are exceptions to these generalizations.

If your situation is like Oregon's and you have an opportunity to run an election under the double majority without the unincorporated vote, do it. You will hear people say that those living in the county use the services and therefore should help pay for them, so they should also vote on money measures. However, I am of the opinion that the unincorporated voter keeps those of us in a city from getting what we want. If you feel that the city folks will resent subsidizing those in the county, think again. We subsidize county residents every day: They use city streets, parks, and whatever else your municipal government has in its empire. City residents, through county taxes, pave the county roads to service those living in the unincorporated areas but those in the county do not pave city streets.

There are five reasons why you should try to limit those voting to voters within the city limits:

1. The assessed valuation (AV) is greatest per acre within the city, so even if you include county residents in the overall funding scheme, it won't have a huge impact on the cost per thousand of the property tax.
2. People within city limits have a higher voter turnout than those in the county, so you're already ahead if you have to meet a double majority rule.
3. It is easier to run an election and bring in votes within city limits because of the density of population.
4. The percent of people favoring taxes for *anything* is higher in city limits than in the county. Obviously, people living within city limits want what government has to offer or they wouldn't be there.
5. By holding your voting district to the city limits you eliminate many "sinners" because of the possible voting tendencies of those living in unincorporated areas.

Avoid Competing Measures

There are all kinds of things that have to go to a county-wide vote or a vote larger than a city, but city schools and library buildings aren't among them. Be creative. If you're an elected official in the city, you get to make the rules. When road blocks are placed in your way, keeping your community from having great schools, open spaces, and libraries, don't take that road.

Before the double majority rule, there were tax measures, sometimes two and three, on each and every ballot. The schools would need a new gym, the parks department needed to continue funding for the pool, the fire department needed a ladder truck, the county needed operating and maintenance money for the library, the sheriff needed more deputies for patrols, the bus system needed more routes, and so forth. Now, because of the double majority, everyone is afraid to place anything on the ballot except in the even-year general election when the double majority doesn't apply.

To have a ballot where only one money issue is presented to the voter allows that single issue to get lots of light, air, dialogue, debate, and media attention. It also gives campaigns working for the issue a chance to turn out the support without another election poking a sleeping dog somewhere else.

The Super Majority

A super majority requires that two-thirds of those voting approve a tax measure for it to take effect. Here your objective changes dramatically from a double majority. The best chance you have to pass anything with a super majority is to place your money measure on an election with the lowest voter turnout possible and no competing measures. Then you must ID your supporters and have a top-notch GOTV effort to get them to the polls or to return their absentee ballots.

A few years back, in Marin County, California, supporters of a school facility plan used an interesting tactic to pass their bond measure under the super majority rule. The supporters of the bond measure determined that those sixty-five and older were both "no" votes and voters who were very likely to vote. To move this age group over to the "yes" column, the bond measure excluded them from having to pay, but did not exclude them from the vote. The campaign then worked hard to turn out that age group, who had nothing to lose by voting "yes." The facility plan passed.

> "Experience is not what happens to a person, it is what a person does with what happens."
> —Aldous Huxley

Given that many seniors are two generations away from having children in public education and that they have probably paid enough, this seems like a happy compromise.

13

The Campaign Flowchart

In this chapter
Building Your Campaign Flowchart
The Campaign Calendar

You have now almost completed this handbook; based on your time, resources, and volunteer base, you have decided what campaign activities you are capable of doing. You are now ready to create a campaign flowchart, which actually marks the beginning of your campaign. Start by listing the tasks you need to complete before the election. These might be canvassing, brochure development, media, phone banks, and lawn signs. Your choice, of course, is dictated by your resources and the type of campaign you are running. For example, you may not be able to afford direct mail even though you'd love to use it, or you may have decided you do not want to use lawn signs because they are unnecessary in the ballot measure election for which you're campaigning.

Once you have the list of campaign tasks, transfer them onto your campaign flowchart in the proper sequence. A mockup of a campaign flowchart appears in figure 13.1, and there is a blank flowchart grid in Appendix 1. Please feel free to copy it for your campaign use.

Building Your Campaign Flowchart

A flowchart is an essential tool in any successful campaign. It is helpful for the campaign team because members can see the plan of the whole campaign. Flowcharts keep the campaign organized. I have also found that the chart can have a calming effect on the candidate and staff because it clearly outlines exactly what needs to be done and when. I like to do my flowcharts in color.

To construct your flowchart, you will need a long, unbroken wall, and you will need to gather the following items:

"Simply reacting to the present demand or scrambling because of tensions is the opposite of thoughtful planning. Planning emphasizes conscious, disciplined choice."
—Vaughn Keeler

- Five or more sticky-note pads in assorted colors
- Butcher or freezer paper
- At least six different colored marking pens
- A yardstick
- Masking tape
- One or two key campaign people (no more) to help you think

If possible, pull in someone who has worked on other campaigns to help you. An experienced campaigner will be an invaluable aid in building the flowchart.

To begin your chart, unroll about ten feet of butcher paper and tape it to a wall. On the far right bottom of the chart, place the date of the day after the election. On the far left bottom, place the date of the beginning of your campaign. It may be the date that you start your flowchart or the date when your first "formal" campaign activity (such as your announcement) is to take place. Draw a single line along the bottom between the two dates.

Divide the line into fairly equal monthly or weekly parts and print in all the dates between the day that your campaign begins and the day your campaign will end. Next, using a sticky note of a different color for each campaign function, brainstorm with your helpers and attach the appropriately colored sticky note to the butcher paper above the date on which you want to do that particular campaign function. For example, if lawn signs are represented by green notes, put one that says "take down lawn signs" on the day after the election because you know that your crew will have to take down lawn signs on that day.

Work your way backwards from the end of the campaign, making decisions as you go. For example, you know you will need to repair lawn signs the day after Halloween, so put that on a green note above October 31. Lawn signs go up usually one month before an election, so put that up next. You'll need a work party to get the signs stapled if you're using poly tag. This is a clerical function, so choose a different color. Write "staple lawn signs" on the sticky note and put it up somewhere in the week before the signs are to go up.

Keep working your way back, thinking through each of the campaign activities you have on your list. Review the chapter titles and headings in this manual. Think in terms of the progression of an activity and all the sub-activities needed to support it.

To continue the lawn sign example, you will need stakes before you can start putting up signs. Decide on a date that doesn't clash with other lawn sign activities, such as stapling, and label the note "get stakes made." Ask yourself when the signs will be printed. Make up your mind and label that note "print lawn signs." Natu-

"The final days are the longest."
—Bill Meulemans

rally, before they can get printed, you must have them designed and camera ready. You might want to allow two weeks for this. So, on the date that is two weeks before the lawn signs are due to go to the printer, affix a sticky note that says "design lawn signs." Continue in this fashion for each and every function. Some functions will overlap with others. For example, fund-raising goes everywhere. The clerical team supports a number of activities, some of which may be happening at the same time. Use an arrow from the clerical line down to the appropriate activity line to show the connection. Should dates start to bunch up, move your activity dates around and keep track of them with your sticky notes.

Spread Out the Activities

With this method, activities that have been allowed too much or too little time become apparent immediately. For example, if you find by the concentration of multicolored sticky notes that brochure development, two direct mail pieces, and a phone bank for an event are all happening at the same time, you may consider moving something to another time slot. Brochure development could move up and be finished sooner, and the direct mail pieces may be handled by a mail order house or be prepared earlier or later. Your sticky notes are mobile for a reason, and you want to take advantage of this during this campaign planning activity. Spread out the activities so you and the volunteers do not get overworked or burned out. If nothing can move, it will give you an opportunity to line up extra help to organize the work.

By placing colored sticky notes for every function in a campaign on the chart, you build a visual representation of the campaign. Some of the functions will end when others begin. For example, your brochure must be done in time to canvass. If canvassing will take you two months, working each day after work plus weekends, then your brochure must be developed and back from the printer by this time. Therefore, your sticky notes for brochure development and printing will end on the flowchart before your canvassing begins.

> "A perfection of means and a confusion of aims seem to be our main problem."
> —Albert Einstein

The Activities

Following is a partial list of activities that should be represented on your flowchart:

- Ads: print, radio, and TV
- Lawn signs, big and small
- Coffees, fund-raisers, special events
- Letters-to-the-editor

- Direct mail
- Brochure development
- Canvassing and precinct analysis
- Phone banks

When your sticky notes are up where you want them, you are ready to put together your permanent campaign flowchart. Take another ten feet of butcher paper, your colored marking pens, and a yardstick. Lay the butcher paper on the floor in front of the flowchart. If there is room, you can hang the new chart on the wall directly below the old one. Fill in and make permanent your campaign commitments on the dates listed. Follow your color scheme; for example, if lawn signs were on green sticky notes, use a green marking pen for lawn signs on the flowchart.

Above the various dates, write the activity that is on the sticky note for that date, then draw a line in the same color to the next date or activity and continue until you have transferred everything from the first chart. By using colored lines, at a glance you will be able to follow a particular activity across the whole campaign. Figure 13.1 is an example of a typical flowchart for a general election race. It's not as difficult as it sounds, and a flowchart is definitely well worth the effort.

The Campaign Calendar

Many campaigns lay out the activities and duties of the process in a campaign plan. Nearly every book on campaigning makes reference to campaign plans and examples of how to set them up. I have tried to use them and have found that they are for a different type of person than I. However, if you prefer a campaign plan you may transfer your flowchart to 8 1/2 by 11 inch paper, listing activities and dates from most recent up to election day and post-election activities.

While I prefer a campaign flowchart, I have also had great luck using a campaign calendar (see figure 13.2). All you need for a calendar is a large sheet of tagboard, a straightedge, and a pencil. Map out your activities from election day backwards, this time on a large calendar that the committee can see and access. I start with pencil, then once things are set, go over it in ink. However, if time does not allow that, just put down the information as quickly and easily as possible and hang it up.

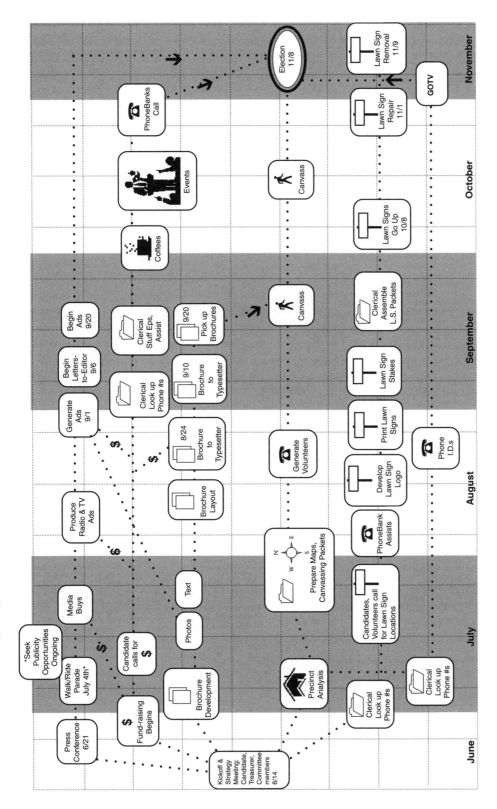

FIGURE 13.1   Example of Campaign Flowchart

254

Sunday	Monday	Tuesday	Wednesday	Thursday	Friday	Saturday
15	16 Committee working on Brochure wording Lawn Sign to Graphic Designer	17	18	19	20 → Lawn Sign to Printer	21
22 8PM Campaign Team Meets	23 Brochure copy to Graphic Designer Call for Volunteers to put up Lawn Signs	24	25 Review Brochure with Committee	26	27 Pick-up Brochure from Graphic Designer	28
29 8PM Campaign Team Meeting	30 Brochure to Printer	1 11AM Ground breaking for Senior Center 4PM Opponent on Ken Linbloom Show KCMX Call for $	2 10AM Temple Emek Shalom Ribbon Cutting Golden Class: Meet the Candidates Candidate call for $	3 Pick-up Lawn Signs fromPrinter Organize Lawn Sign Cards	4 Clerical Party to Staple Lawn Signs - Bundle Stakes	5 8-10AM Lawn Signs Go up 12 - firefighters 2 - Carole, Ken 2 - Bill Street Canvass?
6 Canvass 8PM Campaign Team Meets	7 Candidate Calls for $	8 5:30-7PM Chamber of Commerce - Meet the Candidates, AHI	9 12 noon LWV Lunch at the Mark 5-6 Canvass $ Calls	10 Canvass Ashland Mine 6:30-10PM Kathleen Brown Dinner SOWAK, Red Lion	11 12 Noon Welcome Leadership Conference 4-6 Canvass	12 10AM Canvass 3-6PM Make informercial SOU for Cable Access $ Calls
13 Canvass 12-3 3-5 Canvass 8PM Campaign Meeting	14 5-6 Canvass $ Calls	15 7AM Lithia Springs Rotary Debate 5 min. + Q&A $ Calls	16 4 PM Office Hours 5-6 Canvass $ Calls	17 10AM Meet the Candidates 1023 Morton St. DEBATE - AAUW/LWV	18 Letter-to-Voters Ad to Graphic Designer 4-6 Canvass Kennedy Roosevelt Dinner	19 10-1 Canvass 4-6 Ribbon Cutting of Environmental Center Design and Write Experience Ad
20 10AM Crop Walk 12-3 Canvass 3-5 Canvass 8PM Campaign Meeting	21 Experience Ad to Grahic Designer Camera-ready Letter-to-Voters Ad to paper 4PM Ken Linbloom	22 7PM Cable Access Debate	23 5-6 Canvass	24 Camera-ready Experience Ad to paper Run Letter-to-Voters Ad Noon Rotary Debate	25 Run Letter-to-Voters Ad again 4-6 Canvass	26 Bob Miller 2-1001 Welcome Lions Club AHI 10-1 Canvass 3-5:30 Canvass Letter-to-Voters Ad again Call for EndorsementAd
27 12-3 Canvass 3-5 Canvass 8PM Campaign Meeting	28 Run Experience Ad Layout Endorsement Ad Canvass	29 Run Experience Ad Camera-ready Endorsement Ad to paper Canvass	30	31 Run Experience Ad	1 Run Endorsement Ad Lawn Sign Team Clean-up 4-6 Canvass	2 Run Endorsement Ad Canvass 10-1 3-5:30 Canvass
3 12-3 Canvass 3-5 Canvass 8PM Campaign Meeting	4 Run Endorsement Ad	5 - ELECTION DAY -	6 Lawn Signs come down			

FIGURE 13.2   Example of Campaign Calendar

14
After the Ball

There are many things you must do to put your campaign to bed, win or lose. However, before taking down your lawn signs, bundling your stakes, paying your bills, finishing reports for the state, closing out bank accounts, and reassembling your house, you must first face election night.

On election night, if you are not in a well-known location with other candidates and their volunteer teams, you should let the press know where they can find you. I have held campaign parties in restaurants and at my home. I prefer my home. In the last days of the campaign, I let my volunteers know that I will be home and throwing a party in honor of them and a great campaign. I live in a small town, so people call and stop by all night. It is difficult to stay home and watch returns alone if you have been involved in a campaign, especially a winning one. Most people drop by to share the excitement, even if it is just for a few minutes. My home is open.

If your campaign covered an area larger than one city, you might need to go to a more central and public location. Again, tell all your volunteers where you will be and invite them. I try to spend election day or even the weekend before the election calling and personally thanking my volunteers. This is also a good time to remind them to join me on election night. Don't wait to thank them until after the election. If you lose, volunteers are anxious to talk and reflect and comfort, and you are anxious to sit alone on the floor of a dark closet with the door closed.

There is no preparing for a loss, and I'm not even sure people *ever* get over it. It will change your life, just as winning will. But win or lose, you must be prepared to face the media and do it with class.

In one election on which I worked, I sat with the candidate as the first big returns came in. The shock that went through us as we realized we were losing is indescribable. I remember cameras pointing at our faces. There is something predatory and morose about our society when it comes to watching a leader fall. We had expected a win and were not prepared for what was before us.

"Always let losers have their words."
—Francis Bacon

The next day our pictures were in the paper. I looked for shock, disbelief, upset, disappointment. None of it was in our faces. We just sat, stunned, looking at the huge TV in the restaurant. In the story that followed, the candidate thanked his volunteers, his campaign team, his supporters. He thanked everyone for a chance to serve. The end.

> "The two happiest days of my life were the day we moved into the White House and the day we moved out."
> —Betty Ford

Win or lose, that is the speech. You must be graceful and appreciative. If you win, you must be humble and immediately begin mending fences that might have been broken during the process. Win or lose, you thank your family, volunteers, supporters, and the community for support. If you lose, there is one more call you must make, and that is to your opponent. Congratulate that person and say that you are on board to help make his or her time in office as successful as possible.

In my second bid for mayor, we won handily, by nearly two to one. On election night my house was full of friends and volunteers. Well wishers phoned. Everyone brought something to eat and drink. Then a reporter called. He said that one of my opponents was convinced that he had lost because of a damaging letter-to-the-editor that accused him of criminal wrongdoing twenty years before. The reporter said my opponent had suggested I was responsible for the letter.

Although I had nothing to do with this letter and the accusation was without merit, it made me feel like the campaign wasn't over.

Have you ever watched a game after which the coach for the losing team says, "It's no wonder we lost. We made mistakes and didn't play our best"? While it may make that person feel better, it makes the losers feel guilty and the winning team feel slighted.

Be graceful. If you lost, say you put together a great effort but that your opponent put together a better one. Give your opponent a little of the limelight if you won and a lot of the limelight if you lost. Don't blame your loss on insufficient campaign effort. That translates into "My volunteers are responsible for my loss." The most common feeling of volunteers after a losing campaign is "What a waste of time that was." Say you had a great campaign team who put in countless hours and that the whole thing was a ball, challenging, instructive, and fun from beginning to end. Take heart in the fact that you have come to know yourself and the democratic process better.

Should you ever run for office again, you will be glad you acted magnanimously.

Afterword

You are now prepared to begin on the time-honored path of a political campaign. Campaigns are enormously fun and exhilarating. If you do everything right, you are almost assured a win. Just a few reminders before you begin:

1. Know the law.
2. Stay on your campaign theme or message, and you will be in control.
3. Deliver that message to your targeted voters; "aim at the souls that can be saved."
4. Redirect negative campaigning at your opponents and use it as an opportunity to restate your message.
5. Work hard and others will work hard for you.
6. Be humble and listen more than you speak.
7. Know who you are before others find out.
8. Smile. Always look as though you're having a great time.

> "The great use of life is to spend it for something that outlasts it."
> —William James

Win or lose, you will emerge from the process a different person, a leader within your community.

Appendix 1:
Forms for Photocopying

> "In this world there are only two tragedies. One is not getting what one wants, and the other is getting it."
> —Oscar Wilde

ELECTION DATA FORM

Candidate _____   **County** _____

Election Date _____   **Page** ____ **of** ____ **Pages**

Pre-cinct	Reg. voters	Reg. Dems.	Dem. T/O	Reg. Reps.	Rep. T/O								Dem. U/V	Rep. U/V

PRECINCT TARGETING WORKSHEET

Support	Turnout
H/S	**H/T**
M/S	**M/T**
L/S	**L/T**

From *The Campaign Manager* by Catherine M. Shaw. © 2000. Westview Press. (303)444-3541

PRECINCT PRIORITIES WORKSHEET

(1) H/S + L/T = High Priority	(6) M/S + H/T = Medium Priority
(2) H/S + M/T = High Priority	(7) L/S + L/T = Low Priority
(3) M/S + L/T = High Priority	(8) L/S + M/T = Low Priority
(4) M/S + M/T = Medium Priority	(9) L/S + H/T = Low Priority
(5) H/S + H/T = Medium Priority	

From *The Campaign Manager* by Catherine M. Shaw. © 2000. Westview Press. (303)444-3541

TARGETING PRIORITIES AND STRATEGY WORKSHEET

Prio-rity	Pre-cinct	Reg. voters	Party density	Support	T/O	U/V	Precinct location	Campaign strategy

From *The Campaign Manager* by Catherine M. Shaw. © 2000. Westview Press. (303)444-3541

BALLOT MEASURE FORM

Precinct	Reg. Voters	Turnout	Count yes	Count no	Turnout %	% Yes	% No	UV

From *The Campaign Manager* by Catherine M. Shaw. © 2000. Westview Press. (303)444-3541

SAMPLE FORM DETERMINING
BASE PARTY SUPPORT

A	B	C	D	E (D × C) × B)
Precinct number	Percentage of votes same party candidate	Current voter registration	Percentage expected turnout	Number of voters who won't leave the party
TOTAL				

SAMPLE FORM FOR DETERMINING
AVERAGE PARTY TURNOUT (REPUBLICAN)

Precinct number	Party turnout 1st election	Party turnout 2nd election	Party turnout 3rd election	Average party turnout (B + C + D/3)	Current Republican registration	Average # Republican turnout (E x F)
A	B	C	D	E	F	G

From *The Campaign Manager* by Catherine M. Shaw. © 2000. Westview Press. (303)444-3541

SAMPLE FORM FOR DETERMINING SWING VOTERS

Precinct number	High Democrat win by percent	Low Democrat win by percent	Percent of swing (B − C)	Projected turnout	Current voter registration	Number of voters who could swing (D × E × F)
A	B	C	D	E	F	G

From *The Campaign Manager* by Catherine M. Shaw. © 2000. Westview Press. (303)444-3541

SAMPLE FORM FOR DETERMINING THE VOTES YOU NEED TO WIN

Precinct number	Total registered voters	Projected turnout (%)	Projected turnout (#) $(B \times C)$	Percent swing vote (calculate above)	Votes up for grabs $(D \times E)$	Percent your support	Number your support $(D - F) \times G$	Percent opposition support	Number opposition support $(D - F) \times I$	Votes you need to win $(J - H) + F/2$ plus 1	Votes left $F - K$
A	B	C	D	E	F	G	H	I	J	K	L
									Total		Total	

VOLUNTEER SIGN-UP SHEET

Name (please print)	Home Phone	Canvass neighborhoods	Phone Banks	Lawn Sign Location (address)	Donation	Letter to the Editor	Endor. ad?

From *The Campaign Manager* by Catherine M. Shaw. © 2000. Westview Press. (303)444-3541

FLOWCHART GRID

Appendix 2:
The State Initiative and Referendum Process

Types of Initiatives

1. *Direct Initiative.* The completed petition places a proposed law or amendment directly on the ballot, bypassing the legislative process.
2. *Indirect Initiative.* The completed petition is submitted to the legislature, which then may enact the proposed measure or one substantially similar. If the legislature fails to act within a set time, the proposal is placed on the ballot.
3. *Advisory Initiative.* The outcome provides a nonbinding indication of public opinion to the legislature.

Kinds of Referenda

1. *Mandatory Referendum.* State laws vary; however, in general, with a mandatory referendum the legislature must refer all proposed amendments to the constitution as well as measures regarding tax levies, bond issues, and movement of state capitals or county seats.
2. *Optional Referendum.* The legislature may refer to the citizens any measure that it has passed. This is often called a referral.
3. *Petition Referendum.* Measures passed by the legislature go into effect after a specified time unless an emergency clause is attached. During that interim, citizens may circulate a petition requiring that the statute be referred to the people either at a special election or at the next general election. If sufficient signatures are collected, the law is not implemented pending the outcome of the election.
4. *Advisory Referendum.* The legislature may refer a proposed statute to the voters for a nonbinding reflection of public opinion. This is becoming a way for state legislatures to go around a governor's veto of proposed legislative law.

"The ax handle and the tree are made of the same wood."
—Indian proverb

Initiative and Referendum Procedures

1. Preparing the petition. Preparing the initiative petition and organizing the collection of signatures are the responsibilities of the chief petitioner(s). The text of the proposed measure is drafted by the chief petitioner(s), with legal assistance if desired, and filed with the Secretary of State for state initiatives and the local election office for local initiatives.

2. Filing the petition. Any prospective petition must include the names, addresses, and signatures of the chief petitioner(s), a statement of sponsorship signed by a certain number of registered voters and verified by county election officials, a form stating whether or not the circulators of the petition will receive payment, and the complete text of the proposed measure.

3. Obtaining the ballot title. State statutes usually provide strict timelines for moving a filed petition through the process to obtain a ballot title. For state-wide initiatives, all petitions are filed with the Secretary of State and two additional copies are sent to the Attorney General, who prepares a draft of the ballot title.

4. Preparing the cover and signature sheets. The chief petitioner(s) must submit a printed copy of the cover and signature sheets for approval prior to circulation. The cover sheet must include names and addresses of the chief petitioner(s), the proposal itself, the ballot title, and instructions to circulators and signers. The cover sheet must be printed on the reverse of the signature sheet and contain instructions to signature gatherers. Notice of paid circulators must be included. Signature sheets must never be separated from the cover sheet and the measure's text.

5. Circulating the petition. As soon as approval is obtained from the election officer, the ballot is certified and may be circulated for signatures. Usually you can withdraw the petition at any time. Any registered voter may sign an initiative or referendum petition for any measure being circulated in a district where the registered voter resides. All signers on a single sheet must be registered voters residing in the same county.

6. Filing the petition for signature verification. There is a deadline for signature verification state-wide (usually four months) and locally (usually less time).

7. Filing contribution and expenditure information. Within a specific time period of filing petition signatures for verification, the chief petitioner(s) must file a statement of contributions received and expended by them or on their behalf.

Before a political committee receives or expends any funds on a measure that has met the criteria for being placed on the ballot, the committee treasurer must file a Statement of Organization with the Secretary of State, and subsequent contributions and expenditures must be reported. Sometimes this must be done even if a petition is withdrawn.

Figure A2.1 lists states having citizens' initiative authority.

STATES WITH CITIZENS' INITIATIVE AUTHORITY
for Constitutional Amendments and Statutes

State and Date Adopted	Constitution Signature Basis	Statutes Signature Basis	Amend or Repeal by Legislature	Restrictions
Alaska 1959	Not allowed	10% votes in general election from 2/3 districts	After two years can repeal or amend	No revenue measures, appropriations, acts affecting judiciary, local, or special legislation. No laws affecting peace, health, or safety
Arizona 1910	15% of vote for governor	10% of vote for governor	Yes	One subject only; leg. branch only
Arkansas 1909	10% of eligible voters	8% of eligible voters	2/3 vote each house	Limited to legislative measures
California 1911	8% of vote for governor	5% of vote for governor	With voter approval	One subject only
Colorado 1910	5% of votes for Secretary of State	5% of votes for Secretary of State	Statutes, yes Constitution, no	One subject only
Florida 1972	8% presidential election; 8% from 1/2 cong. dist	Not allowed	Amend, yes Repeal, no	One subject only
Idaho 1912	Not allowed	10% of vote for governor	Yes	No provisions
Illinois 1970	8% of vote for governor	Not allowed	No provisions	Limited to leg. branch; structural and procedural subjects only
Maine 1908	Not allowed	10% of vote for governor	Yes	Any expenditure in excess of appropriations void 45 days after legislature convenes
Massachusetts 1918	3% of vote for governor. No more than 25% 1 county	3% of vote for governor. No more than 25% 1 county	Yes	Not for religion and judiciary, local, special legislation or specific appropriations

FIGURE A2.1   Initiative Process in Various States

(continues)

FIGURE A2.1 (continued)

State and Date Adopted	Constitution Signature Basis	Statutes Signature Basis	Amend or Repeal by Legislature	Restrictions
Michigan 1908	10% of vote for governor	8% of vote for governor	Yes, by 3/4 each house	Applicable to statues that leg. may enact
Mississippi 1992	Qualified elector 12% of vote for gov. 1/5 from each congressional district	Not allowed	Yes, with voters' approval	No modification of bill of rights, modification of pub. employees' retirement or labor-related items
Missouri 1906	8% of vote for governor. 8% each of 2/3 congressional district	5% of vote for governor. 5% each from 2/3 congressional district	Yes	One subject; not for appropriations without new revenue; not if prohibited by constitution
Montana 1904	10% of vote for governor. 10% from 2/5 state leg. districts	5% of vote for governor. 5% from 1/3 state leg. districts	Yes	One subject; not for appropriations; not for local and special laws
Nebraska 1912	10% eligible voters. 5% each from 2/5 counties	7% of vote for governor. 5% each from 2/5 counties	Yes	Limited to matters that can be enacted by legislature. No more often than every 3 years
Nevada 1904	10% total votes last general election. 10% each from 3/4 counties	10% total votes last general election. 10% each from 3/4 counties	After 3 years	No appropriation or require an expenditure of money unless a sufficient tax is prohibited
North Dakota 1914	4% resident population	2% resident population	After 7 years except by 2/3 vote each house	Not for emergency measures. Appropriation for support and maintenance of state depts. and institutions
Ohio 1912	10% of vote for governor. 1.5% each from 1/2 counties	3% of vote for governor. 1.5% each from 1/2 counties	Yes	One subject; not for property taxes. Legislation only
Oklahoma 1907	15% of votes cast for office with highest # of votes	8% of votes cast for office with highest # of votes	Yes	Single subject; legislative matters only

(continues)

FIGURE A2.1 *(continued)*

State and Date Adopted	Constitution Signature Basis	Statutes Signature Basis	Amend or Repeal by Legislature	Restrictions
Oregon 1902	8% of vote for governor	6% of vote for governor	Amend and Repeal, Yes	Single subject; legislative measure only
South Dakota 1898	10% of vote for governor	5% of vote for governor	Yes	Except laws as nec. For immediate preservation of public peace, health, or safety support of state govt. and existing public instruction
Utah 1900	Not allowed	10% of vote for governor. 10% each from 1/2 counties	Amend, yes	Lesiglative matters only
Washington 1912	Not allowed	8% of vote for governor	After 2 years, 2/3 each house	Legislative matters only
Wyoming 1968	Not allowed		Amend, yes. Repeal after 2 years	No earmarking, make or repeal appropriation create courts, define jurisdiction of cts. or ct. rules, local or spec. leg. defeated initiative w/in 5 yrs. or legis. prohibited by const.

SOURCE: Oregon League of Women Voters, 1996.

Appendix 3:
Directory of Campaign
Web Sites and Other Resources

Campaign How-Tos

Online how-to-run-a-successful-campaign sites:

- Political Resources Home Page http://politicalresources.com/
- Campaign College Online http://campaigncollege.com/
- Your help is vital! Romanian Site http://haven.ios.com/~dbrutus/diaspora/contribute.html#toc

Non-Partisan Special Interests

Political organizations that have strategy pages and campaign tools online.

- AARP Webplace http://www.aarp.org/index.html
- League of Women Voters of the United States
  http://www.lwv.org/
- Welcome to the NAACP Home Page http://www.naacp.org/
- HRC's Campaign 98 Tools http://www.hrc.org/campgn98/tools.html

General and Political
General Sites on the Internet

- America's Active Political Community Votenet
  http://www.votenet.com/
- Congressional Quarterly
  http://newsalert.cq.com/FreeSites/freesites.htm

Political Science Resources on the Web

- http://www.lib.umich.edu/libhome/Documents.center/polisci.html
- Vote Smart http://www.vote-smart.org/img/pvs.gif
- Shepherd Center Legislative Alerts http://www.shepherd.org/disres/JFA/
- Politics http://www.politics1.com/

General Campaigns and Elections Sites

- Campaigns & Elections http://www.camelect.com/
- Elections U.S.A. http://www.geocities.com/CapitolHill/6228/
- FEDERAL ELECTION COMMISSION http://www.fec.gov/
- Historic Presidential Campaign Information http://www.vote-smart.org/campaign_96/presidential/index.html
- Project on Campaign Conduct http://www.campaignconduct.org/bkgrd/
- The FEC and the Federal Campaign Finance Law http://www.fec.gov/pages/fecfeca.htm

Election Results

- National Association of Secretaries of State (links to all states' Secretary of State Web pages) http://www.nass.org/
- http://www.webwhiteblue.org

Advertising and Media

- Direct Mail Made Easy! http://www.horah.com/
- Internet Resource Guide Advertising http://www.adweb.com/home.html
- CDC's TIPS – Media Campaign Resources http://www.cdc.gov/nccdphp/osh/mcrc/index.htm

Campaign Software

- FREE Campaign Software http://www.votenet.com/governet/

Electorate

- Committee for the Study of the American Electorate http://www.epn.org/csae/index.html
- ELUCIDATING THE ELECTRONIC ELECTORATE http://www.cda-idaho.com/jhaner/articles/voting.htm

- Kettering Foundation http://www.kettering.org/
- Record of American Democracy (ROAD) Project http://data.fas.harvard.edu/ROAD/
- The National Election Studies http://www.umich.edu/~nes/
- The Voter in American Film – Undergraduate Research Paper http://ccwf.cc.utexas.edu/~jpowers/thesis.html

Fund-raising

- Fundraising with the Fund$Raiser Cyberzine http://www.fund-raiser.com/index.html
- Fund Raising Methodology http://www.giftedmemory.com/method.html
- Fund-raising assistance and information to boost results for non-profit organizations http://www.drcharity.com/fund-rai.html
- Non Profit Marketing and Fund Raising http://www.drcharity.com/marketing/nonprofit_marketing.htm

GOTV

- GOTV Tips http://www.lwv.org/internal/gotvtips.html

Political Methodology

- Polmeth Homepage http://polmeth.calpoly.edu/

General Reference Information

- Call the reference desk at the local public library or the nearest university or college.
- Try the government documents department at the library.
- Check out the Web page of Project A (http://www.projecta.com) for approaches to Internet research.
- Try the search engine guide at http://www.sou.edu/library/cybrary/search.htm
- Try the main library page to get online access to the Library of Congress at http://www.sou.edu/library
- Try Image Bank's Web site at http://www.theimagebank.com

Other Resources

- Dubois, Philip L., and Floyd Feeney. *Lawmaking by Initiative: Issues, Options, and Comparisons.* New York: Agathon Press, 1998.

- Salzman, Jason. *Making the News: A Guide for Nonprofits and Activists.* Boulder, Colo.: Westview Press, 1998.
- Shea, Daniel M. *Campaign Craft: The Strategies, Tactics, and Art of Political Campaign Management.* Westport, Conn.: Praeger, 1996.

Index